PRAISE FOR *WING (*

"Jacqueline Hollows is a force of nature, and this book will renew your faith in what human beings are capable of when given the time, love, and attention to bring it forward. In the stories of prisoners awakening to who they really are underneath the hand they've been dealt and the choices they've made, you may well find your own true self quietly awaiting your return."

Michael Neill, Los Angeles, USA
Bestselling author of *The Inside-Out Revolution* and *The Space Within*

If you believe that there are "some people" in this world who are not worth saving and need to be locked up, this book will summon you to question that belief and touch your heart beyond your thinking. If you believe you are irredeemably broken and there is no hope for you, this book will reawaken your hope and nurture your true soul, like spring rain opens the flowers to bask in the beauty of life. If you wish you could reach out to people in trouble and make a difference in the world, but you don't think you have it in you and you are insecure and frightened, this author's story will lift you on the Wing of an Angel to follow your calling and dream beyond your limitations. This is a beautiful revelation of our common humanity, no matter what we think. It will leave every reader inspired.

Judith A. Sedgeman, EdD, California, USA
Mental Health Mentor

The book touched me deeply. It is a beautiful and very realistic testament to the true nature of all human beings and especially the ones considered "broken" by most people. It clearly points to extraordinary resilience and freedom from habits and thinking that is available to us all. Jacqueline's unconditional love and hope for the men behind bars shine from every word.

Martin Jotov, Prague, Czech Republic
Vice-Chairman of Porozumeni mysli z.s,
Managing Director of IQ Structures,

After reading the first few chapters, my thought was, "Everyone who works in addictions and criminal justice will benefit from this book." A few more chapters and my thought was, "Everyone who's experienced childhood hardship will benefit." A few more and, "Everyone who has ever judged another will benefit." Everyone. Period.

On the surface, this is a book about one woman's courage to initiate change in an archaic prison system, one woman's parallel uplift from her own harsh childhood, and one woman's struggle to run a non-profit business with a mission to guide "criminals" beyond recovery to the fullness of their potential.

You will meet yourself in down-and-out prisoners. You will meet yourself in a vulnerable author, a helper who struggles with insecurities but keeps on keeping on. You will meet your own power to have insight and to change.

Linda Sandel Pettit, Ed.D. Phoenix, USA
Mentor to Intuitive-Creative Women; Business owner, author,
consultant, and speaker; Retired Counselling Psychologist;
40-year career in mental health work

Like other universal teachers throughout the ages, Syd Banks unequivocally stated that, without exception, at the core of every human being is perfect mental health. Our personal mind covers it up as we go through life, which leads to the many mental dysfunctions and associated behaviours. Can every human being wake up to their mental health no matter how badly "damaged" they appear to be?

Wing of an Angel answers this question and more. Whether or not you are familiar with Syd Banks' work, read this book to deepen your understanding of the hidden treasure inside all human beings. It is truly transformative.

> **Dr Shadrick Mazaza, Cape Town, South Africa**
> Professor of Personal Transformation and Leadership, University of Cape Town; Founder: African Consciousness Institute

---

Wing of an Angel is a beautifully written, personal, and incredibly insightful book. It highlights the miracle of insight and, in the process, offers us so much hope. I feel privileged to be part of Jacqueline's story and to have shared so many magical times. Thank you, Jacqueline, for all you have done, your gentle, unwavering determination, your immense love and kindness and your unique ability to show us all that there is a *Beyond* for everyone.

> **Paul Lock, Artist, London, UK**

The book is a fascinating read and difficult to put down. It documents the fact that we can all make a big difference in the world. The book is about following your inner wisdom, trusting the next step, and then enjoying the beauty of how life unfolds. The book is about overcoming challenges and adversity. The book is about miracles, true rehabilitation and preventing future victims. The book is about finding love, sharing love, and creating hope when there was none. And saving lives, beginning with your own. The book is about true forgiveness of oneself and others. Oh yes, the book is also about being stubborn!

The research Jacqueline undertook, first supported by Jack Pransky and Tom Kelly, was ground-breaking. The outcomes showed statistically significant improvement in mental well-being, purpose in life and behavioural issues while at the same time significantly reducing depression, anxiety, and anger. Had they been able to track drug use and recidivism, I'm highly confident that Beyond Recovery programs would have shown significant improvements in these outcomes as well. I'm focused on finding and developing scalable 3P research projects, and Jacqueline's program was the first scalable one I've seen because of her vision of inmates becoming mentors and then coaches and instructors. This has now happened, thus providing a scalable solution to rehabilitation and recidivism. Or, in other words, a miracle.

Ron McVety, Florida, USA
Founder Three Principles Research and Consulting
(3PRC.com) and Innate Health Research (IHR.org)

"In a world of prejudice and stigma, Jacqueline inspires us as she negotiates the criminal justice system to find innate well-being where most of us would see none. Thought-provoking and insightful, *Wing of an Angel* is full of real-life stories of men who have found freedom and peace of mind literally 'inside'. Unlike all the other programs available to prison inmates, Jacqueline doesn't bring it to them; she shows that they already have it themselves by her own incredible example. This book is truly an inspiring read for us all."

Chana Studley, Jerusalem, Israel
International speaker, coach, and author of *Painless*.

Will this book change the world? No. But it may change the perception that people who have served prison sentences are sub-human. Wing of an Angel should be required reading for all who think prisons are holiday camps which could not be further from the truth. It is about time for a more realistic approach, and this book, with its message of well-being, is at its heart.

I am proud of the work Jacqueline and her team do. Wing of an Angel is of its time and should be required reading for all who work in prisons, all who are or have been within the criminal justice system and, importantly, the public at large.

"The degree of civilization in a society can be judged by entering its prisons" — Fydor Dostoevsky

Lady Val Corbett, London, UK
Founder The Corbett Network

I am struck by the feeling that this is really an important book and will make a big difference in this world, helping open people's eyes to how we are all the same and how love is the answer. Such a depth of wisdom shared, so honestly and without pretence, and written in such a compelling way. Thank You!

Jane Tucker, Salt Spring Island, British Columbia
Author of *Insights: Messages of Hope, Peace and Love*

Wing of an Angel is a marvellous read of everyday transformations: the author, her work in the prisons and more than likely, you, the reader. You will be taken on a journey of exquisite storytelling and enlightening moments. Jacqueline Hollows is an angel amongst us who has revealed hope for humanity's most troubled. Freedom from an imprisoned mind is what everyone hopes for. The answer to prison reform is in this book. It is a must-read for new perspectives, fresh ideas and hope for all of humanity.

Karen Miller Williams, Vancouver, Canada
Former Three Principles Nurse

Jacqueline Hollows is a source of inspiration for me and many others. It's just like the explosion of a supernova where the light will go on through generations and generations from one awakened person to another – and hundreds of years more. People who will turn their lives around and will follow the path of wisdom will be enjoying their innate emotional resilience, amazing endless potential, and freedom even as inmates. The hatred will be no more.

The influence of Jacqueline's work will surpass her life here on earth, it will go beyond, and it will never stop giving.

Masha Liashenko, Ukraine
Transformative coach, mentor and speaker

Jacqueline Hollows is what we Jews call in Hebrew a *tzadaikes* – 'a holy and righteous woman'. She goes about her work, of transforming the lives of those suffering in prison humbly, lovingly, compassionately and without desire for reward or credit. Jacqueline simply lives a life of service. And our world is the great recipient of her kindness and love.

The stories she tells, including her own, are so full of hope, so full of possibility, so full of meaning, wisdom, and human greatness. I defy anyone to read this book and not shed tears – multiple times. Tears of hope for humankind. Tears of love for the greatness of the human spirit. Tears that you shed when you see something beautiful in others that reflects your own beauty back at you, and you remember how privileged you are to be alive.

Thank you, Jacqueline, for this book – a gift to humankind.

Rabbi Shaul Rosenblatt
Director Better World Charity, London UK

Wing of an Angel is a remarkable book that will alter the course of the life of every person that reads it. JB Hollows bares her soul's journey as she discovers her own essence and wholeness while freshly seeing the same in the men and women in prison she was inspired to serve.

As her personal awakening occurs, she experiences the awakening of innately present love, compassion, wisdom, peace and wholeness in so many who had been mistakenly labelled by others and themselves as Broken and Lacking.

JB witnessed prisoners serving long sentences and having many years of criminal and violent behaviour after reading Sydney Bank's The Missing Link, sharing, "An incredible peace washed over me. Tears flooded my eyes. I started having answers to questions I never knew that I had… For the first time in my life, I felt free."

As her own journey continued, JB states ".I feel free. I saw my parents were innocent. I'd never seen that before… I saw that I could have more freedom. That I could let go of the pain and move on.

In summary, the author states with a quiet certainty that emerged from her personal shifts and those of the prisoners, "I believe the world would change if we all took a moment each day to be kind to each other if we all stopped and listened to each other, if we were kinder and listened to ourselves."

Warning: if you read this book with an open heart and mind, it will appear to you that the external world has changed substantially. In truth, it will be your eyes. whose lenses have effortlessly shed cataract-like conditioned thinking, are seeing the world and those in it with a new-found clarity and appreciation.

William F. Pettit, Jr., MD, Phoenix USA
Retired Psychiatrist / Three Principles-based Wellbeing Coach &
Mental Health Educator; Adjunct Clinical Professor, Creighton
University School of Medicine, Department of Psychiatry

JB Hollows ability to write about seeing health and trusting Mind was very inspiring. I was engaged and wanted to read the whole thing! Unusual for me if there is no sex or suspense!! I will buy this and get it for my program as the stories are so good, and the awakenings are so powerful! Her writing is great as her sweet, joyful feeling comes through.

Christine Heath, Hawaii
Ex. Director Hawaii Counselling & Education Center

WING OF AN ANGEL

WING OF AN ANGEL

An Exploration of Human Potential
in the Back of Beyond

JB HOLLOWS

IW
Press

First Published in Great Britain by IW Press Ltd 2023

Cover design by Andrew Hollows
Page layout by Catherine Williams | Chapter One Book Production

ISBN-13 978-1-916701-00-7 (Paperback)
ISBN-13 978-1-916701-01-4 (Hardback)
ISBN-13 978-1-916701-02-1 (ebook)

IW Press Ltd, 62-64 Market Street, Ashby de la Zouch, LE65 1AN
www.iliffe-wood.co.uk

Out Beyond Ideas

by Rumi

Out beyond ideas of wrongdoing and right-doing,
there is a field. I'll meet you there.

When the soul lies down in that grass,
the world is too full to talk about.
Ideas, language, even the phrase 'each other'
doesn't make any sense.

(translated by Coleman Barks)

To Angel, I'll meet you there.

—————————————————

Contents

Act II – Insight on the Inside (2015–2018)

Act III – Each One Teach One (2019–2020)

Foreword

by Joseph Bailey

When I first met Jacqueline, I was struck by her inner beauty—a radiant smile, a kind look in her eyes, and a joy unmistakably real and contagious. I was giving a talk in London, and she invited me to lunch with a group of others she worked with in the prisons. Much of my work has been in the recovery field as a prevention director, trainer and therapist, so our paths were parallel. In addition, both of our lives were transformed by studying with Sydney Banks. I knew we would become colleagues and friends immediately.

I love my wife's first poem: "There are no mistakes, there's only the revelation of the inner Self." In reading *Wing of an Angel* this weekend, I realise that this pretty much sums up the central theme of Jacqueline's book. Throughout the accounts of her work in corrections and teaching the Three Principles, Jacqueline weaves in stories of her immense personal challenges and pain. All of which give us tangible situations we can relate to and learn from, including Jacqueline taking on the status quo of the corrections field with a revolutionary understanding that will upend the way we treat criminals and the incarcerated.

She has done it with unwavering faith in seeing that the unknown is nothing to fear but to be embraced whole-heartedly. By sharing her deep understanding that mistakes and challenges are pointers to new insights that will always appear at the right time when we let go of the fear of the unknown, she has given new hope and a path of transformation to many.

There is a Universal Intelligence that guides all of life—knowing that it exists and can be trusted and that acting on the insights it gives us removes our fears, insecurities, and self-doubt. It guides us to mental health, inner peace, and our true purpose in life.

In Jacqueline's inspired book, *Wing of an Angel*, she shares her transformational odyssey with us in the most personal, eloquent and simple way. Her raw honesty about her life struggles, and her journey of taking her realisations to those less fortunate in our correctional systems, informs the reader of how their mind works. She shows how to trust our inner guidance as we face the uncertainty and unknowns of our own lives. Her life is her teaching, and from her real-isations about the nature of our psychological functioning and how life is created from the inside out, she was able to move through one of the most resistant systems—prisons and correctional institutions, with grace, ease and tenacity against all odds.

I had the honour to speak to one group of prisoners at one of the correctional institutions she worked with in Rugby, England, many years ago. What struck me about Jacqueline most was her love for the men and her non-judg-mental acceptance of them—seeing past the scars, the tattoos, and the rough exterior to the truth of who each of them is. Through her seeing their natural health and resilience, they began to see it in themselves and others.

Prisons are dangerous, depressing, and uncomfortable places to be. Our society sees criminals as "bad people" who need punishment to change their ways. Jacqueline brought hope, love, understanding and acceptance to these men in many prisons all over the UK and other parts of the world, sharing the same simple message of love and compassion coupled with an understanding of The Three Principles Psychology that shows people the path to personal transformation and mental health.

I love the raw honesty of her writing. She openly shares her times of despair, wanting to give up on her work in the prisons and her struggles in life. As she shares realisations and insights that transformed her life, she demonstrates to the prisoners her humanness and how we are all capable of the same transformation. Here is a quote from her book that expresses more clearly her philosophy of working in corrections: (she often quotes from her personal diary as in this example)

PRISON NOTES

We did the first Notts group this week. There's a thorny pleasure to starting to work in a new prison. Knowing I have an elixir the residents all want but don't know they want it. Waiting to see the tiny sparks of hope fanned alive. They think we're crazy, talking about peace of mind, the miracle of life, and how our world is created inside out. It's not a conversation a group of men in prison are used to having. Some might have read self-help books and attended many courses, but still, they're not used to unconditional love. You can tell by how they come into the room, chatting about how the system has f**k*d them over, how this man needs to be beaten up, and how they used to enjoy this drug or that lifestyle. And then there we are, all smiles and warm handshakes. Encouraging space and silence and meaningful conversation. It's a weird juxtaposition. But I love it. I know it's strange to say, but I love that uncomfortable feeling, a mix of being a bit scared, insecure, daunted, and out of my depth. I love it because I go with it; it doesn't stop me from doing what I'm doing, and the reward, wow, the reward, it's incredible! To see men have insights that prevent them from being big scary hairy creatures and turn them into gentle giants has got to be the best reward in the world. To start with, people grunting at me and then having them fall over themselves to make me a cup of tea or turn a fan on to cool me down because they've found their gentle selves inside is the sweetest feeling in the world.

This book has the power to transform you. I know because, as I read it this past week, I was in the midst of a significant challenge in my life. We found out we needed to move out of our home of forty years due to a mould contamination issue. I was heartbroken and upended emotionally. But reading this book while going through that brought me back to my understanding and faith that the unknown is nothing to fear, but to know that life is benevolent if we listen within to the wisdom and insights that come to us when we trust our inner voice of wisdom to guide us to the next steps into a new reality that is better than the one we are leaving.

Open your heart and mind, and you, too, will be transformed by this book.

Joseph Bailey, Licensed Psychologist and Author of
The Serenity Principle, Slowing Down to the Speed of Life, his latest, *Thriving in the Eye of the Hurricane—Unlocking Resilience in our Turbulent Times,* and many more.

Prologue

I never thought I'd come to much. That's what my dad told me anyway.

The story of me was based on negativity, abuse, neglect, and a belief that I was stupid.

It was all so wrong! Who'd a thunk it?

In my life, I've achieved. I've just never thought of it that way.

I dropped out of college at sixteen to care for my mum and sister when our father left us. A mum in hospital with a smashed-up leg from a car crash. A sister at fifteen, who'd turned into a wild child. A heap of debt. And a cat with fleas.

Even then, I was resilient. I blagged my way into a job in a bar. I sat on the hard plastic chair at a housing association until they provided us with a home. I discovered disability benefits for my mum and moved us lock, stock and barrel for a fresh start.

It wasn't a fairy tale ending, but that is a story for another time.

For thirty-nine years, I thought I was a failure, a fake, and not worth loving. In that time, I'd achieved two degrees, climbed mountains, won awards, been a loving mum, and succeeded in my career. And yet nothing filled the gap that ached inside me.

Not therapy, not sex, not booze, not chocolate, not certificates, not love, not work. And I tried them all. Jeez, did I try.

One day I woke up. Just like that. I didn't know I was waking up. I just knew that something clicked inside of me. I realised I'd lived my life under the shadow of someone who couldn't stand me: my father. He'd never wanted the kid that forced him to marry my mum. He'd used all of us, me, my sister and my mum, to satiate his anger, lust, and emptiness. He never found his dad gene.

I was standing in the freshly decorated living room of the two up, two down I'd struggled to buy. I was about to have a hysterectomy, and a phone call with my dad showed me the light. "I love you, you bastard," he said. Those words messed with my head. He'd just told me he wouldn't come to see me because he didn't want to upset his wife. I stared at myself in the black-rimmed mirror above the fireplace. I could hear the birds in the garden. My sweaty hand held the phone tight. "Goodbye," I said.

And in that moment, everything was different. Overnight, I lost my shadow. The world changed when I saw myself anew. I found a diamond beneath the layers of crap that had stuck to me all my life.

For real!

I'd been playing the part of a woman who had to pretend to be good, who had to work harder than everyone else to achieve, who had to self-medicate to cover the cracks. Beneath the movie I'd been living in was a bright, vibrant, warm, loving, creative human being. One that deserved love and was love.

I went on a mission. To discover my true self and help others find their true selves.

I re-trained as a life coach. I soaked up everything I could find about what makes people tick—and devoted the next two decades of my life to helping others. Many of the teachings I discovered would fix a particular problem or solve an issue, but I never felt that they were the complete answer. I researched addiction and found that the existing paradigm was based on the premise that people have a disease that does not account for the innate health within all people.

When I discovered The Three Principles uncovered by a man called Sydney Banks, I didn't need to look any further. The Three Principles explains how the human experience works. One hundred percent of the time. It showed me what everyone is looking for, but no one talks about. Who we are at our core, and how we get so lost.

It's simple because it already exists from when we are born.

It's profound because everything changes once we glimpse our true nature.

It's holistic because we don't have to solve each problem separately.

It took a minute, but eventually, I ditched my career in IT and set up a social enterprise, Beyond Recovery. With a mission to radically review the way we view and treat addiction, mental health, and offending behaviour. And to end the stigma associated with these issues.

My goal was to share the understanding of The Three

Principles with people in prison and the community. I went on to create a curriculum, write research papers, and train others, but in the beginning, I just had hope in my heart and eyes that saw innocence.

I feel blessed to have found this path.

Don't get me wrong; prisons are brutal. Racism and sexism are alive and kicking. It is a dog-eat-dog environment. Cruelty is the order of the day.

And yet. I met amazing people. Creative people. Resilient people. I've seen that anything is possible regardless of the circumstances in which we live. I've discovered that human potential is infinite. And each time I found these aspects in another, I uncovered them more in myself.

I found out that love is the answer.

Always.

I met Angel, a gangster who scared the bejesus out of everyone. I met Derrick, who believed he was a career criminal. I met Wilson, who thought he had to be tough to protect his family. I met Chris, who just wanted quiet time.

And in the murky world of addiction, I met Pete, who tried to end his life of trauma by jumping off a bridge.

I met many men and women who'd followed a path of misguided thinking which led them to do wrong deeds and hurt others. I realised they were hurt. And hurt people hurt people.

I saw over and over again that people's true nature is loving, compassionate and kind. It just gets clouded by stinking thinking and a misunderstanding of how our experience of life is created.

I've written this book to honour the people I met and the transformations I saw. It tells of my journey of getting into this work and conquering my demons because that gives the context of why I think the problem we face as a society is not restricted to one cohort of people.

I worked with many outstanding individuals along the way who were all part of our great work in Beyond Recovery. I've simplified the story, so they are not always mentioned for the significant contribution in which they worked.

Many of the incidents are so personal, I've had to disguise them to protect people from being identified. I've also amalgamated some of the characters to preserve identification further. However, all the words used, and the stories told, are things I've seen or heard on the wings of the prisons I've worked in.

There is the thorny question of what term to use for the people in our prisons. The terms inmates, residents, prisoners, and offenders are used in various ways. The guys I've asked don't feel what word is used makes a difference because it doesn't change how they are treated. I've chosen to use residents in most places in this book. I hope that this does not offend anyone.

This story is about me and what led me to work within the UK criminal justice system. It's about the people I met along the way. It is a story of redemption and hope. I sincerely hope you find redemption and hope for yourself and your loved ones within these pages.

Introduction

Imagine. A world with no crime. A world full of kindness. A world of hope and compassion.

Imagine a world where people have unlimited potential for change, regardless of their circumstances.

Now pause in the quiet for a moment and imagine a world where prisons could become centres for rehabilitation, where people who exit prison contribute to making the world a better place, and where children do not grow up to become criminals.

This book is about how invisible judgements shape what we see.

The book charts my story and the story of Angel, who represents the many people I've met within the walls of the prison system.

I'm an ordinary woman who overcame childhood traumas, abusive relationships and emotional difficulties to make a difference in the lives of hundreds of people in the UK who have been locked up, marginalised and treated as 'others.'

Some of the stories sound unreal, straight off the TV. Some of the men sound like 'bad guys.' Some of the situations sound too dramatic to be true. Some of the lives sound far removed from our own.

I can assure you they are not. I may have disguised some facts to protect identities, but I witnessed or experienced every word, story, and situation.

Our paths run parallel. Our traumas are real. Our freedom is found from within.

THE UK PRISON SYSTEM

My intention for this book is to:

◆ Demonstrate that people in prison make the mistakes we can all make and that their stories could be ours.
◆ Ignite hope that transformation is possible for anyone.
◆ Inspire others to be the change they want to see in the world.

The prison population in the UK is a growing problem that continues to be ignored and misunderstood through inappropriate media attention and an archaic system creaking at the knees. Most people who arrive in prison have already been living on the fringes of society and have experienced early childhood trauma, lack of education, undiagnosed mental-health conditions, homelessness, and addiction issues.

Humanity faces numerous distressing issues. These issues are not separate; they are not disconnected. They are all different strands of the same thing: we *fear* change, we *fear* others, and we *fear* that we can't do anything to make a difference. This book aims to show that when we use love and compassion as our guiding principles, we can create, develop, and implement systems that have the power to build a world that is fair and loving.

My journey, and the journeys of the people I've worked with, describe how we can overcome our difficulties, insecurities, and challenges. And we can use the adversity to create sustainable solutions to society's problems.

I've experienced how we can rise again with resilience, passion, and determination.

I've seen how inner strength doesn't come from what we think we know or have been through, but rather from our essence.

This book is a story of everyday transformations. When we concentrate on the struggle, we miss the miracle of life.

When we see the miracle of life, we have a happier experience.

Natural Intelligence

by JB Hollows

They are not dumb, these men, these people.
Not dumb at all. They've been lost, for sure, they've
been in a battle in their mind, in their hearts, with life.
But they are not dumb.
And they are not broken.

They don't need fixing. I can hear their wisdom. I
see it in their eyes. They light up when they feel the
unconditional love I offer. They can taste it.
And each week, their warmth grows. They are learning
to trust again. They are starting to trust me, trust what
they hear and most of all,
Trust themselves.

They have woken up to themselves. They have started
to see that wisdom was there all along.
And not in some far-off place.
Or unreachable God.
But within them, and through them.

I could see their souls today as they left the room. Their eyes sparkled and they looked straight into my soul. They are alive.

They've heard it for so long—how broken they are—sometimes they are vulnerable and scared and can't quite believe it's OK.

But when they hear something else at a deeper level, they soon realise it is their own spirit speaking to them, welcoming them home.

Act I

The Quest for Purpose

1974 – 2014

ANGEL 1990

"I'm scared," Angel's mum whimpered. She was curled into a ball behind their new brown sofa with soft cushions. He could smell the flowers in her perfume, the leather from the couch, the sweat from his father, and the piss that had dribbled down his right trouser leg. "Shut up, yer upsetting the lad," his dad spat in a forced whisper and handed Angel a Colt '45. "If anyone comes through that door, shoot 'em in the leg," he said. He used the gritty voice he used for the men in his gang. His dark eyes glinted like steel. His cheekbones were flushed.

Angel felt the cold black metal of the heavy gun in his tiny white hands; his six-year-old face tinged with pleasure at being part of this grown-up game. The mix of fear and excitement churned in his stomach. The fists on the door beat in time with his heart. The sound drowned out all sense. "It's the police. Open up, or we'll have to break in."

The shiny gun felt good in Angel's hand, although his wrist ached with his attempt to hold it steady. His little pudgy fingers barely reached the trigger, even with two hands wrapped around the butt. He wondered what it would be like to shoot a copper in the leg. Would the blood splatter everywhere like it did in the Zombie films? Would he enjoy the copper's scream? Or would he end up shooting the light bulb? Like when his sister had made him mad, he'd picked up his dad's gun. He'd been shocked at the power of it as his little arms ricocheted upwards. The bullet was still embedded in the cracked magenta ceiling between the light and a red blood stain.

"Good lad," his dad said. Angel's arms shook as he mustered all his strength to be a man. The police didn't break in that day; something to do with a warrant.

The next day, Mum made Angel go to school. Her eyes were red and swollen. The large blue bruise on her cheek looked like it was gonna be a corker. Angel fetched the frozen peas as soon as he saw her. "Don't leave Mum," he said as she started to cry again. He'd heard his dad threaten to kill them if she kept on. She'd screamed that she'd leave and take Angel with her. He'd listened to the thump of her head against the wall and knew his dad was holding her by the throat. He liked to do that. Hold them up by the throat. Like chickens. Legs dangling, arms scrabbling, eyes bulging. His dad once said he liked to let go just before their eyes popped out. He'd snorted with laughter at the thought that one day he might go too far. It had been Angel's sixth birthday that day.

"Go on to school, Pumpkin," his mum said and kissed the top of his head, his black hair gelled down like his dad's. "I'll be OK; tell Miss I've got a bug."

Angel dragged his grey rucksack down the broken paving slabs all the way to the school on the corner of his road. He knew his teacher disapproved of him turning up without his mum by the scowl on her face, but he didn't care. He was a man now. His dad trusted him with a gun. All morning, he sat throwing blue Bic pen tops at the other students' heads and daydreamed about cops and robbers. "I'm going to have to ask you to leave," the teacher snapped.

"Fuck you!" Angel shouted.

"Right young man, down to the Head," the teacher fumed, red face matching her red jumper.

"Alright, Rudolph," Angel said. The other boys laughed. They always did.

The Head Teacher kept him waiting. Sweat dripped down the back of Angel's neck as his confidence slipped. He liked the Head; he'd always been kind to Angel. One time he'd even given him one of the green lollipops from the glass jar on his big desk. Angel picked at the stuffing on the old chair outside the Head's office and fixed a scowl on his little face.

"Come," the Head called out.

Angel stood in front of the vast mahogany desk. He felt like he'd shrunk as he stared at the large Head Teacher. The room smelled stern. A red bubble gum wrapper lay on the floor by the bin. A loud clock ticked and tocked and measured his time away. "What do you want to be when you grow up?" the Head Teacher asked with a smile. Angel's mind flashed back to the feeling of the heavy metal gun in his hand, the cold black glint in his dad's eyes, and the sense of excitement as the police pounded the door.

"A Gangster," he said.

Lock 'em Up &
Throw Away the Key

"Everybody has the capacity to be remarkable."
~Lord Michael Young

Imagine we're sitting outside a café, on a bustling street in Camden, London, on a blazing hot sunny day. The small rickety tables and chairs are crammed so close together we can smell the coffee on the breath of our neighbours and eavesdrop on their intimate conversations.

Our straw hats shade the glare of the sun. Our skin glistens with sweat. The heat from the pavement scorches the paws of dogs as they lap at the now-warm water set out for them in metal bowls. Behind sunglasses, we watch people on the busy street with bohemian clothes shops, vintage jewellers, and eateries.

The beautiful weather has filled the street with London's diversity: old and young, pink and brown, students and professionals. They walk down the road, and their chatter and laughter float above the noise of horns and traffic.

18

People browse, and workers skive. They eat multicoloured ice creams that drip from corn cones. They stand close to each other and gaze into shop windows.

The people on this street wear summer clothes: short dresses and white shirts, linen jackets thrown over shoulders, and bangles jangle from wrists.

Some people have been victims of crime.

Some of them have been perpetrators of crime.

From where we sit, we can't tell the victims from the perpetrators.

There are no signs above their heads. We only see people. And we see them through the shades of our judgements and filters. We wonder what that man is up to, the one with the gold front tooth and long dreadlocks. We notice the nervous tick and grey pallor of the woman who just sat down. We smile at the cute waiter in the blue cotton apron. The stories we create about them all are immediate and sticky and yet are born from perception.

Have you ever driven when drunk[1]?

Have you ever taken a towel from a hotel room?

Have you ever acted out of anger?

Have you ever found a wallet and kept it?

Have you ever felt like you wanted to kill somebody?

Dear Diary (Feb 1990),

I'm a terrible mother. I knew I would be. What chance did I have? I was dragged up. I did it for a reason, though. I did it for my baby boy, my little Darren. I did it for love. It snowed so bad I couldn't see the end of the street. I've never seen snow like it. Well, maybe once when Darren's dad was still here, but I don't want to think about that. My eye is still swollen from the last attack. I thought about leaving Darren home alone. But he cried out. The guilt pierced my heart with its shard of iced fear.

So, I took him with me. Darren was almost invisible, with every inch of skin wrapped up and a little pair of sunglasses to protect his eyes. I pulled him backwards in his pushchair through the knee-high snow. I limped to the corner shop. We'd run out of baby food, and without anyone to help, what else could I do? I thought about Mum when I was walking. I wondered if the snow was as bad in Leicester, all those miles away. Snow blinded me in front and around and behind us. Cars were lost in an icy white blanket; shapes that used to be trees were now covered in crystal white cloaks.

I shopped for the essentials I could carry back home, but picked up more than I meant to. When I got to the shop, I took my time to thaw out for a moment and to cuddle Darren. I placed the large tin of baby milk formula in the pushchair basket. While I paid, all I could think about was the horrendous walk home.

> I didn't mean to steal the baby's food. I just forgot
> it was in the basket. I'd been so focussed on getting
> Darren home again. I stood at my kitchen counter,
> staring at it for a long time. My tea went cold in its aban-
> doned cup. My heart sank as I thought about having to
> go back out and pay. I told myself I'd do it another day
> but knew I wouldn't. I'm not just a bad mother; I'm a
> terrible person. But you already know that.

I never did pay for the baby food. I'm a shoplifter.

I've driven while I've been drunk. I'm grateful I never killed anyone.

I've found money in the street and kept it. It's called Theft by Finding.

I've had a parking ticket I tried to get away with. The insurance company called it: Morally Bankrupt.

Am I a criminal? Should you lock me up and throw away the key?

I've been robbed.

I've been mugged.

I've been violently attacked.

I've been sexually abused.

Am I a victim? Should you pity me, lock up my attackers and throw away the key?

Why am I telling you this? Because I'm offering you an invitation to join me on a journey. My journey. And the travels of the people in prison that I have worked with over the last five years. I will tell stories from my life and experience as a woman, an entrepreneur, a human who has made mistakes. I will share stories of people in prison. People like me and maybe like you. People who have made mistakes. People who have been lost. People who have hurt others and people who have been hurt.

The media feeds us a single story about prisoners. That they have different wiring; rotten apples; evil; bad to the core. So, we feel scared and treat them as if they were "other" than us. We want to feel safe. However, this is one angle of a very complex view. The result is that, as a nation, we tend to have two responses to prison and the people in it:

1. We have a vague idea of how horrible and scary prison must be, and so must the people who go there.
2. We don't think about it at all.

As a victim of crime or wrongdoing, we want retribution. We lash out in anger and pain. Me too. However, for this time we are together, I'll ask you to consider the other stories for a moment. You may get a different insight into the people's lives and hearts behind those thick walls and steel bars. These are the stories that demonstrate the humanity, the tears and the fears of those people. The stories that open our eyes to hope and potential and love. I share stories of the men and women I work with. I don't say that they shouldn't be in prison or that what they've done should be forgiven.

Can we forgive the killing of a child? Fats did.

PRISON NOTES – SPRING 2017

Fats was in the group today. As my mum used to say, he's like a strip of wind. He's got a wild afro haircut, and his clothes hang off his skinny body. He talked about how his life of crime was due to anger over the murder of his daughter. He couldn't bear it. He told us how he lost the plot when she died. He turned to drugs to help him blank out his pain. Turned to crime to feed his habit. Turned to us for help. Blamed his mum, his environment, himself.

Fats had a daughter. A drunk driver ran her down. Fats wanted to kill him. I've only ever seen him sad, until today, in the group, when he told us a funny story about chips. About how angry he got when no chips were left at lunchtime and the tantrum he threw. He wanted to find someone to blame, caught himself, and burst out laughing at his own created misery about CHIPS! We laughed so hard at the way he told it. There were nine of us laughing at Fats' funny story.

As he finished his tale about chips, with tears, snot, and his head in his hands, he said, "Ting is, if I got that wrong, then maybe I got other stuff wrong." He told us it made him think about how he saw the events of his baby's accident. And that he no longer blames his mum, himself, his daughter, the driver or God. He saw that he used all those things to hold on to the girl he had lost, to somehow honour her memory. He saw that letting go of the anger was not disrespectful to her. And as soon as he let go of that blame, he started to have happy memories of his time with her. Memories that a wall of pain had blocked were now available to him. He forgives the driver. He forgives himself.

He hopes others can forgive him too.

I share these stories because I've found more similarities than differences between us and the people in prison. I've come to realise that "There go I but for the grace of God…" One mistake too many, one wrong decision, one sliding door moment, and it could've been me in prison. I don't want to be judged for my mistakes. Who does? I want to let the world know that there is always more than one view and that our undeserved stigma is created from the narrative we've heard and never questioned.

When I look beneath what makes us different, I see a wealth of what makes us the same. I share these stories because it makes me a better person when I challenge my invisible judgments and discover what my neighbour is like.

PRISON NOTES – SUMMER 2018

We've been working with Fats for a year. Today he told his story again about how he forgave the man who killed his baby girl to a group we ran in the prison chapel. We had forty guys in the room, and everyone was spellbound. This scrappy little guy was there, Jimmy, a lifer; he's already spent nineteen years in prison for killing someone. He could have got parole ten years ago, but he's been fighting everything. His prison life consists of spending as much time as possible in the "block" [2] for beating up staff and flat packing [3] his cell. With no family contact (unwilling to let them visit as he'd have to have closed [4] visits) and a drug addiction that kept him numb coupled with an attitude of "I'll die in here," Jimmy had given up. He told me we couldn't teach him anything. He'd seen it all before. He

24

ain't interested in our new bullshit. I asked him if he could sit for the day. He agreed but said he couldn't promise to return each three days. When Fats started speaking today, all of that changed. Fats' story landed on Jimmy like a thunderbolt. "If he can forgive the man that killed his daughter, maybe I can be forgiven too," he said. His eyes misted up; his shoulders relaxed; his face grew soft. He felt a spark of hope for the first time in nineteen years.

I invite you to view these people in prison from a new perspective. Prison is gritty but also full of potential, creativity, and possibility. And we can find solutions in this gritty place. Answers to the problems we face as a society; solutions to social injustice; solutions that will protect our communities; solutions that will resolve the underlying cause of crime.

I invite us all to put aside our judgments and beliefs for now. Let's see what we can uncover about the human condition and life.

Notes

1   In 2020 in the UK: 140,000 drivers admitted to driving while over the limit; 28,171 convictions for drink driving; 7,800 people injured or killed in an RTA involving a drunk driver. https://www.quittance.co.uk/uk-drink-driving-statistics

2   The Care and Support Unit – is a place where prisoners are isolated for infractions such as violence. It is used to protect prisoners who need to be segregated and punish prisoners by isolating them. More commonly known as The Block or Seg (segregation).

3   Prisoners who act out by smashing up their cells will remove sinks and fixed items from the wall and use these to barricade themselves in. Referred to as 'flat packing' by the guys in prison.

4   The family is only allowed to see the prisoner behind a screen and speak through a communication system such as a telephone. High risk prisoners or those likely to smuggle drugs into the prison, must have closed visits.

Who Are We Not to Shine?

"Believe you can and you're halfway there."
~Theodore Roosevelt

What would you do with your life if you knew how brilliant you were?

How did a woman with no experience in psychology, mental health or prison become passionate about being the voice for the voiceless? The story of my childhood is sad but not unusual: neglected, abused, and mistreated.

Dear Diary (July 1974),

For a bit this morning, I wondered what to feel about the way they made such a fuss over my birthday. I hadn't dared dream they would make it memorable. I stood in the doorway of our front room in my blue-striped pyjamas. I picked at the thread on my right sleeve. A warm glow slipped into my heart and lit up my hope.

"Well?" my mother said. Wide-eyed, I took in the battered dining table and chairs against the walls to make space for a large parcel wrapped in brown paper and tied with string. Blue and red balloons dotted the ceiling. Homemade posters pronounced "Happy Birthday," A pink birthday cake with ten candles sat beside three red plastic cups and a stack of pretty paper plates on the old dresser. I wondered at the absence of the fourth cup. A half-chewed dog biscuit, almost invisible, lay next to the dresser's legs. Mum's brown eyes danced. Apron tied at the waist, red hair pushed back, and a smidge of flour on her flushed face. I let myself hope that maybe ten is such a grown-up age it meant an end to childhood pain.

"Take the edge off?" Dad asked, his face a question mark. The pungent smell of whiskey in the missing red cup told me how stupid my hopes were.

As an adult, I was determined to claw my way out of the gutter I'd been born into. I wanted to be better than the way I was brought up. I designed a new identity for myself.

In 1984, I worked as a 'data input clerk' in a Builders Merchants. An office of eight women took the purchase notes from the counter where all the bricks and tools were sold, and we typed them into a computer system. This was the pre-Microsoft era. Everything was manual.

The colossal computer disks whirred in a large room

just behind us, and I'd see the Computer Manager, Ruth, going in every evening to remove the daytime disks and carry them down to an iron safe in the basement. Ruth was only about five feet four inches, so I would often help carry the disks, and we got to be friends. "I need an assistant," Ruth said one day as we sipped our sweet tea. The gigantic printers whirred and clicked as they spouted out the end-of-day reports. "I'll apply," I said and hugged her.

"What makes you think you can do the job?" The general manager sat behind his elephant desk; squinty eyes pierced me over the top of his silver-rimmed glasses. His thin hair was greased back from his stern, pale face.

"Well," I stuttered, my face hot from the closeness of the room and the threat of humiliation. I wished I could disappear and never have to face this man again. A sudden flush of indignation spread through my body and washed away the insecure thoughts. *Who am I NOT to do this job? What makes you think I can't?* I found a voice that didn't seem to be mine, that told him why I was capable and what I was capable of.

"You won't get your old job back if you fail," he warned.

"I won't fail!" I said and sat up straight in my chair.

That drove me.

I worked and studied for the next twenty years, went to night school and then university. I gained a Computer Science & Ergonomics degree, a master's degree in Networking Technologies and Management and the confidence to succeed. I started my own Project Management consultancy and climbed up the career ladder. By 2010, I'd got the Head of Operations and Customer Services position for a Premium Finance company. I showed him!

Despite my success and the life I'd built for myself, I'd painted myself into a corner. I was always worried about being found out as a fraud. I never felt good enough or that I knew enough. I spent more than I earned. I partied as hard as I worked and couldn't seem ever to feel good enough for the relationships I had. Something had to give.

Then several things happened: the Premium Finance company I worked for went into liquidation, my father died of cancer, and the housing market crashed. My world turned upside down. My life, already teetering on insanity, descended into chaos.

Yet there was a tiny spark of hope. I glimpsed my life behind me, as it had been, and apart from the birth of my son, I saw no meaning. I'd been living a life of masks and struggle. I believed that money and qualifications would fix the pain inside. I'd made no difference in the world.

The light from the path ahead was blurred. I couldn't see what would come, what I'd do, what difference I'd make, but I wanted to try.

I reflected on the months after my father died. The mixed emotions of grief, anger and confusion. The inability to cry. The stern refusal that the last five months of my time with him had meant anything.

"What the fuck?" I said out loud to the empty room in my father's two-up, two-down rented terraced house on a quiet street in Derby. His ex-wife and brother had swept through the house before his body was cold, taking anything they'd considered valuable. I'd been left with pots and pans in the kitchen and boxes of paperwork stacked on an old, chipped desk in the tiny bedroom he'd called a study.

The view from the window was of a graveyard behind

a church. Spring sunshine lit the room with rays of dust. I breathed a quiet into my body that I hadn't noticed before. A red paperclip under the desk caught my eye.

"Good luck finding a will," his ex-wife had said as she banged close the front door.

I plopped down on the floor, back against the cold cream wall, in the tight space between the desk and the window. I picked up a random sheet of printed paper that had escaped the boxes and hid under the desk on the thin brown carpet. The sunshine warmed my skin. I giggled at the heading, "Why should I forgive you?" It was by a Life Coach in Los Angeles called Michael Neill[5]. It talked about how holding a grudge is like drinking poison and expecting another person to die. It was a simple, funny little story, followed by a quip or two and an invitation to Supercoach, a training programme for new coaches.

Big fat juicy tears marked my cheeks with mascara as I sobbed out my pain.

I'd thought the whole thing was a bit silly; I didn't believe in all that spooky stuff, but I couldn't deny the relief I'd felt in that snug little corner.

I subscribed to Michael Neill's newsletters, and within a few months, I'd signed up to go to LA and participate in the Supercoach Academy training programme. I sold everything I could get my hands on to afford it. I even took an extra job. But somehow, it felt right. I wanted to discover myself and lead a meaningful life; this might help me do that.

Dear Diary (April 2011),

Supercoach is over! Today was the final day of the six months of training with Michael Neill to be a Life Coach. It's been one hell of a journey. I've loved flying to Santa Monica every month and the whirlwind of all the different teachers from around the world, and I've loved, loved, loved the other students. I like myself so much more now, and I've made friends for life. The Supercoach faculty has been amazing; so cool to hang out with them all. I think I fit in here; I think I've found a place I can be comfortable. I'm excited to see what I do next. I know now that I'm worthy and have such a lot to offer to the world.

That moment in Santa Monica reminds me of how little I knew about the journey ahead. I had no idea what I would do with my new qualification. I'd completed fifty hours of coaching to earn it, and I had experienced various techniques during the six months. And yet I felt unsure, unsteady and underqualified. But not like in the past. Not like the girl who was scared to get found out. There was a big difference. And the difference was I had learned to like myself.

Notes

5   Michael Neill's website https://www.michaelneill.org/

What's Stopping Me?

"When we do the best we can, we never know what miracle is wrought in our life, or in the life of another."
~ Helen Keller

In the moment of a good feeling, like the one I had on the way back from Supercoach Academy, I think the world around me will transform like magic, and I'll "know" what to do next. Yet that wasn't my experience. Yes, I now had a new direction, and a renewed sense of purpose, but I still didn't know how to earn a living. Well, not the one I was used to. I had an executive apartment with a baby grand piano and a convertible Audi TT on the drive, but I no longer earned enough to pay the mortgage or even put fuel in the car. I spent the next couple of years trying to figure out what to do next and how to keep up the lifestyle I'd been accustomed to. That didn't work out!

Starting a brand-new business is hard, and it takes a while to build trust and credibility. Time I didn't have. I soon realised I needed to get a paid job and do a drastic downsizing. I'd built a fortress made of sand. All the time I'd accumulated material goods, I'd just added to the anchor around my neck. It took me a while to see this. Because I'd been so busy in my head worried about "how" to make it work, I couldn't know that I didn't need a solution; I needed to reframe the problem. I'd been so concerned that if I didn't live in a posh area or drive a nice car, it would say something about me — that I'd failed, that my father had been right about me all along: "know all, know nothing,"

I spent a year trying to figure out how to stay where I was until one day, I woke up and saw that the only way to move on was to do something different. That meant giving it all up and starting with a clean slate.

It sounds scary, right? Well, it was, until I realised what I was doing to myself was painful. I was peddling backwards, trying to hold on. And when I stopped peddling, I found a flow I didn't know existed.

As I let go of the old me, the masks I'd worn all my life started to fall away. When my job didn't define me, I could do any job! When I wasn't being judged by the house I lived in, I could live anywhere. When I wasn't being defined by my qualifications, I could begin again.

I decided to minimise my life and do something I was passionate about. It was during this time that I met Rob, my future husband. I wasn't interested in dating; I was too busy redesigning my life, but he seemed nice enough, so I agreed to have a meal with him. One mild day in April 2012, he came to pick me up to take me out for dinner. I'd called him the night before and warned him not to be fooled by the appearance of my living standards. "My flash car and the posh apartment are an illusion," I told him. "They are not me." He told me later that my vulnerability and honesty appealed to him.

By our second date, I'd started to sell my worldly goods, so there were gaps on walls where art used to hang and marks on the plush cream carpet where the piano used to stand. "I've got news!" I said.

Rob was sitting on the burgundy leather sofa in the open-plan living room of my executive apartment in Solihull. April sunshine flooded through the double doors that led to the patio and open fields beyond. His long legs took up much of the sofa, and he sat with a bemused look on his handsome face, blue eyes intrigued and attentive.

I held a gigantic rolled-up map in my right hand and a wad of Blu Tack in my left. I knew I had finally broken months of stalemate with a master plan of adventure. "I'm going to travel the world!" I announced.

I unrolled the map and fixed it to one of the big empty spaces on the wall, and that sad corner of the room was transformed into a land of dreams. I outlined my plan: "I met many people at Supercoach who live all over the world — the States, Europe, Scandinavia, everywhere! I'm going to hand over the keys to the properties I own that are all in negative equity, hand the keys to the car over to the finance people, and I'm going to get the hell out of Dodge. I'll get a job, save every penny I can for the next six months, and then get a job on a boat or something and make my way across the world. I'll work where I need to, coach people where I can, and visit all of these people I know. What do you think?"

Rob said it was a crazy plan and accused me of being "as mad as a box of frogs," but he smiled and, with a wink, said, "I'll track you down."

I did save every penny I could. The bailiffs fetched the keys to my house and car. I downsized to a flat in Moseley and got myself a job as an administrator for an Estate Agent. I found bits of work I could do in the evenings to build up my savings. Wherever I saw the possibility of putting another pound or so in my savings pot, I did it. For instance, if I bought something and returned it, I would save the money from the return. I would put the money in my savings if I wanted a coffee, but didn't buy it. It surprised me how these few pounds and pence built up. Like my mother used to say, "Look after the pennies and the pounds look after themselves." My mindset went from one of lack to one of abundance. Instead of repeating affirmations about how wealthy I was, I was making my life happen, penny by penny, step by step.

While my head was focused on this new plan, my heart had other ideas.

After many years of being single and only dating for fun, I cherished my weekends with Rob. He would leave on a Monday morning, back to his busy job and life, hundreds of miles away from me, and my spirits would sink. Our times together were full of laughter and conversations, and joy. I'd fallen in love. Drat, I hadn't planned for that! My world tour would have to wait. I wasn't going anywhere without this fantastic creature.

I wondered what I could do instead.

The Catalyst

"There's magic in stories, magic in hope,
and magic in coming together."

~ Sharad Vivek Sagar

A chance meeting, a look in a new direction, is all it takes to discover a new path.

During the days of creating myself as a Life Coach, I'd signed up for lots of business network meetings. These events are often held in the early morning hours when it seems the rest of the world still sleeps. They're hosted by one organisation, and other businesses send a representative. Everyone stands up and "pitches" for sixty seconds about their business. It's an opportunity to network with other companies over breakfast or, less often, lunch or dinner. One wet Thursday morning, I dragged myself out of my cosy bed and dressed up for the breakfast meeting called BOB (Business Over Breakfast).

As I walked into the venue, a squat man in an open shirt and dark jeans said, "Hello." His thick blond hair was swept back, and dark-rimmed glasses framed a young-looking face like a cartoon character. "I'm a filmmaker and a recovering drug addict." I was intrigued.

The restaurant was bright with tasteful chandeliers and decorated in calm tones. Tables had been moved together to create one extended eating area in the middle of the room, big enough for thirty people. Smells of bacon, eggs, and buttery toast exuded from the kitchen. A shiny penny stuck out from under one of the table legs. A light buzz of chatter and laughter came from the business people who stood around in groups. "Hello," I said and smiled at the filmmaker.

I'd only ever met "suits" at these events before. People with businesses who wanted to sell something. This guy was different. Over the next two hours, he told me his story. He'd been in recovery for three years using the 12-Steps[6]. He'd been addicted to most drugs, including crack cocaine and heroin. He'd also spent time in prison and stated that his life had turned around from "death, destruction and disease" to putting all his skills into creating a social enterprise to make films and to help socially disadvantaged people learn the intricacies of film production. I was fascinated.

We found an immediate connection and chatted like old friends. His attitude and determination inspired me. I wanted to know more. We met again a couple of weeks later. Within a few months, I'd taken a voluntary position on the Board of Directors for his community interest company to help him in any way I could. He helped everybody. He did home detoxes and volunteered to help people turn their lives around. I was often by his side, so I met many other people with addictions and mental health issues. Many had been in prison, had traumatic lives, and experienced homelessness. And they were all amazing! They were resilient, persistent, determined, and creative, but they couldn't see this about themselves. Their stories helped me overcome the shame I'd felt. Shame for things that'd been out of my control. Shame for being a girl.

Dear Diary (July 1977),

I can't believe my cousin would be in on it. I've always loved Elizabeth; I thought she was my friend. My thirteenth birthday is next week, but instead of giving me a present, she just fired instructions at me. She didn't seem upset about getting me ready for those beasts. My skin crawled with anxiety as she washed and scrubbed me in the bathtub. I wish she would scrub my skin off and make it bleed. "Don't whimper," she said. "Just do as you're told, and you'll be OK." I tried to keep still while she fixed a sheaf of oak leaves to my crotch as a makeshift thong and taped a leaf to each of my rose-pink nipples. She said I looked like Eve and patted some light foundation onto my cheeks.

I'm so ashamed. I should've run away. I should've screamed. I should've refused. But I was so scared I didn't know what to do. I didn't know if it would be worse if I played up. So I decided to suck it up and get on with it. My "job" today was to serve Dad and his work buddies at their celebration lunch. "Come on, girl!" he shouted when I stood in our narrow dining room doorway – holding the blue china gravy boat, filled to the brim with hot brown, steaming gravy.

Heavy red velvet curtains drawn tight across the bay window blocked the sun and any nosy neighbours. The dining table in the centre of the room was stacked with plates of meat, steaming vegetables and bottles of red wine, "Bulls Blood", they called it. My "guests" faces were flushed with the first hit of the wine. Excitement hid the shame.

"OK," I said. I forced a bright voice and approached the table of greedy eyes.

The people in the recovery community welcomed me as one of their own. I felt like I'd come home. I was humbled by their stories and decided that my problems and traumas paled to insignificance next to what they had faced. I was in awe at their strength. I noticed how stigmatised they were and how they felt the brunt of this stigmatism. They told me they felt limited and lonely and that their self-esteem and confidence had been ground down.

I admired them and knew I could help them see they didn't need to restrict or limit themselves. Something I had learned about the mind could be the key to unlock the potential I could see in these fantastic but forgotten people.

For the whole of that summer of 2012, I worked in an estate agent's office and, in my spare time, read everything I could on addiction. I researched addiction and how it is viewed and treated, and I was shocked. I discovered that ninety percent of all interventions assume addiction is a disease. That people never recover. The best you can do is educate people to stop them from harming themselves[7] and keep them medicated.

Or enrol them in a 12-Step program for the rest of their lives.

I knew there must be another way. I didn't believe that people could be broken. I knew there was something more hopeful than what these papers alluded to. I found some research and books on asset-based recovery, but these findings were few and far between. I thought *someone had to do something about this.* If addiction was a product of Thought, as I knew it to be, it meant more people could recover; there would be more understanding of addiction and less fear of relapse. Someone needed to tell the world about this.

The stigma individuals faced would be eliminated if the general population saw how normal it is to experience obsessive thinking. Someone needed to shout about this and create a different reality for all of us.

I noticed that the shame people faced was often made worse in their reality through their own beliefs and feelings about themselves. They found it hard to excel when they believed the world was against them. Someone needed to help these fantastic people see their true selves and uncover the resilience, creativity and potential within them. Someone needed to show them that there is always a greater potential available. Someone needed to end the stigma and the suffering and help them see that our thoughts create our reality.

That someone turned out to be me.

Notes

6   The 12-Steps, also known as Alcohol Anonymous or AA. The AA program has helped a lot of people all over the world find sobriety and serenity. It was co-founded from an insight by Bill W (Wilson)

7   A particular philosophy known as 'harm reduction', is where instead of getting people clean, you keep them on medications and teach them about how different substances interact with each other physiologically. https://www.hri.global/what-is-harm-reduction

You Can Do Anything

"The cave you fear to enter holds the treasure
you seek."

~ Joseph Campbell

The Supercoach Academy with Michael Neill had introduced
me to an understanding of mental wellbeing called the Three
Principles[8]. It's based on people finding solutions through
personal insight. It seemed too simple, so I disregarded it at
the time. I'd even wondered if it could be some sort of cult!
This understanding is based on the premise that all human
beings have everything we need within us and that our true
essence can never be broken. To be honest, I could see that
might be true for other people but "it ain't true for me." If all
the answers are inside me, why can't I find them? There was
a lot of talk about insight, and I couldn't really get to grips
with what that meant. It didn't seem to me I'd ever had an
insight, or that I was even capable of these huge transformational type insights others talked about.

Then, when I started volunteering in the recovery community, I noticed they had "lightbulb" moments with ease.

We'd have deep conversations about how our experience of reality is created in our own minds, and I saw them have insights they hadn't considered before about situations they were in. It was clear that when people were caught up in their heads they couldn't see solutions, were more likely to become frustrated, angry or agitated, and feelings of hopelessness would limit them. On the flip side, when they got reflective or were light-hearted, they were more hopeful and could see more potential, which led to seeing opportunities.

In short, when our minds are not focussed on our problems, we find new solutions we hadn't considered before. They taught me that life gets easier when you don't think so much! I became curious about how this Three Principles understanding could help people more than I'd first realised, and I noticed that my own life seemed easier, despite my dramatic change in circumstances. Disregarding what had struck me as the "woo-woo," I boiled down the understanding to: "When people feel inspired, they take positive action; and when they feel daunted, it's easier to give up." I wanted to know more.

In spring of 2013, I went along to the annual Three Principles conference (3PUK) in London. I'd been before, but this time I listened with different ears. Instead of being judgmental and trying to figure things out, I was curious and open. I stopped trying to fit in what was being talked about with what I already knew and was willing to hear something fresh. I mean "every day's a school day" right? So why wouldn't I quiet my mind and see if I could learn? That quiet space helped me to listen as if I were a child. I just soaked it all in. I didn't try to understand. I didn't try to remember. I didn't try to see if I agreed or disagreed. No analysis or comparisons. I just listened.

One of the speakers, Elsie Spittle, was doing the final presentation of the event. I had enjoyed the weekend and was ready to go home. Still, for some reason, I stayed. "Oh wow!" said Elsie, a little round lady with a beautiful big smile that lit up her gentle face. Her grey trousers were complemented by a loose, midnight blue top, a tiny daisy pinned to the buttonhole. She stood very still on the stage in her cute little red shoes, hands folded in front of her. The large auditorium was packed with around five hundred people sitting on plastic chairs lined up next to each other, about ten rows deep.

I was flushed with the socialising and conversations of the last few days and felt sleepy in the hot room, so I wasn't really listening to Elsie's talk. My mind drifted, and then inside my own head, I heard these words: *You can do anything.* I tingled all over. The rest of the room faded. I felt clear and confident. I sat bolt upright in my hard chair. The words seemed so commonplace – "You can do anything" – and yet they felt huge. Like I'd suddenly realised it meant I could do ANYTHING I wanted. I drove home that night in a fog of tired inspiration. It was like I had won the lottery or discovered a secret no one knew. Everything felt different in a way I couldn't put my finger on and couldn't explain.

I found out a couple of years later *that* was an insight. It made me laugh to see that insight is so commonplace we don't even know what it is. Even without knowing that it was an insight, my life changed. I didn't know what it all meant, but each step I took revealed more about what to do next. I felt inspired and somehow lighter. I considered how

45

I could turn my passion to uncover the potential I had seen in marginalised people into something I could do full time.

Another strange thing was that as my mind focussed on this new possibility, I met people who helped me along the way. I just followed what was in front of me, doing whatever seemed like the thing to do next. The more I did this, the easier life was, and the more things worked out. My whole way of life had turned inside out. It went from being driven to be good enough and to have enough, to seeing that I already am enough and have enough. My mindset switched from aiming to achieve, to seeing where I could be of service.

That year, 2013, I'd had a knee operation that laid me up for six weeks to recover. It gave me a lot of time to reflect. I had all sorts of worries about how I could follow my passion but still pay my rent. I was insecure about whether I knew enough about this new understanding to be able to help people. But I knew that it didn't help to dwell on insecure thoughts.

Out of the blue, I volunteered to interview people for a film about the upcoming Recovery Walk in Birmingham in September. I'd still be walking with a stick, but it felt right to do it. I didn't know about an inner voice, or that my life was about to take another turn.

Notes

8   The Three Principles of Mind, Consciousness & Thought as realised and taught by Sydney Banks https://sydbanks.com/

The Insight in the Park

"We make the path by walking it."

~Simon Morgan

I loved volunteering at the Recovery Walk in Birmingham on a beautiful Saturday in September 2013. The walk is a celebration of people who are in recovery from any form of mental anguish, including addiction and alcoholism. It's held every year in the autumn in the United Kingdom and thousands of people turn up from all over the country to be together, march together, sing together and demonstrate that "people can and do recover." I met with the film crew at Victoria Square early in the morning to get our orders for the day. I'd brought them all bacon butties[9] and we got fresh brewed coffee from one of the market stalls close by. A feeling of joy and celebration filled the air as busloads of people turned up from places as far and wide as Scotland, Lancashire, and Cornwall.

My job was to interview people on the two-mile journey to the park where the Recovery Celebrations would be held. My walk was slow, with a walking stick to support my knee, but my heart was full. I interviewed people and cheered others as we went along.

When we got to the park, I took a breath to let it all sink in. I'd just finished an interview with a lady who sat on a bench at the edge of the park. "It's just been lovely," she said. I could feel the softness of the green grass beneath the soles of my sturdy trainers. The trees that surrounded the wide-open space sparkled with rays of warm sunlight, imbuing the edge of the inner-city park with a magical aura of beauty. The air vibrated with songs of hope from the bandstand. Smells of coffee, cake, samosas, and cheese caressed my senses. Chatter and raucous laughter came from groups of people sitting on blankets and coats. A squished piece of gum had stuck to the bottom of my long brown walking stick. I'd forgotten the pain in my swollen knee and the sweat on my back from the tough walk.

"Thank you," I said. A whoosh of light and sunshine exploded inside me. I felt drenched in love. My heart expanded and raced so fast I felt it was about to burst out of my chest, like a cartoon character who'd fallen in love. I stared at the ragtag groups of people in the park and love for them exuded from my every pore. I felt blinded by this light and love. In that moment, I could only think of one thing: I wanted to work with them. I wanted to serve them; I wanted to show them the beauty I saw in them. I didn't know how to do that, or why I wanted to do it, or how this would pay my bills, or even how I would start. But I didn't care, I just knew that this is what I had to do.[10]

Seconds later, I saw a tall man with a shock of dark hair who stood alone, watching the crowd. Full of this incredible force, I struck up a conversation with him. He told me his name was Simon and that he hated crowds. He asked if I would walk with him to get a coffee. We'd only just met, but words rushed out of me that I didn't even understand myself at the time. I told him that our reality is created by our own thoughts, that nobody can be broken. His face crinkled into a frown, and I rushed on about how the potential to thrive is always alive inside every human being. Simon's face softened, and the frown turned into curiosity. He was a Recovery Activist, a Socialist and a student of psychology and philosophy. He was the service manager of an addiction organisation and ran a group for people in recovery in the city of Coventry. "You should come and talk to my group," he said.

A couple of weeks later I did go to see his group. A diverse collection of individuals in recovery from all sorts of drug and alcohol related issues. They called themselves the Coventry Recovery Community (CRC), and they met once a week on Tuesday evenings, on the top floor of a tall grey building, due to be demolished, in the centre of Coventry.

The first night, I walked in full of nerves and I walked out with loads of new friends. Each week, this group met to support each other, and Simon and his team were there as volunteers, providing tea, coffee, biscuits, and interesting topics to discuss. All sorts of community projects were started out of that little group: a cooking project; an outreach to the local homeless population; an art class; and many others. On that first evening of my visit, I just told them why I was so happy to be there and that I'd stumbled across something that might be helpful to them. My words tripped over themselves with anxiety, but the people were gentle and supportive. I felt accepted. I walked away that evening flushed with the conversation and with a feeling of hope that maybe I could do something meaningful.

After that, Simon would send me people he knew struggled with their recovery from alcohol or drugs. The people who found life difficult. He said, "Summit different may help these guys, they're desperate." Each time, I was pushed out of my comfort zone—I often felt like I didn't know enough, or I couldn't deal with this particular situation. I just slowed my mind down and listened, and if something occurred to me, I would say it. I pointed them back to their own advice and showed them where I could see they'd got answers but hadn't realised it. I felt hope for all of them. I saw the purity in all of them, the psychological innocence. I knew they were all OK despite what they'd done, or what they'd been through. They felt inspired. They felt heard. They felt hope.

I wondered about ways I could support them more. I was able to get some part time work as a Support Worker[11] at a university, so I could offer my "coaching" to these guys free of charge. People often ask me about how to follow their dream or purpose and still be able to pay their bills. My advice is do something that pays the bills. That way you don't have to think about money. If there is a way of doing what you love and being paid for it, it will show up along the way; not when you think it should, but when the time is right.

I kept going to Simon's group, and I did several days of one-to-one coaching with his tribe. One day, I walked into his office and Simon said, "It's Beyond Recovery!" I frowned with misunderstanding. "The guys and girls you've worked with say you don't help them to get into recovery, you show them that there's life BEYOND recovery." I liked the story and so the name stuck.

Each step I took uncovered a deeper sense of purpose and meaning for me. Each moment of resilience seen in another person's eyes revealed to me my own resilience, my own creativity. In each moment of clarity, someone had defined my own path and shown me that I didn't need to run away or travel around the world; that all the time the path had been there, waiting for me to see it.

Notes

9   Buttie – slang for a bacon sandwich.
10 A video of the Volcano moment https://youtu.be/tqidMLuVa1s
11 A Support Worker works with people who need help at university, taking notes in class, helping with research, organisation and deadlines.

Getting Comfortable
with Being
Uncomfortable

"If the only thing people learned was not to
be afraid of their experience, that alone would
change the world."

~Sydney Banks

I continued to volunteer my time with Coventry Recovery Community (CRC), and work part time at university. And it felt as though I'd discovered a whole world of possibility. I created programmes and a methodology. I researched what sort of businesses had social values. Every time I got stuck or felt unsure about what I was doing, I would just do something simple: like concentrate on the student support work I was doing, or take a walk, or fix up a nice meal for Rob. I felt like an adventurer in an unknown land of immense and incredible beauty, in shoes that weren't quite fit for the job. I'd get overwhelmed with how much I didn't know, and then I would feel overjoyed at new discoveries or at small steps forward. I'd get frightened that I didn't have a clue what I was doing or why. And then, I'd feel like I was a pioneer creating a brand-new world. I'd get insecure at how small and insignificant I felt. And then I'd feel like I was going to change the world. I rode the different emotions the best I could, strapping my seat belt in and holding my breath when it was turbulent, then relaxing again as things calmed down.

Dear Diary (July 1978),

Uncle Paddy's back in Winson Green prison. I heard Dad taunting Mum again earlier. "Being a drunk runs in the family," he said. Mum sat on the edge of the wooden stairs, her head in her hands, auburn hair spilled over her face. Puke lined the grey washing-up bowl beneath her. "You make me sick," he said.

I don't know why they're so horrible about Uncle Paddy, he doesn't mean any badness. He just gets carried away and ends up in a fight. He's always kind to me. My favourite day in the whole world was when we had a picnic in the garden on blankets. We laughed and laughed, and everything seemed right in the world. He said I was "a bright bairn," It was the kindest thing anyone's ever said to me.

A fella I met at one of the recovery groups was a facilitator at Birmingham Prison[12] for SMART Recovery[13]. He introduced me to Trevor, the Head of Substance Misuse at the prison, and invited me to sit in on one of his groups. I was excited, although nervous, at the idea of going into the prison my uncle had been in, so I jumped at the chance.

After going through the security gates and having my bags scanned on the huge grey metal scanner, I sat and waited for Trevor. I had no idea what to expect and jumped every time a gate clanged or a bell rang. Trevor, a tall, gentle man, picked me up from the security gate and gave a bit of a tour as we walked through the prison. He pointed out various buildings with thick barbed wire, where the residents lived. We even passed a group of residents on their way to one of the work buildings. "Hello miss," said one of the guys. A broad smile displayed off white jagged teeth. Long locs tied up in a blue cloth. High vis jacket bright against the grey day. I was so relieved he'd been nice!

"Hi," I said.

I asked Trevor, "Is it OK to speak to the guys?" He told me it was. I laugh now at how naïve I was. I'd no idea what the protocol was or what goes on inside a prison.

It took forever to get to the group room in the substance misuse block. It seemed there were hundreds of big metal gates and huge, long corridors. When we arrived at the dull room with blue chairs and a small kitchen area, Trevor offered a cup of coffee. "Ah," I thought. "Home comforts," but that was before I tasted the foul-tasting drink! My surprise and disappointment made me laugh. What was I expecting? A Vanilla Latte with chocolate sprinkles on top?!

A group of residents filtered in, all of them chatty and all of them interested in why I was there. Once the guys were inside the room, I relaxed. Conversations with these guys were what I loved doing. I soon forgot where I was. Time passed and no SMART facilitator turned up. More time passed. And more time passed. I enjoyed talking to the guys and felt comfortable until Trevor said, "Oh well, why don't you run the group instead?" BOOM.

Twelve pairs of eyes waited in the hushed room. Sweat gathered on the back of my neck beneath my blue polo shirt. I could feel the cloth chair beneath my hands, now tucked under my legs to keep them steady.

"Life is easier than we think," I began. With no preparation, there I was in Birmingham Prison, running my first group. Before that moment, I'd always said I couldn't run groups. In that moment, I forgot all that and had the time of my life. Soon it was time to leave, and I didn't want to stop. I loved being with the guys, and I loved our discussion about life and how it works.

As we left the unit and walked back down the long corridors to the main gate, I was aware of Trevor's chit-chat, but all I could hear was my own excitement. "I can run groups! And I love it." Being thrown in the deep end like that had shifted my mindset. All the insecure thinking I'd had prior to that moment was washed away with the new awareness that running a group is just like having a conversation with more than one person. Even when my little insecure voice tried to add doubt, I didn't mind. I saw those doubts for what they were, just my ego trying to protect me when there was nothing I needed to be protected from.

In short, I got comfortable with being uncomfortable. This has been a recurring theme in my life and in my journey with Beyond Recovery. Each time I'm uncomfortable and have my insecurity telling me I'm not good enough, or that I can't do something or that I'm afraid, I just sit with that feeling – I know that if I try to fix those wayward thoughts, I'll just buy into the idea that they are real. When in fact, just being OK with being uncomfortable shows your mind that you are not afraid of feeling afraid, and clarity soon follows.

Notes

12   Also known as HMP Winson Green (or The Green).

13   SMART Recovery is an international non-profit organization that aids individuals seeking abstinence from addiction. SMART stands for Self-Management and Recovery Training. The SMART approach is secular and science-based, using cognitive behavioural therapy and non-confrontational motivational methods https://www.smartrecovery.org/

And Death Came Third

"The mind is its own place and in itself can make a
heaven of hell, a hell of heaven."

~John Milton

There are moments when I get a glimpse of infinite poten-
tiality. A flash of what's possible when my heart expands to
the bursting point. They are quick and powerful and raise
my little mind to look beyond time, space, and matter.

One warm Autumn Day, I drove home from my tiny
attic office above the hairdressers. It was a typical day. My
mind drifted with the slow traffic. As I pulled onto the
drive of the apartments I lived in with Rob, I had a random
thought: "This is bigger than me."

"Yes!" I said. "This is not about me coaching people one-
to-one; it's greater than that. I don't know what it is, but I do
know I need people around me who can help." Four names
popped into my head at that moment. Three of them became
my first directors; the fourth became a client!

I love how life unfolds.

A couple of weeks later, on the same drive, I thought, "I'll
be talking about my work in front of thousands of people."

"Whoa!!" I said out loud to no one. "You've got the wrong girl here."

That couldn't be possible. My lifelong fear of public speaking has been reinforced time and time again.

I remember when I excelled at an application for a dream job at a university.

After weeks of interviews and application forms, all the candidates were invited to a *Dragon's Den*-type interview. We spent the day together and were given several tasks to complete. The assessors evaluated us on a list of attributes. At the end of the day, each candidate gave an individual presentation. That was the part I dreaded most. But I'd prepared well and planned to look them in the eyes and do my best. I guessed there would probably be a panel of around five; even I could cope with that.

"We are doing this in alphabetical order," the coordinator stated. As Bennett, I was first.

My crisp white blouse stuck to my body with sweat. The inside of my mouth felt like the bottom of a bird's cage. I tried to steady my nerves.

"You'll be OK," she said as she fitted a Madonna-style microphone to my head.

I walked into the two-hundred seat auditorium to find it was packed with people from all over the university. "Here's the clicker," the coordinator said. The impressive bright room was theatre style, with endless rows of plush red velvet seats. People sat with their packed lunches and bags of crisps. A low-level hum of chatter filled the room. Eyes bulged at me from every corner. Red mouths opened and closed and chomped—judgements perched on every seat. My naked body was laid bare, revealing all its dark secrets. My leaden tongue lay useless. Shame dripped onto the sodden notes in my shaking hand.

"Hello," I said.

The thing I'm most proud of now is that I made it to the end without wetting my knickers. It was close! The sweet interviewer lady called a few days later. "I'm sorry you didn't get the job." I was relieved.

"What happened?" she asked. "You excelled in every area, apart from the presentation. You were, in fact, our front-runner up." I gave some lame excuses and reminded myself that I would never be able to get over my fear of public speaking.

It's not an unusual fear, is it? A study from 1984[14] on social anxiety concluded that death came third on the list of people's biggest fears. The first two are "walking into a room full of strangers" and "speaking in public."

So, imagine my surprise at that thought from earlier, "I'll be standing on stage, talking about my work in front of thousands of people." I saw the applause, the lights, and the podium. I even imagined myself apologising for my nervousness! I woke up out of this day-mare with a shudder. "No way!" I said. "Not me!" I said. "NO WAY!" I said again.

The trouble was the thought kept occurring. And occurring. And occurring. I couldn't shake it. I wasn't doing anything spectacular with my life, so why would this public speaking malarkey be relevant to me? In time, I wondered if I should get some training or practice or something. I still dreaded the idea, but I'd rather be prepared than keep saying, "I can't."

It amazes me that when I stop thinking about why I shouldn't do something, ways to get it done come to mind.

Not long after I'd had this change of perspective, the idea occurred to me to look for opportunities to speak, present, tell my story, or tell any story. I discovered that many breakfast meetings liked having someone with inspirational stories at the start, and most of the speakers were quite dull, so I felt in good company. Of course, I wasn't that good either. I'd feel sick to my stomach each time. But I saw it all as practice, as an experiment. I tried different topics, different styles, and different audiences. I still felt the nerves, my hands shook, and my mouth dried. I'd have all the insecurities, but I tried to concentrate on what worked instead of what didn't.

Each time I learned something new. I forgot the nerves when I enjoyed the subject. I noticed people were interested when I told stories. I saw it went better when I spoke from the heart. I also learned to forgive myself when it didn't go so well and move on.

I noticed I could get over feeling bad.

Some gigs were worse than others. I remember one occasion when I cried because it seemed so terrible, and I vowed I would never do it again. I volunteered to do a short presentation for Recovery Month.

"We are all diamonds inside," I said. The old theatre in the centre of Newcastle was packed to the gills with people. Every room and every space was utilised for talks and activities. I'd been given the foyer on the second floor, right in the middle of a sweeping set of double staircases. The small space was jaggedy and awkward. With its curved breast, a dark mahogany bar took up most of the room. Stools and small tables were placed ad hoc for the audience of people hungry to hear something useful that would help them on their recovery journey. I held little white crib cards in front of my blurred eyes. Anxiety washed over me in waves. I wondered if I could dash it.

"Sorry," someone said as they crashed and clattered around the bend of the stairs.

I bombed. I was nervous. My words came out wrong. The audience looked bored. I felt ridiculous. I kept going, reached the end and said. "Thank you."

The kind audience clapped. I took my props and escaped. I ran down the stairs, out of the building, past the people who wanted to chat, away from everyone, everything. But I couldn't escape myself. I slumped onto a low wall, head in hand.

I called Rob. "Did anyone die?" he inquired.

A small giggle escaped my sobs. "No," I answered, "but it was awful."

"Is it you who thinks that, or did someone throw tomatoes?"

"Stop it!" I said.

A girl said, "Wow, I never knew I had a diamond inside. Thank you so much." I told Rob.

"So, what's the problem?" he asked. "If you've impacted one person, I'd call that a job well done."

He was right. The only thing that hurt was my ego. I licked my wounds and decided to try again and see if I could improve.

So, I did. I kept putting myself forward. I tried different things, and after about a year of many talks and presentations, I started to find my voice. The voice that had been muted as a child. The voice that spoke with compassion and love. The voice that had been hiding inside all along.

Notes

14 And Death Came Third, by Andy Lopata & Peter Roper.

Addiction is Not a Disease

"I realised that my thoughts of using drugs in prison are just thoughts."

~ Beyond Recovery Participant

The people I'd met and my experiences with public speaking showed me repeatedly that reality looks different to different people at other times. I wanted to know if this was true, and if it was, what the impact would be if everyone knew our experience of reality is temporary. My research took me to a book by Dr Jack Pransky, *Somebody Should Have Told Us.* The book describes "separate realities", and I was startled to realise that everyone on the planet lives in their separate reality created by the thinking and the mood in each moment. For instance, I can get annoyed at another driver on the road for being inconsiderate, but that driver may not think his action is selfish. He may not have even noticed that he did something. I'm in my reality of seeing the bad behaviour, and he is in his reality of thinking about a dinner date (or something else). Understanding this was a massive help for my relationships: I'd always assumed everyone understood what was going on in my head or could see what was "obvious." Now I started to get curious about what was going on for them.

I followed Jack's work and was delighted to find a post on one of the social media platforms asking for help to turn his book *Modello*[15], into a documentary. I reached out to see if I could assist, and out of the blue, he mentioned he would be passing through Birmingham on his European book tour. "We have a spare room if you need a place to stay," I said, my tongue stuck into my cheek. I mean, I barely knew the guy! The lush green trees outside my window were full of sunshine and birdsong. I stared at the bird poo on my window ledge. "That'd be fantastic," Jack replied.

Jack was friends with another lady in Birmingham, so I planned for the three of us to meet for coffee. The afternoon was full of laughter and deep conversations about how the world is created within our minds. They helped me see that we use the power of Thought to experience what we see. I'd always imagined that we see the world and interpret it. They told me it was the other way around. "But this chair is real," I said, tapping the back of his ornate seat at the Syrian-style cafe in Moseley village.

"We can say the chair is real," Jack said. The soft glow from the gold lampshades lit up his gentle face. The aroma of coffee and honey filled the air. "But how you experience the chair comes from you. If you even notice the chair at all. How many times have you walked past it and not seen it? One person may think the chair is comfortable; another thinks it's hard. One day it's just a chair; another day, it's an important chair; another day, it's in the way. All these feelings come from within your mind. They are not emitted from the chair."

We talked about how that was true for people, too, that they cannot make me think anything; they do not create my feelings; they are just people. How I experience people and their actions is within my mind.

By the end of the afternoon, my head spun, but I felt better than I had in a long time. I wanted to skip back to where Rob and I lived.

The months passed, and I talked to everyone about this new way of understanding life and addiction. I met with countless addiction agencies; none of them were interested. I spoke to my 12-Step friends; they were sceptical. I volunteered with clients; they were impacted! Seeing their faces light up after years of trauma was all I needed to keep going.

PRISON NOTES – DECEMBER 2015

I asked the guys what they thought about addiction today. Osman put his hand up. It surprised me as he is so shy, but he's getting out next week, and he said he wanted to let us know how much had changed for him. "I thought I had an addiction on drugs an' crack an' heroin an' that. But when I came to jail, I realised that I didn't have an addiction cos when I came to jail, I couldn't get hold of the drugs and I knew I didn't have an addiction because I weren't running around to get it! So, in my mind, I thought I had an addiction. But now I know that was just in my head; when I was buzzing, I wanted to get buzzed and drunk and whatever. So now,

> I feel that addiction is just an excuse to take drugs. I
> know that me, myself, don't need it. I feel better without
> it as well. And I can get on with my life."

It's not just what I've seen with the guys and girls I work
with. I come from a long line of addicts. If anyone had a pre-
disposition for addiction, that'd be me and my son, Darren.
My mother, uncle, and father have all had issues with alcohol
and addiction demons. Back then, I was just a party girl and
partied like I did everything else. Hard. I was proud of my
ability to drink others under the table. Drink made me the
life and soul of the party and took away my anxiety and
nerves. I'd hated what booze did to my parents, the rows, the
noise, the debauchery. The first time I got drunk at fifteen, I
ended up flat on my face in a neighbour's garden at the end
of our street. But none of that stopped me. I could never drink
one glass. I didn't see the point. So, every time I drank, I got
drunk. Blind drunk. Falling over drunk. And I made a mess.

I remember the day that booze became a staple of my
life. I'd got myself into Aston University to prove I wasn't
stupid. I was a mature student and hung out with a group of
drinkers. After a heavy party session in the dark students'
bar, I walked through the sunny streets towards the bus
stop, towards home. I thought, "Life's so much nicer when
drunk." For the next fifteen years, I was either drunk, hung
over, or thinking about a night out. I functioned well; I
secured two degrees, held down good jobs, and even started
my own business. I never thought I was a problem drinker,
but I never went an evening without a drink.

When I met Rob in 2012, we both partied hard. It caused
issues in our relationship with insecurities and jealousy.

We'd row, and I'd cry. It did nothing for my self-esteem, so I wondered about giving up alcohol but couldn't see how I'd have fun without it. I'd also started hanging out with many sober people through my work in the recovery community, and I'd been seeing the devastation substances cause. By then, I'd also attended many "dry" events, parties, and dinners without alcohol. Although it had seemed strange at first, I'd become used to having a night out without a drink.

Unnoticed, my attitude towards alcohol had shifted.

"I will be with you in half an hour," Rob said. He was on his way from his home in Hemel Hempstead, to spend the weekend with me. I'd prepared a delicious steak dinner; the kitchen was filled with exotic smells. Soft music played in the background, and bee-friendly candles dotted the small tables in the living room. The tiny dining table, crafted from old pallets, was laid with my best paper tablecloth, napkins, and crystal glasses I'd rescued from a charity shop. I wore my favourite red, swirly dress with velvet kitten heels, my long ginger hair piled high on my head in a twist. Excitement coursed through my veins.

"Wow!" I said. I'd clocked that there was no wine. At that moment, I realised we hadn't had an alcoholic drink for over three weeks. It was never a conscious decision; it just happened. I'd stopped buying alcohol. We hadn't been out, and Rob had stopped asking. "Who will get the wine in?"

We both stopped drinking. Just like that. Without any effort or even any decision. Since then, I've tried a sip of champagne, a cocktail, and sometimes even a sip of wine. But I wouldn't say I like the taste. I'm not interested. I wouldn't say I like the buzz that seems to happen straight away, the one I used to chase. My drinking was never the issue. It was what I thought of myself that was the issue. I'd tried to hide behind the mask of booze to make me more interesting because it seemed to me that the woman under the mask was dull. When I started to like myself more, I no longer needed to drink to numb the pain in my heart. I could live with the emotions I experienced without having to fix them.

Notes

15   Modello: A Story of Hope for the Inner City and Beyond: An Inside-Out Model of Prevention and Resiliency in Action by Jack Pransky

Sally's Story

"I'm Sally, and I'm not an Alcoholic."

~ Sally

I've had the good fortune to meet living angels. Jo McKinnon,[16] was one of them. A kind, strong, determined woman who was a visionary in business. Tall, curvy with a smile as broad as the equator and a laugh to match, Jo stood out in a crowded room. I met her at a network event and discovered she was a Trustee at the Welcome Charity, an organisation that supports people with addictions. She was dedicated to helping people in any way she could. We clicked straight away. "Come and see our new Recovery Centre in Shard End," she said.

A week later we sat having coffee at the refurbished church hall she'd named "The Welcome Change," She'd proofread an application I'd written for a grant to run workshops. "What do you think of the place?" she asked me. The bright room was full of sunlight that danced off the butterflies painted on the walls. Tables and chairs had been sourced from the local second-hand shop and upcycled to look vintage in pastel colours, shabby chic style. The sound of the onsite chef and Smooth radio filtered through from the large kitchen.

"I love it!" I exclaimed. Jo had campaigned for National Lottery money to turn the old church hall into a wonderful, bright cafe for people in recovery to meet, and for the local community to hold events.

Her next question was, "Why don't you move in?"

My mind buzzed with possibility. Her open face was lit with love and compassion. "Yes, please!" I said.

I could have a desk in the shared office and use the group rooms for a year, rent free. I offered to run groups for her team in return, and we shook hands on the deal. At the start of 2014 I turned up with my box of stationery, favourite coffee mug, battered laptop, and moved in.

One of the plus factors was that the area was closer to Coventry. This meant that Simon Morgan was able to send clients to me who needed support, which is how I got to meet Sally. A friend of hers I'd been working with told me, "If you can help her, you can help anyone." I grimaced at the judgement and prayed I could be a support.

Sally was a sweet, petite lady in her fifties. Her down-trodden look came from a lifetime of drinking. She'd been in eight different rehabs. The last one, a few months previous, when she'd realised she couldn't drink anymore but felt like her life was worthless.

At five years old she'd discovered wine and drunk a whole bottle after yet another shouting match when her mom screamed, "You were never wanted anyway." She was taken to the doctor's and diagnosed with an anxiety disorder at six. Her reliance on external fixes took hold, as did her reliance on thinking that everything wrong with her life was the fault of others. Very bright and funny, Sally still managed to succeed in her career. She'd landed a good job in a school and bought herself a small house. But her drinking never stopped. If her dog was ill, she drank; if someone upset her, she drank; if her work was hard, she drank.

She started to lose control. First, she was charged with drunk driving and lost her licence; then, found drinking at work and lost her job; then, her family distanced themselves from her. "I lost everything," she said, "but I still couldn't stop. Alcoholics Anonymous (AA) helped me for a while, but then I would go to the pub after a meeting for a last drink." Sally spent thousands of pounds on rehabs that would clean her up and send her on her way, but she'd always keep a bottle or two of booze in her home, "just in case."

Late 2013, Sally found herself in her mum's garage at six o'clock one morning, forcing gin down her own throat. Unable to keep the alcohol down because she was being sick at the same time, she screamed out at the shadows on the wall, "Someone help me, please!" The next moment it occurred to her to call an ambulance, and within minutes, the paramedics came screeching to her door, blue lights flashing and horns sounding. They took her to a warm bed in the hospital because it turned out her body was shutting down from hypothermia and acidosis, her organs were shutting down. She was dying. It really was her last chance, and she knew it. She checked herself and her dog, Tilly, into yet another rehab in Southampton. She got sober, but she was miserable. She knew she could no longer drink and felt like her life was over.

When Sally was introduced to me, she just talked. The words would tumble out in one big story for the entire hour we were together. It seemed that nobody had listened to Sally for years. Each week, as she talked, she started to resolve her own questions. I would watch her little face as she would tell me how dreadful something was and how she didn't think she could cope, and then, as she talked it out, something fresh would occur to her about the situation and her face would light up with an answer or an insight.

I helped her to see that her experience was coming from within her own mind, her own perceptions and views. I encouraged her to see where she was doing well, where she was already coping, where she was already having insight. Each week, a little bit of the real Sally got revealed – her brilliant sense of humour, her kindness, her intelligence.

At the same time, Sally attended AA meetings and "worked the Steps," which she had never done before with real intent. "Do you know something?" she asked.

We were sitting on the orange foam chairs in the therapy room at the Welcome Change Cafe. The walls were decorated with art and a super-sized, framed mandala Rob had bought me for Christmas. Spring sunshine filled the room with a gentle warmth; the smells of coffee and toast wafted up from the kitchen. It felt like home.

Sally was sitting up straight, hands on her knees, in her blue jeans and yellow hand-knitted jumper. Her short blonde hair was ruffled from the spring wind and her face clean of make-up. "I only think of booze when I go to AA!"

Sally realised that all week she would just be living her life, which seemed to be getting easier, and then she would go to AA. She'd hear all the stories of drinking and all the focus on how many days someone had been sober and all the determination in the room to be called an alcoholic. And she'd go home and think about drinking and have drinking dreams and wake up in a sweat. After that moment, Sally gave up AA and continued to blossom and grow.

She went on to be a public speaker, sharing her story with others. And to live a life she'd dreamt of, doing the work she loved and surrounding herself with friends who loved her.

Notes

16   Jo McKinnon passed away from cancer in 2019. She continued to support people in recovery right up until the end and beyond. She is always in our hearts.

It's Not About Forgiveness

"All human psyches are rooted in universal truth and no person's psyche is better than any others."
~ Sydney Banks

Forgiveness is never about the other person. It's about accepting our story and embracing our own life. And letting go of what holds back the light we are meant to shine. It does not mean that the acts done to us are acceptable. It's about realising that an act forced upon us doesn't define us. We are not our behaviour, nor what's been done to us. If we were, we'd all be f***ed!

It's not about forgiveness. It's not about empathy. It's not about compassion. These feelings are all products of PEACE.

Here's what I mean.

Forgiveness, empathy, and compassion all came to me AFTER I realised from the depth of my being that I am OK. No matter what.

I came to see that nothing. **Not One Thing** can harm my spirit. Nor anyone else's.

I realised everything I am, everything I can be, and everything I've learned are merely pointers to the infinite potential of who I am. And that this is true for all human beings.

Dear Diary (June 2004),

I'm done with Peter Bennett. He's supposed to be my dad, but does that mean anything? I'm going into hospital next week for a hysterectomy to get rid of these enormous fibroids in my body, and he doesn't want to know. My sweet boy was so worried about me that he wrote to Peter and asked him for help. I think he's afraid he won't be able to look after me now; we are alone, and he's only fifteen. Bless Darren.

Peter called today and was weird; nothing strange there! At first, I got that scared feeling I always get when I hear his voice. I crumple up as small as I can inside and feel ten again. Then, he started talking shit about how his wife was jealous of me, and I felt disgust rise in my throat. They've been married for twenty years; you'd think she could get over herself. He tried to be all stern and annoyed, but for the first time, I didn't take the bait. I got stronger, not smaller. And then he started to cry. My stomach turned.

"I love you, you bastard," he said. I was in front of the mirror in my living room; phone pressed hard to my ear. Disbelief painted my face white. I could feel the steady pulse of life in my veins. I could smell the fragrant wisteria growing up the outside of the window.

"Goodbye," I said. As I snapped the cover closed on my mobile phone, I felt a rush of something new through my body. At that moment, I realised I was no longer scared. I've lived my life dominated by him. My relationships, self-esteem, and ability to love—were all tied to him and what he'd done to me. I looked deep into the hazel eyes in the mirror and said, "You're thirty-nine years old, woman; grow up!" I'm cutting Peter Bennett out of my life.

At that moment on the phone, I became aware that I'd been holding myself back all this time. I couldn't forgive myself for letting my dad hurt me as a child. I thought that my three-year-old self could have done something to stop him from holding my hands in the fire when he wanted to punish me. I thought my twelve-year-old self could have said "No" to the humiliation of being spanked with his belt before his friends. I thought I'd not done enough to prevent these things. When I realised that I was innocent and did the best I could as a child, I was released from the torture of blaming myself.

Dear Diary (November 2008),

What a pickle! I sat in the travel agent's office, booking a week away with my friend Sarah, and I got a missed call from an unknown number. My heart dropped to my boots when I listened to the voicemail. "Jacq, it's me, your dad. I'm dying of cancer, and I want to fix things."

It's so funny that he introduced himself as my dad! I spent the next two days and nights sleepless and soul-searching. I don't need the pain of him in my life anymore, but dying? I went round and round with all these questions: Would I regret it if I called him? Would I regret it if I didn't? I couldn't decide, so I did it anyway. I called him back.

"I've got Stage Four cancer and five months to live," he said. "I've changed, Jaq. I've had hypnotherapy and regression therapy, and I know I've done bad to you. I need you to forgive me. Can we meet?" The old bastard wants to die in peace. It makes me laugh; it's still all about him.

I knew that if I had this relationship with my dad, I'd need to go into it with an open mind and heart. I couldn't spend the next five months hating him or holding onto the past. I realised I needed to let go.

But it was more complicated than I'd imagined. We had a rocky five months together. Both trying, both failing, both dying. I met him where he was at. Went to his house in Derby, met his girlfriends (he had three), and listened to his stories. He came to my house and met Darren, his grandson, whom he hadn't seen for over five years. The three of us even went to Australia together because he wanted to see his long-lost family who'd moved there. There were laughs and some softening of the feeling between us. But he was still a bully and still wanted his way. And he was dying in front of my eyes. We all tried our best to be kind, to forgive, to love. I learned things that helped me understand why he'd been the way he'd been. I learned the truth that people are only doing the best they can in the level of consciousness they are in. I learned tolerance.

ANGEL 2008

"One last job," Angel said. Susie's cold black eyes stared back at him. Her face remained blank. Angel's elbows rested on his knees, hands clasped in front of him; his knees touched the king-sized bed she lay on. His bear frame blocked the early morning sunlight streaming in through the hotel window, his elbows resting on the ripped thighs of his Louis Vuitton jeans. His huge hands were clasped, prayer-like. Angel didn't believe in God. He'd given up ideas of redemption after his baby died. A lipstick-stained cigarette butt was squished beneath his foot. "Shit," Angel said.

He looked around the room. A bomb site. They'd partied hard for a fortnight. The red and gold carpet was strewn with champagne bottles. Debris of silver foil, brown stained spoons and discarded needles were scattered on every surface. Angel's philosophy had always been "Go large or go home." He knew he only had a few months to live it up between each nicking, so he went at it big time. Going to prison was an occupational hazard at the best of times. The trick was to do as many drugs, booze and women before his collar was felt. This time, he knew without a doubt they'd get him. He'd been walking backwards on his fingertips for far too long.

He limped over to the toppled dressing table stool. Breath rasped in his throat when he spotted the diamond engagement ring juxtaposed with the broken mirror. The whole thing had smashed when the cork from one of the bottles of Verve Clique had ricocheted around the room, bounced off the corner of the four-poster bed and crashed into the glass.

"Shit," Angel repeated. Scraps of moments from the past couple of weeks flooded back through the fog in his head. The engagement party was in the vast ballroom with crystal chandeliers. The coked-up argument with the shifty guy who'd mauled his sweetheart's arse. The disappointed look on her face. The sound of cracked cartilage. The screams. The splatter of blood as the tosser decked and stayed there. The car chase. The sounds of metal on metal. The escape back to the hotel room. "What a bleedin' rush," Angel had said.

He glanced back at the body on the bed. "Sorry," he said. She was a stunner in her cream Agent Provocateur knickers. One stockinged leg bent at the knee. The other leg bare. Suspender belt dangling free. Her pale almond skin looked luminescent in the morning light.

"Shit," Angel said. He felt himself get hard. His eyes flicked to the black and blue bruises around her neck where the belt had taken her last breath. The image scorched into his brain. The sound of sirens stopped, and heavy footsteps pounded down the corridor.

"Shit," Angel said.

Follow the Breadcrumbs

"Life shrinks or expands in proportion to
one's courage."

~ Anais Nin

In early 2014 another piece of incredible luck came my way. I was introduced to SD the manager of the substance misuse team at HMP Onley,[17] a prison near Rugby. I was invited to meet with him and the Head of Healthcare, Beth, to discuss the idea of bringing my innovative programmes to their service users.

I knew this was a chance in a lifetime and dressed with care the morning of the meeting. I was too nervous for breakfast.

I'd invited one of my clients along, Will, who'd been impacted by our sessions together and was keen to give back. As we sat in the grubby reception area, looking at the officers behind the security glass and watching for our escort, I thought, "I want to work here." Just then SD appeared on the other side of the airlock and waved at us through the thick glass. The heavy metal door to the airlock slid open, we stood stock still while one door slid shut and the door to the prison opened to let us through. Just like that we were locked inside the prison. My head buzzed with anticipation.

As he walked us to our meeting room, SD talked about the prison and his passion for providing quality services to the inmates in his care. His solid feel and his kindness struck me.

He led us to a lovely room in the Healthcare block with a mini kitchen. "Could I use the toilet?" I asked.

"You stay in this room," SD said to Will, then escorted me down the long corridors and through some double doors to the female toilets.

"I'll wait for you," SD said. As I washed my hands, an alarm pierced my ears. My brain felt scrambled. It didn't stop. A man shouted and banged hard. Anxiety and panic stunned my senses. My throat tightened.

"We have to get you back," SD said as I rushed out. "Someone has pushed the panic button." There was some confusion about where the emergency was, and in the mounting tension, we hurried back into our meeting room. Officers, decked with keys, batons, tasers and radios on their black prison belts, raced passed us to resolve the situation.

After a time, when an alarm is not resolved in prison, the situation gets escalated to headquarters, which has a standby Tornado Squad[18] ready to disperse. In addition, all other prison duties are stopped so full attention can be focused on the crisis.

As we walked through the meeting room door, Will said, "You know that big green button on the wall? It's not a light switch, is it?" Disbelief and relief mingled as it dawned on us that Will had pressed the Panic Button! I stood in silence, white-faced and shocked. Had Will just blown our chances of working here?

"All sorted," SD said as he returned to the room, and the sirens stopped.

It wasn't easy to get the meeting going. I was jittery. SD wanted to know how people change and what I do to facilitate that. I just kept saying, "I have a conversation, and they change. That's it."

I'd developed my "intervention" in a very organic way. I knew that sounded lame, but I struggled to articulate what I'd been doing and how it'd been helping. I hadn't yet grasped what was causing the change and didn't know how to explain it. I just knew it worked.

After a painful thirty minutes, I needed a breather. "Could we have a coffee?" I said.

Over coffee, stood at the kitchen sink with SD, I chatted away about how Thought creates our reality and that when people elevate their consciousness, they uncover their natural feelings of compassion and resilience. Something about the way I talked about it this time got him interested. He suggested to Beth that we could do a twelve-week pilot programme to see how it would work out.

I was so excited that when the next question came, I made another big boo-boo. "How much will it cost?" SD asked. A reasonable question, right? But I'd not even considered how much to charge.

I tried to wing it. "Fifty pounds?" As soon as it was out of my mouth, I knew it was ridiculous; driving there would cost me more than that! However, not wanting to pour cold water into this promising situation, I said nothing. They asked me to write a proposal; we said our goodbyes and were escorted back to the gate. Now I wondered how I'd make it work.

Notes

17 HM Prison Onley is a Category C Men's prison, operated by Her Majesty's Prison Service, that houses up to 750 prisoners. The prison is named after the lost village of Onley, which is located next to the prison. Onley Prison is in the county of Northamptonshire, close to its border with Warwickshire in England.

18 Tornado teams are units of elite officers sent into prisons to bring riots under control. They are usually made up of 50 officers who dress in Robocop-style black boiler suits. The squads are armed with batons and protected by shields.

Destiny or Just the Next Steps

"With a change of perspective, the impossible becomes possible."

~ Beyond Recovery Participant

I remember writing that proposal for HMP Onley. I agonised over it. I wanted it to be perfect. I'd already designed the methodology, so I could lean on that to flesh out ten separate sessions with objectives and lesson plans. It was the costs that got me; after the faux pas in the meeting, I turned to Rob for help.

"I told them the cost was fifty pounds." I said. The proposal was ready, but I couldn't overcome the anxiety of looking stupid over the costs. We were going down to Southampton to visit friends on the Isle of Wight. I sat in denim shorts and an orange t-shirt in the passenger seat, laptop perched on my knee, notebook under my leg.

"Say you meant fifty pounds an hour," Rob said. Bingo! That made perfect sense. Each of the ten weekly sessions would be three hours long to fit in with the prison regime. I finished the proposal, proofread it over the weekend and sent it off with my fingers crossed first thing Monday morning.

I got a phone call from SD a couple of weeks later. "The mental health team love your proposal. The psychologists, not so much," he said. I basked in the first part of the sentence. The mental health team LOVE my proposal!

I was buzzing! I brought myself back down to earth. "What's next?" I asked. The committee wanted me to prepare some background information and research for the psychologists to review to show that "this stuff" works and that I hadn't just made it up. Fair enough. I wondered where I'd find research for this brand-new understanding. I knew I had a difficult road ahead, but, at that moment, on the phone, looking out at the traffic outside my window, I felt grateful just to be having this conversation. It felt exciting. It felt like the numerous rejections I'd received were a thing of the past. I knew I had a chance to provide something that would give me a chance and be a lifesaver to many people. I was overwhelmed with joy.

"One other thing," SD continued, "Could you do a twelve-month pilot instead of twelve weeks?" I could hear the birds above the traffic. Looking out, I saw the weak Autumn sun glisten on the church opposite to dance in sparkles off the windows. I felt like I was standing at the edge of a vast landscape. "Yes," I said, "I could do that."

I came off the phone and just stood there, stunned. One of the committee members who had reviewed the proposal was Ian, Commissioner for the local Drugs and Alcohol team in the local council. He had an underspend in his budget for 2014/2015 and felt my project would be a good fit for the clients, funded by the underspend. He'd requested that I write a Business Case and present it to him in early December to be reviewed at the next committee meeting in 2015.

Wow, I had just got my first major project. I knew I had some work to do, but WOW. I'd never been asked to write a proposal before; this was GOOD. Once I had climbed down from my high at this fantastic opportunity, I realised two things:

1. The proposal would need to be appropriately costed, as this now would be my work for a year.
2. I didn't know what the flirt a Business Case looked like.

Number one was a beneficial insight. It meant it was no longer about what I was worth; it was just business. At this point, I'd never worked in prison and didn't know anything about how stable the population was; how difficult it would be to get people into rooms; how difficult it would be to get rooms in the first place; how often the regime must change because of an incident; and a whole raft of other challenges that came after I started. I always think it was a good thing I didn't know anything. Otherwise, I might never have jumped in! I got down to writing a bid that would deliver excellent service to the residents at HMP Onley.

The Business Case was like writing a dissertation for university. I reviewed existing programmes that had been evidenced and found papers relating to them. This meant I did a lot of reading. I got to know tons about the history of the Three Principles Understanding, where it had come from and how it had evolved to the current paradigm.

Then I designed a year-long Programme: how many groups there would be; how long it would be; how long each session would be; how many people would be in each session; what were the selection criteria; what were the expected outcomes, and how I would measure results.

Next, I described the Operational Support I would need; what I would need help with; what resources I would need; how I would manage risk.

It felt to me like a work of art. I had a love/hate relationship with that Business Case over the next two months. I dreaded sitting at my computer to write things I didn't know about, and then I'd have breakthrough ideas that gave me a buzz and inspiration. I asked everyone questions, I spoke to people, and I read. But most of all, I wrote. I wrote and rewrote and agonised over the writing. I designed a delivery plan. I tried to imagine what twelve months of working in prison would look like and how I would achieve it. I spoke to Will, and a woman named Tracy, who'd also been a client, and asked if they would like to volunteer to help me deliver the work. They could learn on the job and then be part of the team, creating a virtuous circle.

One morning I decided to call Jack Pransky and tell him what I was up to. He was delighted, "Make it a Research Project,"[19] he said. I knew he was right. I'd seen from my investigations evidencing the impact of this approach was very light on the ground. I had a little understanding of research from my university studies, which meant I understood we needed a "control group" and statistical significance and other "research" type things, so I agreed. Little did I know just how much time and effort this aspect would be.

I missed the first deadline because now I had a whole other area to investigate and write about. I called Linda Ramus, a researcher who had worked on delivering Three Principles programmes to jails in the USA. We designed a research protocol between Linda, Jack, and a professor, Tom Kelley. This included what we would measure;[20] how we would engage the "control group"; how we would deliver the measurements; and what our Hypothesis was: "That an increase in understanding the Three Principles would lead to an increase in well-being and purpose in life, and a decrease in anger, anxiety, and stress."

I delivered my Masterpiece to the commissioner's inbox on 22 December 2014. His response was immediate: "This is better than I could ever have imagined. Thank you." I breathed a sigh of relief and felt the rush of satisfaction of having completed such a feat. Now it was time to kick back and enjoy Christmas.

Notes

19   A Research Project is a scientific endeavour to answer a research question. Jack suggested that I measure the impact of our program against people who were not receiving the program but who were in the same circumstances (called a Control Group).

20   See the appendices on the research protocol.

Start Close In

"In the beginner's mind are many possibilities, in the expert's mind, there are few."

~ Shunryu Suzuki

I've heard the question, "How would you live if today were the last day of your life?"

I like to ask, "How would I live if this were the first day of my life?" What would I do now that I know I can do anything? What would I be willing to try if I believe there is no such thing as failure? What would I follow if I trusted that we never know what's in store for us?

When I offered to volunteer in the community of people recovering from addictions, I never knew I would find a quest and purpose and start a social enterprise.

When I offered my room to Dr Jack Pransky, I never knew he would become a research partner and help me produce three research papers.

When I offered to do a pilot project at HMP Onley, I never knew I would win a twelve-month contract and still be there five years later.

When I offered to speak at a networking event, I never knew I would present in front of thousands or travel worldwide, sharing stories.

I just followed what was in front of me. I just took each step as it occurred and enjoyed each moment as it was happening. I celebrated the little wins and picked myself up after the stumbles. I entered each day ready to learn, hungry to experiment, and eager to explore. I listened to myself and followed my intuition as best I could.

I've had doubts, I've had insecurities, I've had moments of despair. I lived in those moments for as long as they lasted, and then I got up and got on with it again.

I'm not a special person with a special purpose. I get in my way with my insecure thinking, and then I get inspired by ideas that seem commonplace but turn out to be beyond my wildest dreams.

I've learned to have no expectations and to look at what is, not what isn't. I've learnt to forget my timelines and understand that everything happens when it's meant to happen, not when I think it should. I've learnt to enjoy the moments as they come. I've learnt to cherish every day and start each morning as if it was the first day of my life.

Act II

Insight on the Inside

2015 – 2018

ANGEL 2015

Angel barged out as soon as the screw unlocked his door; his six foot four inch frame blocked the light from the tiny, barred window behind him. "Watch it, son," said the burly officer. He'd been watching Angel since he was inducted onto the wing two days ago; he knew he was trouble by the stories that went around the staff mess when they heard Angel was back inside. The screw was waiting for an opportunity to show Angel who was boss, but he had his rounds, so a quick "accidental" elbow to the ribs would make do.

"Oi," said Angel.

Angel watched the officer stomp onto the next cell; heavy keys jangled on the end of a long metal chain. He weighed the guy up in two seconds flat; five foot six; about one hundred and eighty pounds; muscled arms but spindly legs; single; a smoker and a boozer; most likely not bent, more interested in bullying the inmates. Angel's fighter instincts summed up what he'd need to do to knock the guy down before he could press the red alarm button on the comms radio on his belt to call for help. He decided to leave it this morning. He had other things in mind. A new group was starting on the wing, and he needed to get down there and suss it out.

Angel loved being in prison. This was where he made most of his money. At thirty-one, he'd learned to maximise while in the joint. As a drug dealer, he could quadruple the money he usually made weekly while inside: drugs and mobile phones were his main currency. Men on the wing were desperate for contact with their families, and everyone wanted to self-medicate. Easy prey.

He was new to this wing, so he'd yet to make his mark, but they'd soon find out who he was and realise they'd better not mess with him. He loved the challenge; a nasty fight made him feel alive. Sometimes he'd kick off just to get jumped by the seven or eight officers who'd come running at the opportunity to get a few digs in. They all wore cameras these days, but rarely turned them on until after they'd managed to land a few jabs to his face and groin. He relished the taste of blood as he felt his jaw, or some part of his head, get smashed. It was the only time he felt fear, and it smelt like Lily of the Valley, leather, sweat, piss, and gunmetal. Always taking him back to that moment behind the sofa and the glint in his dad's eyes.

Angel limped along the landing towards the group room. His left leg had never healed properly after a drug deal that had gone wrong when he was ten. On a job with his dad and a tough crowd from the Northeast, Angel had dropped a bag of smack he'd stolen. He'd thought his dad would be pleased; he'd felt the packet close to his chest on the inside of his jacket, and his heart thrummed with pleasure. The deal got nasty. His dad was squaring up to the three Albanian drug dealers in front of him when Angel tripped, and the smack tumbled out of his pocket. All three dealers pulled their guns in one sharp snap of breath. Angel lost consciousness as he felt the heavy weight of his dad smash him to the ground. His left leg twisted like a pretzel beneath him, and his mind turned black. The next thing he remembered was waking up in his mum's arms, her tears on his cheek. She begged his dad to take him to the hospital. His dad had pushed her out of the way, snapped Angel's leg back into position, then wrapped it with a plank of wood and his favourite blue striped sheets from the bed. The pain made his scream sound like a siren, and a hazy mist formed before his eyes. His dad shouted at him to hold still as he pushed a long, thin needle into his arm. Angel felt the warm blanket of heroin surge through his veins before being carried on soft fluffy clouds to a happy place he'd never known existed.

Angel wiped the memories from his mind. Thoughts about his childhood made him angry, and he needed to charm this morning. He'd even put his Louis Vuitton outfit on. Blue jeans with a wide cut. LV belt and matching buckle. LV white T-shirt and his favourite LV high-heeled pumps. The bright white of the pumps was in stark contrast to the grubby state of the prison floors, but he loved the extra inches they gave him, and women liked to see him dressed up. His focus was on wheedling his way into this new group. It was an ideal place for doing business. Inmates from other wings would come to attend the group. This allowed Angel to spread his net further, increasing his exposure to his ideal customers, other inmates with a drug habit. He could see the curvy redhead standing in front of the open door to the group room. She looked fake in her blue polo top. She held a black clipboard and a big smile on her silly face. Angel had seen her type before. Do-gooders. Think they come to save the inmates or help them change. Angel hadn't yet decided if he'd use her or hurt her. He liked the red hair, but her fake smile put him off.

"Oi gimp boy," said a loud cockney accent. The guy was behind him. Angel stopped. His cock hardened at the thought of a fight. A fresh kill. The blade tucked into his white socks reassured him.

"Hello," said the redhead.

The Chicks

"Prison shouldn't be about society's revenge but rather a chance to change the direction of a life."
~ Lord Robin Corbett

It's the smell that hits you first. Stale sweat and burnt toast.

After all that effort and expense of training to be a life coach, I thought I'd be flying to exotic destinations like Hawaii to work with rich clients in swanky hotels, dainty jewelled sandals on my pedicured feet. Sweet, scented air dusting my tanned arms. Cool cucumber water to sip between sessions.

But life had different plans. My road to meaningful work led me to prison. Hawaii would have to wait.

Instead of the sound of waves breaking onto bright white sand, my days were filled with the shriek of alarms and a backdrop of barbed wire and filth. The bangs, shouts, and clangs niggled my nerves. The two's[21] landing of putrid air on K Wing[22] at HMP Onley was an insult to the senses. Rows of cells lined up next to each other like a string of cages. Each one just big enough for a childlike single bed frame or bunk bed, lined with an inch-thick mattress, one sheet and a thin grey blanket. Each cell contained a toilet with no door and a stained brown sink. Each cell door opened onto a walkway flanked by a thick steel railing overlooking the lower landing.

Sometimes the prison residents throw themselves off the railings in a cry for help. The ceilings are high, and the strip lights provide a doomed glow over the off-white walls but fail to hide the grime and dirt engrained into the corners and cracks.

I never thought I would end up working in prison. It never crossed my mind. It was not on my radar at all as being something I either wanted to do or ever would do. Sometimes life is like that. We follow the first steps of a path that leads us to something more than we could ever have imagined.

I never wanted to change the world either. Now that I think about it, it wasn't that I didn't think I could; it was just not something I ever thought about. I was too selfish, too wrapped up in my own little life, and too obsessed with how I was doing to think much about other people except for how they related to me. I never saw the invisible layer of thinking I had about myself or about others. Yes, there are LAYERS of thinking! Judgments, insecurities, beliefs, and stories – are all thoughts. And they were thoughts about myself and the world that I believed were true. Prison broke all that. A nameless random man brought my illusion crashing down and saved me from myself.

"It's just like TV," I thought. I was petrified. I didn't think I would feel like that. I'd done months of preparation. I had my notes. I'd done my training. And yet, as I stood there outside the classroom on the drugs wing of the prison, I was petrified. There'd been an incident at the weekend. The men were 'banged up'[23] for longer than usual on that morning. They were agitated. Sounds of plastic cups and fists banged on cell doors filled the wing. Angry shouts of pissed-off voices battled to be the loudest. Smells of old boots assaulted my nostrils. "No, it's worse than TV!" I thought.

At that moment, I wondered what on earth I was doing. I mean, there were other things I could do to make a difference in the world. Why this?

I tried to calm myself down. I waited, clipboard in hand, for the cell doors to be unlocked and the released men to turn up to the group. The list of names on the printout of those coming to this session told me nothing about the men. I wondered what they looked like. I knew they must come and get their names ticked off my list before being allowed into the classroom.

"I wanna see the chicks, miss," said a gruff voice. A big badass guy stood in front of me, his beady eye on the group room. Shaved head, scarred face, tattooed neck, and skin as pale as a ghost. I asked his name and looked at my list. He wasn't on it. I knew he wasn't allowed in. The training had been very strict about that. I knew I was supposed to say "No." I knew I had to be firm. I just didn't think I'd be facing this on my first day.

The heavy prison belt with its keys and radio rubbed at my hips through my black leggings. The shouts and bangs and loud music were relentless in their attack on my ears. Fear froze me to the spot. The inmate stood firm in front of me. Sweat ran down my back under my blue polo shirt, my eyes desperate to find his name. His bright red t-shirt strained over a bulging belly and arms, his grey track pants stained and snug. He looked like a prisoner. To me.

A scrunched up yellow post-it note poked out from under his big feet encased in big brown workers' boots. I wondered what to say, would my voice work, what does he mean by "the chicks'"? My fear stained the air as I knew I was about to break the rules. "OK," I said.

I let him in. "If he wants to stare at the female officers through the window, what am I supposed to do about that? They never mentioned that in the training!" What happened next humbled me. I hadn't realised that I had an invisible layer of judgement about the very people I wanted to work with. I hadn't noticed how much the media and perception of people in prison had affected my own beliefs. I didn't know that people in prison were kind.

The gruff-looking inmate went straight to the window behind my flip chart stand. There, on the window ledge outside, was a nest and some dove chicks. My heart melted; I hadn't even noticed them. The big guy was thrilled to see them and told me how they had grown, how he saw them when they were still in their eggs, and how he will miss them.[24]

I don't know the name of that man or where he went. But I do know this. He's the reason I'm still working in prisons several years on. I had a passion and a desire to "help" people in prison, and yet until that moment, I hadn't seen just how much judgmental thought I had about so many things. It had been invisible to me. But at that moment, it dropped away like melted snow in sunshine. I could no longer hear the noise and the chaos, and all I could see were people. People living in a mixed-up world, just like me.

People with hopes and dreams, just like me. People with doubts and insecurities, just like me. People who may have done bad things, but who are not bad people, just like me.

And so, it began. A girl with an IT background and no training or experience in the Criminal Justice System or the mental health field. A girl with a vision and a passion for eliminating the stigma that goes with mental health issues and behaviour. A girl determined to uncover the potential of the people society had given up on. Somehow, I'd found my way to share an understanding of how the Mind works with prison residents in a group room on "K" wing of a Category C[25] prison in Rugby.

I wasn't there to teach anything. I was there to learn.

Notes

21 Prison landings are referred to by which level they are on. The second landing is the twos.

22 The blocks or units in a prison are often referred to as "wings". This is where the prisoners reside in cells. In some prisons, they are labelled alphabetically A, B, and C so that they can be referred to phonetically Alpha, Bravo, and Charlie over the radio to aid clarity of location.

23 Banged up - Prison slang for being locked in their cells.

24 I tell the story about the man and the chicks in this video https://youtu.be/76xR5wN1ocE

25 Prisons are categorised from A to D depending on the offenders' risk to the public. A is the highest risk, and D is the lowest (usually an open prison).

How Can You Lose a Man in Prison?

"It helped me see what makes me tick."
~ Beyond Recovery Participant

I still had a lot to learn. I started at the prison with three separate groups a week. I wanted to maximise my time there. I thought doing what I came to do would be the easy part. I was wrong. I thought I'd have a captive audience; I mean, where else would they go? I was wrong. I thought I'd nailed it. I was wrong. I thought the commute from Birmingham to Rugby would be a doddle. I was wrong.

When I wasn't delivering the groups, I studied. I read books by Jack Pransky[26] and Joe Bailey[27] and studied the diagrams and exercises. I'd practice the drawings at home on a big, white, dry wipe board in my living room. I kept a separate "prison bag" so that I wouldn't have any accidental prohibited items on me. It contained my security belt with its heavy chains, my prison ID, a box of tissues, a workbook of the drawings, and a bag of Gummy Bears. I took in magic eye pictures photocopied onto cheap paper.

Photocopies of books by Jane Tucker and Syd Banks's book *The Missing Link*. I was always racking my brain for ways to talk about a subject that could only be felt rather than understood!

Each week, I wondered how I would entertain the guys for three hours. All I could do was show up and do my best. If they got rowdy, I'd have to think about where I had taken them and how to quieten them back down. The hours stood at the flip chart, and the miles walked around the prison took its toll on my knees. Every day after the two-hour drive home, I'd spend the evening with my feet elevated on the couch to reduce the swelling in my arthritic knees.

PRISON NOTES – JUNE 2015

Thank God I had Fiona with me this week; she's learning on the job! And so am I! Even after all the training, being in the prison un-escorted is daunting. Every time I walk in, the smell and the noise assault me. I can feel the undertone of violence and discontent. I also feel humble. I know these men want to change. They want their lives to be better. They want to make better decisions. They really feel that the system is against them, that no matter how hard they try, there is a dead end. They feel they have no choice. One guy, Sean, was proud of the ten and fifteen year gaps between getting caught, and never expected to be in prison again at forty-five. They see themselves as warriors fighting oppression. The guys I've had in group have all been caught in the madness of addiction. There are many classes they can attend. Things they can learn about themselves and about addiction, about alcohol, about life. They have access to counselling, individual case workers, the gym. And yet nothing seems to help.

I stood on the two's landing and watched the prison officer walk the floor and unlock the cells (checking his clipboard in case of infringements). The men emerged like creatures that'd been caged. I know their crimes can be unforgivable, but shouldn't we provide help to change them rather than damage them further? Many of them come from backgrounds littered with child-hood trauma, violent homes, and lack of schooling. I imagine that one day we will look back on this archaic system of locking people up and consider ourselves barbaric. The guys that came to the class were surly and suspicious, but that changed when Fiona told them how she'd lost everything—kids, home, respect. They commented later how happy they are to have us with them. Surprised by the fact that we were "let in" when they are used to professionals, "who don't understand, who have never been where we are." These guys feel isolated from the world that they don't understand and that doesn't understand them.

"This is different," I'd say. "You don't need to remember what we say, or even make notes."

"Really miss?" one man said.

"Yes," I answered.

"You can even go to sleep if you want; the calmer your mind is, the better."

They all laughed and jostled each other at that. I explained that insight-based learning is different from what they are used to. They started to relax. And now,

sitting on my bed, with my warm cocoa and favourite
pink fluffy socks, I'm exhausted, but happy. Everything
hurts; my feet, my knees, my voice, my brain, but I know
now I can do it! At the start of the week, I wondered how
I was going to get through it—wiped out by lunchtime
on the first day, I didn't see how the afternoon could
be done. But now, after three sessions, all I can see is
their beautiful faces. As they left the room tonight, I
felt like I could see their souls. I felt blessed to get the
chance to do this work.

The logistics alone would be enough to have put most people
off. But every time I saw a man getting an insight, it was like
watching a light bulb flood a dark, dingy room with hope.
At the start of the group, I'd give the participants research
questionnaires and consent forms, and again at the end. I'd
arrive at prison at 7:00am, after a two-hour drive, to use the
antiquated IT system for the list of men who were participat-
ing in the group. I'd prepare the urn, plastic boxes with tea
and coffee, plastic mugs and spoons, and powdered milk.
I'd arrange the chairs, the flip chart, and try to make the
stark room as cosy as possible. The communication radio
hung on my belt with an earpiece plugged into my ear so
I could listen out for when the "free flow" call was made.
This is when the men are released from the various wings
to the parade ground to make their way to work or groups
or any other appointments they may have. It's one of the
most dangerous times in a prison because the whole of the
prison population is now out at the same time. It's a time
when fights break out for old scores or new debts; anything
naughty, like drugs or phones or shanks, can be passed

between residents living on different wings and messages can be passed between different gang members.

I'd wait outside the big double gates leading to J/K wing with my list of names to check the men onto the wing. Fiona would stand with me to escort the men up the stairs to the room. We'd have a third person in the room and keep the men in there. I was kept on my toes in this chaotic half hour: men would rush up to say they couldn't attend; others tried to persuade me to let them in; others didn't show at all. All of it was logged and reported to the comms team. Freeflow would run for fifteen minutes, and then the comms team would announce, "All prisoner movement must be ceased, and all gates secured." At that point we couldn't let anyone else in or get rid of anyone who wasn't meant to be there.

Every time there is a big movement the prison does a role count to ensure that all the residents meant to be there are still there (just in case someone tries to escape). The system for doing the role count is imperfect to say the least. Each wing, each group and each workshop must do a manual count of their residents and call it through to comms. The mere fact that this is a manual count with several moving parts means it is nearly always incorrect. So, then there is a recount. And another. And another. Until the role is correct.

During this time, nobody can move from the location they're in. This causes problems in group when the guys want to have a toilet break; they must hold on and hold on and hold on. As you can imagine, patience isn't a strong point amongst a group of rufty tufties who feel they need to shout to get what they want. They take full advantage of the tea and coffee we provide and then need the loo. If we can't move due to the incorrect role, the tension mounts.

Even when roll is correct, there is a whole rigmarole of getting permission to move men. Only moving a few at a time and ensuring there is someone in the room to keep the others put.

Here's a typical toilet run:

- Radio comms to get permission to move men
- After a few attempts, comms grants permission.
- I count the men who want to go and lead them out the room, down the stairs to the one's landing. Two gates to unlock and lock to take us all into the foyer. One of me and six or seven of them.
- Check all men are still with me (some like to run off to other cells or to chat with their mates – also prohibited).
- Get across the corridor to J Wing. Two gates to unlock and lock and usher the men through. Up the stairs to the toilet, where only one man can go at a time.
- Keep the others from wandering off.
- Once all have finished, check the toilet for smells of cigarettes or drugs, then lock it up, then back the way we came.

It wasn't quick, and it wasn't easy. I'd often have up to ten men on those toilet runs!

At the end of the session, we'd have a bit more chaos to contend with – getting the men off the wing! All the other men are returning from their workshops; some of the men are wing workers and people who are Keep on Wing[28], so they are out on the landings. It means that our little posse of men who are supposed to be leaving the wing get all muddled up with the others. I'd often be standing on my tiptoes to try and see where one man has run off to while guiding another three off the wing and calling to another four who are still coming down the stairs. Sometimes I'd think I'd counted them out the door, but someone had snuck off and into another man's cell. In the beginning, I was quite naïve. I mean, what's the harm if they want to speak to their friends? But I soon found out that some men use the opportunity to score, settle old debts or other nefarious activities.

I remember one day being stuck in the reception area waiting to leave the prison, and the role still wasn't correct. After several attempts, the prison goes into a Fixed Posts state, which means that not even staff can move around or leave until all residents are accounted for. This time, the missing resident was found in another man's cell on K wing. When the role was counted, the wing staff hadn't noticed that there were two men in the cell instead of one. Of course, the second man turned out to be one of ours from the group! I wish I could say it was the only faux pas we ever made.

Notes

26 Dr Jack Pransky is a first-generation teacher of the Inside Out understanding and created a curriculum called 'Healthy thinking/feeling/doing from the inside out'

27 Joe Bailey's book "The Serenity Principle"' was foundational in my teaching in the early days.

28 KoW or Keep on Wing – This means the prisoner is not allowed to leave the wing for security reasons.

The Learning Curve

"Even behind these prison walls, I feel free."
~ Beyond Recovery Participant

The first three months were a grind. Aside from the logistics and the rules and the noise and the mayhem, there was the actual work, the groups. I turned up each week with notebooks and plans and ideas about how to teach these men and every week I was humbled by seeing that no matter what people have done, no matter how far they've fallen, no matter what pain they've been through, no one is broken. Everyone has wisdom. My only job was to tap them on the shoulder and wake them up to that fact. We taught each other. Each class would teach me just as much about what not to do as what should be done. I used to start the first session of each group, "What are your challenges?" The list was **very** long. But no different from the challenges we all have; worries about children, housing, money, bills, plus how to get a job with a criminal record.

It didn't take too long before I twigged that starting with their challenges was getting them all worked up about the "system," and why they should have this and that, and what was I going to do about it? They would get noisy and start squabbling with each other. When this happened, I would take a breath, look out of the barred window at the sky beyond the razor wire, and calm my own mind down.

When I got still in my mind the guys followed. One of my favourite things to do was to have "quiet time," I'd read a short meditation, followed by a few minutes of silence, and a reading from one of Sydney Banks'[29] books. There was always silence at the end of those readings. All the guys sat still and relaxed. I'd dreaded the idea of introducing quiet time, but I could see that they needed some space, a little oasis of peace. The thing was the guys LOVED it. Over the years I've developed more and more space in our groups, it is this space between the words that does the real teaching, but back then in 2015 I hadn't quite learned that yet.

"Can we have quiet time miss?" Chris asked. It had surprised me. Chris never sits still, is always late and often misses class for football. We sat on the plastic hard chairs in a semi rectangle, in the long narrow group room on K Wing. On one wall was a map of the world. A small bookcase at the back of the room contained brochures on ways to overcome stress, addictions, and anxiety. The small, barred window let in a strip of sunlight and the sounds of the doves on the wire fence. A tiny egg sat on the mottled nest of grey mud and dark brown sticks. The noise from the wing, the shouts and music and the occasional call from comms over the radio system, permeated our room but it all seemed far away from the quiet realm we were visiting. As our minds settled, the sounds of birds and wind could be heard. "No human psyche can be broken," I read.

Despite the challenges and the exhaustion, I knew I was

where I was meant to be. Those moments of peace, where I saw past the masks to the heart of the men's humanity, were what kept me going. The gifts were the insights: a guy would see his own resilience; another would discover hope; another would feel compassion.

Each week at the end of the session I'd do an exercise to ask the guys what they had heard new, how they were feeling, and what were they "taking away with them," I'd be blown away by their comments, a stark reminder that the people in front of me had the same hopes, dreams, and desires as anyone I have ever met and yet their ability to reflect to their deepest part of themselves was more profound than I had ever heard.

PRISON NOTES – JUNE 2015

It's my second week and there was another lock down on our wing after an incident at lunch time. Seems like it's a regular thing. Trouble is the guys came to group an hour late all agitated and noisy. All full of the story of the incident. When I tried to calm them down, they turned their agitation on me. "What difference will all this make?" they complained. I told them there are two games, one called Fight the System and one called Find Your Answers. They said they'd give the second one a go.

One guy kicked off about a situation he couldn't see how to resolve. An unfair decision on his record. I listened and held a quiet space. He ran out of steam and noticed that I didn't argue back. He looked at me for a few moments. I stayed silent. They are used to people jumping in with answers or reasons they should think in a different way. "I know what I'm going to do," he said. "I'll go to my groups and partake in what I must do and the rest of the time I will sit in my pad and read. I'm going to take time out!" he finished.

"Sounds like your wisdom is helping you find some headspace," I said. The frown slipped off his face when he realised I wasn't going to correct him. He tugged his cap over his eyes, leaned back and relaxed.

Another guy described himself as being "in the basement." He sat at the back, head hung low, face pale and tight. The other guys tried to help him, so we talked about how people's own solutions are the ones that have the biggest impact. Three of the guys had insights for their own challenges, which were all different and only meaningful to them. At the end of the session, Joe said. "I think I just needed to sit and be quiet today to let me head clear. I feel a bit better now."

Every time an insight like this happened, I was reminded that people already know what they need to do, what is helpful and what is not. This has nothing to do with our concept of "right and wrong." That concept is battered into these guys in every other group they attend. They think their problem is that they know right from wrong, but they follow wrong anyway. They want to know, "Why do I keep making the same mistakes?" "How do I know when something is right or not?" "How do I follow that inner voice?" They have become conditioned to thinking that something is wrong with them. I noticed that when they are reminded of the fact that they have always had wisdom, they listen to themselves more, and start to find their own answers. Men come to me with situations that I couldn't even have imagined being in.

Fred asked if he could have a word before we went into class. "What's up?" I asked.

"Can I change classes, miss?" His pock-marked face was pinched with agitation. I said he could and asked him why. "Well miss, I'm in the Green Gang and there's a fella lives down near healthcare from the Grey Gang. The rule is that I gotta fight someone in the Grey Gang, as soon as I see them, init? So, if I come this un, I won't see him. Job done, miss," he said with a big smile. Good job I'm not responsible for coming up with his answers!

In group, one of the guys said he felt stressed. "The screws are bullying me. I ain't gotta clue what to do." I asked him if he could put the question to one side and see if he could get any clarity by the end of the session. When the time came, his answer was, "I think I'm walking around with an angry face, and they are responding to that."

Then someone else wanted to know, "The only way to avoid the contract on my life is to get myself in the block. What do you think, miss?" I asked him how he felt about that option. "Gives me time out miss, and I can get a ton of reading done."

Each answer proved to me that my solutions would have no way near the same impact. Each one came up with their own answers. Each one perfect for his own circumstances.

I remember when I was working in IT and leading a team of people, I always felt under pressure to have the answers. I see now that I operated under intuition most of the time, whether it be a staff issue or a business issue. But I didn't know that was what I was doing, and I undervalued it. The thing that took up most of my thinking space was where I was not doing so well, when I felt I should've been the expert, that somehow, I should know all the answers in order to lead. I was always afraid of being "found out" as a fraud. It's such a relief now to know I don't have to know all the answers, and that from a clear mind, all sorts of answers are available to me and everyone else.

Notes

29 Sydney Banks is the founder of the understanding of the Three Principles. He 'uncovered' the understanding through an experience which you can watch here http://sydbanks.com/longbeach/

The Insight in the Bath

"If we face our fears & bring light to our lives, we can hopefully lead the way for others to do the same, and make the world a better place."

~ Beyond Recovery Participant

Sometimes you have to surrender. I loved the work in prison with all my heart. I was grateful. I felt blessed. But it was bloody hard! I was knackered, worn out, washed out, bashed out. Everything hurt, knees, feet, legs, head. I wondered if I could make it easier.

PRISON NOTES – AUGUST 2015

What an amazing day. A film crew came in today to film our graduation for the guys from the first groups this year. It's been such a tough few months, but today made it all worthwhile. The substance misuse support team also came in and brought drinks and snacks to show their appreciation, and the guys were amazing. The crew filmed the end of the group and then did individual interviews for each of the guys. I can't wait to see how that turns out.

At the end of another long, tough week, I lay in a bath of bubbles, letting the week soak off. I looked up at the white ceiling and said, "What am I missing?" The bathroom was full of steam and scents from candles. My achy head rested on a soft towel at the edge of the tub, my knees poked out from the soapy bubbles. "Yes!" I said and sat up; water splashed over the side of the bath. An idea had just popped into my head. After I won the prison contract, I'd signed up to do a "practitioner training" with the One Thought Institute in London. There were about twenty other students on the course. I realised they could be interested in some work experience. The next seminar was in October 2015. Aaron Turner suggested I talk to his students after they'd finished for the day.

"One more thing," he said as the day came to an end. "Anyone interested in prison work, hang around. Jacqueline would like to talk to you." About ten of the students stayed back.

"Where to start?" I said. I'd taken one of the facilitator chairs and placed it in front of the row of practitioners. Ten faces stared at me with a mixture of curiosity and impatience. My voice was quiet with an awkward stutter. The large auditorium felt cool. "Let me tell you about Jago."

Jago, a twenty-six year old guy with mixed heritage, came to group with an attitude. A fighter. Addicted to money and heroin. Confused and lonely. He'd grown up in the care system and had run away at every opportunity. At age eleven, he'd found a foster home he could settle in and then his mother was killed in a car accident. Jago was angry. I told him that addiction

was an attempt at a solution, and he saw it. His eyes
lit up. He scratched his blonde head. He asked me for
a book. I gave him Jack Pransky's "Somebody Should
Have Told Us," He read it in a week and at the next class
he said, "Can I read you a poem I've written, miss?"

I glanced up after I'd read the poem to the students. Tears
stained some of their faces. Soft smiles dressed the room.
"It's God's work," one of the students said. We got up to leave
and most of the students hugged me, thanked me, and said
they'd think about it. Apart from one: Anna Debenham.

Anna, a tall, slender, dark-haired lady in her mid forties,
said, "YES, please. When can I start?" Anna stayed behind
when everyone had gone and even travelled the tube home
with me. She'd always felt a pull to work with people
in prison and was ready to jump in with both feet. I was
delighted with her enthusiasm.

Over the next couple of months three other students
came forward, Susan Marmot, Liliana Bellini and Jacquie
Moses. They all vetted through the arduous prison process,
which was taking up to three months, but I was so relieved
that at least I would now have support from grounded practitioners. I started the autumn programme at HMP Onley
with a spring in my step. The trainee facilitators were eager
to do the work. Having other practitioners around who
understood what I was teaching saved my sanity. They
shadowed me. Observed the groups. And learnt the many
rules of the prison. The men loved having new people
around. They were touched that people would volunteer to
do this work and spend time with them in prison.

I sourced a local farmhouse bed and breakfast to reduce

everyone's travel as we had such early starts at the prison. One evening, Anna and I sat by the warm fire telling stories. Anna had travelled the world with her backpack; explored mountains, monasteries, and the power of her own mind. I was fascinated by her tales. "I know what I'm going to do tomorrow," she said. The glow from the open fire melted the prison off us after our long day. Our sore feet rested on the stool between us. Our stomachs rumbled at the sumptuous smell of chicken casserole on the farmhouse stove.

"Tell me," I said.

Anna outlined her plan to demonstrate a great diagram she had seen. I was sceptical of the outcome, having begun the previous three months sharing "information" and ditching it all to just share simple explanations that came from my own knowing. However, I knew that the team learned their own way of doing things and I was dedicated to helping them find their own voices. "You could try that." I said.

The next day during the group Anna shared her example. The more she tried to remember what she needed to say, the noisier the room got. The guys shouted out questions and interrupted her. The noisier the room got the more on edge Anna got.

"Let's have a comfort break," I suggested. My bum was numb from the hard-plastic chair, and I couldn't think straight with the noise in the room. Anna stood at the flip chart with one hand on her hip and one holding the blue whiteboard marker.

Matt, a large Caribbean man, sat to my right wearing a white shirt and blue jeans, head rested against the wall. "What do you mean?" he barked.

I blushed and stammered, "A break for a drink or to go to the toilet."

He laughed. "Oh, I thought you meant we were all gonna cuddle when you said, 'a comfort break' and I ain't cuddling these fools!" The tension broke as we giggled and started the convoluted journey to the toilets.

Anna and I both learned from that session that when we teach from our "head" i.e., what we have learned or what we think is a good idea, the guys get into their "heads," Then it becomes about opinions and justifications. When we teach from our "heart" or our "knowing" the guys get quieter because they can hear the truth. This is something we learned time and time again, but eventually we became more sensitive to when things were going in the wrong direction, and how to bring them back. We all got more grounded and that brought a quiet confidence. I got over my insecurities of getting it wrong in these groups of boisterous men. They have very well-honed Bull Sh*t meters and will call you out the minute they think they can. I've learned to just stop and say, "I've taken you off track, give me a moment." And they do.

Anna continued to volunteer with me until she emigrated to Portland, Oregon where she setup a non-profit organisation[30] using the Inside Out approach in prisons.

Notes

30   Anna is passionate about helping people and working toward global solutions. I was blessed to have her volunteer with me as part of her training. See some of Anna's work here https://theinsightalliance.org/

Meeting ANGEL

"True Love is True Spirit Power."
~ Syd Banks, Second Chance

The walk through the prison from K Wing classroom, where I'd been running a group, to the gate that let me out to freedom, sobered my mood.

I'd trudge my heavy bag through the grimy parade ground; past all the barred-up windows and dreary buildings; past the streams of rubbish that littered the ditches, and the rats that scurried for cover. I'd be aware of the black crows perched on the razor wire that watched me with their sharp eyes. I'd smell the enormous waste disposal bins and hold my breath. I'd admire the flowers in the memorial garden dedicated to those who died in prison. I'd feel guilty that I'm about to go to my cosy home while seven hundred and fifty prisoners were being banged up in six by four cells until the morning. I'd wonder, "Am I making a difference here? Is it possible that these men can experience freedom of mind that will transcend their circumstances and elevate their consciousness?"

When I first met Angel, anger oozed out of every inch

of his body. His huge frame was always tensed for a fight, the frown on his face a permanent fixture. His jet-black eyes bored into my soft bits. He liked to intimidate. He did it well. "He's a pain in the backside," said one of the facilitators. Beyond Recovery was in a new phase of programmes and the new team sometimes struggled to find their feet. I wasn't in every group at this point because I wanted them to find their own ways of sharing the work, but I'd often join them at the start and end of each class.

I remember one of the team asking, "Do we have to keep him?"

Angel was opinionated, always telling the other guys to shut up. He had ants in his pants, leaning back on his chair and swaying. And he argued with everyone.

"Yes, we have to keep him. We can't say that all humans have psychological innocence and then pick and choose who we allow to be in the room," I replied.

Angel later told us, "I couldn't believe that people could be as happy as these women looked, always smiling, always friendly. I kept waiting for Jacqueline's mask to drop, to show her true colours."

On the second session of that group, the facilitator was drawing stick diagrams on the flip chart to demonstrate what happens when we get into our heads, and we feel as though we've lost our innate wellbeing. Angel kept butting in with how it was different for him, how his issues were worse than anyone else's, how his trauma ran deeper. He couldn't stop talking about all the diagnoses he had of PTSD, depression, and Emotional Unstable Personality Disorder (EUPD). He repeated stories about his violent past and how he'd killed someone and watched someone else get stabbed to death. We already knew he'd been kicked out of several prisons for his aggressive behaviour and how he was escorted by three armed officers wherever he went. He appeared proud and boastful. But, to me, he seemed sad and lost.

His mood swings were stark due to all the medications he was on, and the fact that he was "topping up" with illegal drugs. He'd also steal other inmates' medications. But we could sense that he hid a gentle side, that he wanted to be loved, that he'd misunderstood how life was experienced and that he lived in his own nightmare.

Many of our participants would try to show how their story was so much worse than other peoples', because that's how it seemed to them. And because they were made to repeat their stories and traumas many times, they'd re-live the pain and suffering, and re-experience the torment. Our minds bring these events to life, and that's how we feel the same pain over and over. This keeps the person trapped in the cycle they are trying to find a way out of, and as with any of us, being stuck in this never-ending cycle makes it very difficult to listen to a fresh thought in the moment.

The facilitator put on a CD of Syd Banks and encouraged Angel to forget his story and see if he could be in the present moment, which would help him find calm. This flipped Angel over the edge. He felt like he'd been insulted. He didn't see the kindness in what he was being offered. He was offended and his anger grew at the thought of other people thinking he was a "dick"; each negative thought spiralled his mood down.

The facilitator was mortified. Blood drained from her face and tears sprung to her eyes. The room fell quiet.

In the silence, the Scottish brogue of Syd Banks could be heard. "Forget the past. It's an illusion. Drop your negative thoughts and find something positive. Your life will be happier." Syd's lilt calmed the room with a blanket of peace. The doves cooed on the razor wire outside the window. Shafts of sunlight filled the room.

"Wow," Angel said. He shook his head in amazement. We could see the sunlight through the huge holes in his earlobes where large round metal rings had been before he came to prison. "I've been living in my own negative thinking."

His huge frame sat upright; dark eyes wide open. A tiny smile played at the corner of his straight mouth. One of the guys giggled and soon everyone in the room laughed. The contagious merriment spread as we held stomachs and wiped laughter tears off our cheeks. Angel laughed the loudest. "It's unbelievable," he kept saying.

The next day, Angel strolled down to the gate where I was waiting to let that day's group into a building at the other end of the prison. "I need to read those books," he said. I provided him with *The Missing Link* and *The Enlightened Gardener*, by Sydney Banks. His face didn't crack, but the feeling of intimidation had gone. He was shy and cautious, as if he wanted to be gentle, but wasn't quite sure how to do it. It was like his whole personality had changed overnight.

ANGEL Meets Syd

I owe my life to Syd Banks. I sat in class listening to the Beyond Recovery team blather on about our wellbeing, and one of the women insulted me in front of everyone. I wasn't about to stand for that. She was lucky I don't hit girls, but I couldn't let her get away with it. I felt small and my bad leg ached like she'd pinched it or som'at. The room was hot and crowded and all I wanted to do was get out of there and use the bogs to take the drugs I'd scored earlier. Then a weird thing happened. The buzzing in my head stopped, and I felt a calm wash over me. I felt like I was having an out-of-body experience. I could see the negative thoughts running round my head, bumping into each other. They must've slipped drugs in my tea!

I borrowed the books that Syd Banks wrote and couldn't wait for bang up that night to read them. I wanted more of that feeling I got in group. As soon as I started The Missing Link, an incredible peace washed over me. Tears flooded out of my eyes. I was shocked. I never even cried when me mum died. It's a weird thing to say, but all of a sudden, I started having answers to questions I never knew I had.

The next day, when the screw unlocked me, I didn't barge out as normal. I just waited for him to move on. I felt strange, peaceful, and emotional all at the same time. It was so weird. Some geezer pushed me in the queue for breakfast and I just moved on, took no notice of him! I was a bit worried because it was like all the fight had drained out of me. I just didn't want to hurt no one. Problem was, the others didn't like it. The inmates harassed me, tried to get a rise. The screws baited me, tried to push my buttons. And I just walked around like some Zen person. It got so bad the only thing I could think to do was ask to be banged up behind me door so that I didn't mix with the others for a while.

I knew I could still damage someone if I wanted to, but that was the thing I no longer wanted to. For the first time in my life, I felt free. Free of all the bullshit I'd been telling myself. Free of all the bullshit from me past. Free from all the pain I'd been hiding behind. It was a good feeling, but it came with some surprises.

Like, I started getting emotional when I watched stuff on TV. Stories about people falling in love. I used to think they were moist or find things to criticise about them, but after the change I started to root for them, I hoped they'd find true love. One day I cried at the end of a show. Cried! It happened so much I asked Jacqueline what was wrong with me. She told me it was compassion. Me! Compassion! I've been diagnosed with "lack of empathy" and now I'm feeling compassion. I told her she'd ruined me life, but then I laughed to show her I was joking. I don't want her to be upset.

The other big change that happened straight off

the bat was about me family visiting. I'd been on closed visits forever, meaning I only see my family behind a glass screen and was not allowed contact with them because of all the drugs and phones I got brought into the prison. I'd been addicted to money and material stuff. I never even considered the consequences on the people I was dragging into my shitty business. After reading Sydney's books, I didn't want to hurt me family anymore. I wanted to spend time with them when they visited. I didn't want to use them or anything. It took a while for them to get used to this new me. It took me a while too!

Insight, Simplicity & Change

"Life is not complex. We are complex. Life is simple, and the simple thing is the right thing."

~ Oscar Wilde

It felt like I'd started to nail this business of working in prison. The team were in love with the work. My latest volunteer was Paul Lock, a silver fox with a big heart. I loved sharing with him. The guys liked him, and insights popped like popcorn.

Of course, there were the struggles.

Driving the eighty-eight mile round trip from home to the prison was one of them. In traffic it could add three or four hours to my day.

The research was another. Men in our groups hated the questionnaires and were often suspicious of our reasons for wanting to gather the deluge of data at the beginning of the program.

And then there were the moments of serendipity.

While working at HMP Onley and living in Birmingham, I cut down on the dreaded driving by staying in local B&Bs

each week. One Wednesday evening, I noticed that there was a seminar in London from a couple of first generation[31] teachers in the Three Principles understanding, Jan & Chip Chipman. I hadn't been to any of their talks before, but I knew they'd been close to Sydney Banks and that they were well respected. It'd be a wheeze to go along and hear them.

I pitched up at the coffee shop across the road from the venue to have an early dinner. The door pinged open and the Chipmans walked in. In a heartbeat I introduced myself as, "the girl who works in prisons." They were kind and nodded but were rushed by their host, so the moment was over in the blink of an eye. What I didn't know then was, Jan never forgot that moment.

"We fell in love again," said Jan. They sat on hard plastic chairs at the front of the Friends Meeting House, a Quaker group room the host had rented for the evening. The heat of packed bodies dried the November rain off our coats. Chip Chipman, a rotund chap with a bearded face and big soft eyes, spoke with a boom. Jan, a gentle woman with thunderstorm hair and a smile like a thousand stars, spoke like a hypnotic lullaby. I was mesmerised. Jan told simple stories of how she'd met Syd Banks and how their marriage had been saved. My mind slowed down to a Zen like pace, my heart burst with compassion. Tears streamed from my eyes; I wasn't sure why, but I felt a deep presence and a great love of humanity from these speakers. A random idea popped into my head. "I wonder if they would visit the prison?"

I rushed up to Chip at the end of the talk. I needed to be quick as I needed to get the last train back up to Rugby. I waited in line and bit my cheek while the other delegates spoke to him. When I got to him, I blurted out, "Would you visit my guys in prison tomorrow?" He looked bemused.

"You need to ask Jan," he said.

I turned to see there was a gap in her line of people so I rushed over to Jan, took her hands in mine, and tumbled out, "Would you and Chip be interested in visiting my prison, tomorrow morning, you need to be there at 7:30am, in Rugby. You need to bring your passports." Jan was gracious and responded that she'd love to, but she wasn't sure because she'd need to see if they could make it work. We swapped email addresses, and I dashed out the door to get to the station on time.

As it happened, my train was very delayed, so I ended up getting back to my accommodation at 1:30am in the morning. By the time I'd got into my B&B, I'd had no response from Jan, and I was not really surprised. They had come all the way from Salt Spring Island, British Columbia and they must have a busy schedule and how would they know how to get to Rugby, anyway!

I went to bed exhausted but pleased that I had asked the question. As one of my friends from the Northeast says, "Shy bairns get nowt." At 6:00am I woke to the sound of my phone pinging a message. The tired, fuzzy head I'd felt abandoned me with a sudden whoosh of energy that leapt me out of bed. There, on my phone, was an email from Jan. "We are on the train on our way to Rugby. See you at the prison at 7:30am. Love Jan & Chip." The Chipmans were coming to my prison to see my guys! I couldn't believe it. I'd felt very cheeky asking them to come without assisting them at all and yet they'd figured it out. For most of that morning, I felt like I was in a dream, and I kept having to

131

remind myself it was real. At times I felt sure I was still asleep at Euston Station waiting for my train!

When I was asked later that day how I'd managed to pull off such a thing, I reflected that I never let myself get in the way of an inspired idea. If I have the thought "speak to them" or "do this," I follow it. I don't analyse it or worry about it or try to do someone else's thinking. I just follow it. Sometimes this creates amazing things. Simple.

Later that day. After plenty of rushing around to secure the visit, we had all the guys from both morning and afternoon groups pile into the tiny group room on K wing. Twenty of them in a room that was risk assessed for up to twelve. They were not happy. Knees touched and men moaned. They hated being mixed with men they didn't know. The only saving grace was that they were excited we had people from Canada coming to see them.

Anna held the fort while I went off to the gatehouse to escort the Chipmans through the prison to our wing. They walked into the room and the same lads who had looked so surly minutes before became gentlemen. One offered to make drinks for the Chipmans, one leapt up to get a chair for Jan, and then they sat and gazed at the visitors. Chip, followed by Jan, went around the room, shook every man's hand and asked their name. Once we were all settled, the Chipmans just talked. I expected profundity, but they just chatted, like they'd met old friends. They told stories about their journey to the UK. They talked about Syd Banks and the experience he'd had. They mused about their relationship. They shared snippets about the work they'd done in prisons themselves. But every word uttered seemed to resonate in the room and deepen the feeling of connection.

I felt a twinge of embarrassment when they mentioned Syd Banks[32], and one man said, "Who dat?"

The moment was lifted when the guy next to him said, "You know bro, he dat fella who wrote *Enlightened Gardener*, fam." Everyone laughed. At the end of the session, I escorted the Chipmans back to the gate. I linked arms with Jan and sheltered under her umbrella. "Thank you, thank you," I kept saying.

"No, Jacqueline, thank you," Jan replied. "We've always wanted to teach in an English prison."

That visit was like a supercharged learning curve for me. I noticed the ease and connection that the Chipmans had with the men. How they just listened to them and spoke from their stories rather than making a point. I noticed how the men got quiet and listened, hanging off every word. The men talked about the Chipman's visit for weeks afterwards, and I changed the way I ran my sessions. I no longer spent so much time at the flip chart, making notes or writing down everything they said. I connected with them and learned to listen deeper and deeper. I introduced Sydney Banks' works as soon as possible. In the past, I'd been reluctant to share the story of an enlightened man, thinking it too 'woo woo'. I just hadn't realised the value of sharing Syd's story in his own words. His story offers hope to all of humanity — that it is possible for any normal person in any moment to have an insight so profound it can transform their lives. And the men loved him.

All human beings are hungry for simplicity. All human beings are impacted by universal truths. All human beings change when they connect to their inner selves.

The Chipmans taught me that I'm good enough. That

what I was doing was heartfelt and honest. That my desire to relieve suffering in that population meant that I couldn't get it wrong. That yes, I will learn and continue to learn, but all I needed to do was keep following my passion and my love for these guys and that I would be guided by my own wisdom and insight into what and when to change.

Notes

31   People who knew and were taught by Sydney Banks – the enlightened man who uncovered the Three Principles understanding. Also known as the OGs.

32   Sydney Banks wrote books and had audio recordings, and videos, made of his talks around the world https://sydbanks.com

Keep On Keeping On

"Don't just create a change for yourself, be a centre
of change to others."

~ Richmond Akhigbe

Some days were just hard. Hard to be in a system that sees
people as broken. Hard to have no access to the outside
world — no mobile phone, no email, and no one knows if
we're going to be out late due to another lockdown[33]. Hard
on our feet as we walked miles around the prison, up the
stairs, down the stairs, along corridors, through wings, and
out in the wind from building to building.

Hard on our sleep. Getting in by 7:00am to warm up the
creaky computer system and sort out the many issues with
the paperwork for our men. Getting home by 7:00pm due to
traffic and weather.

Hard on our patience when half the men on the list
didn't turn up, so we tracked them down or report them
missing. Hard on our energy when a man would turn up
"under the influence," and we'd send him back and report
him. Hard on our ears with the comms team barking
instructions into the earpiece while we tried to get our

group to settle into a quiet space.

Hard on our headspace as we navigated being present with little on our minds while being fully aware that we were in a secure environment with lots of rules to follow. Hard on our boundaries with the juxtaposition of immense feelings of compassion and limitations imposed for our safety. Hard on our resilience as one thing after another would go wrong or get cocked up: like the team travelling up from London in bad weather on cold blustery days to run a group that gets cancelled because of a regime issue; like relying on drinks supplies from a third party, to turn up one day and find the coffee had been removed because they "couldn't afford to support us anymore"; like finding out someone we had worked with had been raped or beaten up the night before.

And more, much more, more than I'm allowed to write about.

And then there was the research. I'd entered the research element with a willingness and engagement to evidence the work. Not even to prove it, just to find out if what we were doing had an impact on the people we worked with. Simple. Or so it seemed.

Proper academic research should measure the changes by comparing the group of people you are working with to a group of people with the same circumstances, who you are not working with. So, if twenty men, with addiction issues, residents at HMP Onley who were taking three other interventions were on our waiting list, ten of them would be in the "treatment group"—i.e., they would receive our programme, and ten of them would be in the "control group" – i.e., they wouldn't receive our programme.

Before the programme ran, both sets of men would be

measured for well-being, purpose in life, depression, and anxiety. And both sets of men would be measured after the programme had ended ten weeks later. Then a researcher would compare the measurements to see if the men we were giving the programme to (the treatment group) had changed compared to the set of men who were not getting the programme (the control group).

With enough numbers, the research team can run a statistical analysis that shows if the change is "significant," meaning that there is enough of a difference in the two sets of men that it can be extrapolated out to the wider population of the people you are working with (in our case, all other prison residents with the same criteria).

It was a nightmare. Logistical issues (finding men scattered all over the prison in dusty warehouses and noisy wings); ethical issues (turning men down from starting the program because they were part of the control group); educational issues[34]; crowd control issues (having ten men surrounding us in a dusty workshop, with no tables or chairs, leaning against walls to complete the surveys, with screaming machines drowning out our voices, and trying to help someone with their reading while keeping an eye on the others so they don't wander off).

It was all hard. But. The stories I heard made me want to keep on keeping on.

PRISON NOTES – MARCH 2016

I sat in for the start of one of our groups on K wing today. It's the final day, and I wanted to be there for the check-in, to hear how the guys were doing. Each one of them had got something, each one spoke with a quiet wonder at their insights, each one listened as the others talked. Marcel was last to talk, a man from Albania who was shy to come forward in group, who'd always sat at the back of the room with his arms across his chest. His long legs unfolded in front of him, his white socks showing above his untrendy grey trainers.

"I came to England to become a man, and I did become a man, a road man. I learnt the ways of the road and ended up in prison, where I have been for the past two and a half years. When I got to England, I knew nothing. I learned a new language and a new culture. I did the best I could, even though I did bad things. I was lonely and desperate. I closed down in prison. I wore a mask to hide my feelings. But then I found this programme. This Beyond Recovery. This group of men, all willing to show their inner selves. In this wonderful room, I found love. I found peace. Because of you."

He paused, looked at each person in the room. "I will be a better man, a better father, a better husband. I owe you my gratitude forever."

Notes

33 Some threats to the prison, like a missing man, or someone on the roof, or a threat to life will result in the whole prison going into lock down – all men will be locked up and accounted for and all staff have to stay put, unable to leave or even move around the prison until the issue is resolved.

34 60% of the prison population have literacy issues – https://literacytrust.org.uk/

FRANKIE's Story

"It's all Thought Bruv."

~ Frankie

It's a gift to watch someone have an insight. To see their face glow with a light from the inside. Every time we would run groups in prison, at least one person would get a fresh perspective or have an "AHA" moment. It never failed to give me a rush of pleasure. I love the warm feeling when I see the "click" happen. When their eyes light up, or they realise something for themselves that changes everything. I love the way I learn from it too; I get to see something new; I get to bathe in their elevated consciousness.

On a cold winter's morning, we had a group of fifteen guys in the Healthcare Group Room at HMP Onley on week five of the latest ten-week programme. There were four facilitators in the room that day, sitting amongst the guys in a big circle on the soft blue chairs.

The men struggled to settle. One of them joked around and dragged the conversation down. "On that note," I said, "Let's talk about the nature of Thought." I stood next to the flip chart with a blue marker pen in one hand and a red one in the other. I'd drawn a blue stick man on the off-white paper of the flip chart and two wavy lines to represent a river. The guys were all watching me. "We only ever experience thought in the moment," I said, as I finished off the diagram. The room was still. And then the joker picked up where he'd left off and started to describe how exciting it was to commit crime; how his adrenaline pumped, how he'd felt high, how he didn't regret it. I was dismayed. I'd lost them. My mouth was dry as I regained my patience and considered how to bring them back away from this chatter.

"Oh My God!" Frankie said. Shafts of early morning sunshine sprinkled the stale air. The ridges on the top of the whiteboard pen dug into the palm of my hand. Frankie's pale grey face was flushed pink, as if with a light from within, his brown eyes wide as saucers.

"It's all Thought," he said. "It's ALL THOUGHT! Oh my God, bruv, it really is all Thought." His head shook with disbelief, blonde hair slicked back in place with gel. Waves of relief emanated from him. Each wave crashed over me as his insight got deeper and deeper.

"Nah, mate, when I see that phone box at the end of my road, I get cravings bad man, real bad," Paulo said.

"How can it be the phone box?" Frankie replied. "Think about it bruv, it's gotta be Thought, the phone box ain't done nothin' to ya." The conversation went on with different men coming up with different scenarios and Frankie answered every time, "Thought, bruv!"

Frankie's insight that "It's all Thought" was a defining moment. When the world looks one way in one minute and then a new perspective hits and everything looks different. When that happens, the world changes in such a radical way you can't believe you didn't see it before. Not everyone has such huge defining moments but when someone does, it's like watching a miracle unfold. Frankie saw more about his insight as the next few weeks went on. He saw how things he'd always believed were no longer true. He'd believed he was a heroin addict, yet he stopped taking drugs overnight. He'd believed he wasn't loved, yet he found his family had never stopped loving him. He'd believed his only choice was to be a criminal, yet he started to see potential beyond that.

We Shall See

"We shall see what we shall see."
~ Wilhelm Röntgen

An old Chinese proverb[35] tells the story of how no matter what happens, the master just says, "We shall see."

Every time something unfortunate occurs, his entourage say, "Oh no this is really bad."

And he says, "We shall see."

When something fortunate happens, his people say, "Wow, this is really lucky."

And he says, "We shall see."

Because, in real terms, we never know what will turn out to be the best thing that ever happened or the worst thing for us. People have been made redundant, felt devastated, and within twelve months be travelling the world writing because they had always wanted to do that but couldn't while holding down a responsible job. Someone wins the lottery, goes wild, alienates their friends, and ends up homeless and poor.

My life with Beyond Recovery feels like that Chinese fable. A roller coaster of ups and downs. Moments of, "Yes, we're getting somewhere!" followed by, "Oh no, it's all gone wrong." Through it all, I never knew how things would turn out. There were times it seemed worth it. There were times I wanted to give up. There were times I was lost with no idea what to do next. There were times I felt like we'd save the world. Truth is, I could never tell if the events would be for the good or for the bad. It was always, "We shall see."

The work in prison was exhausting, heart-warming and soul-destroying, in equal measures.

But there were the rewards:

Wonder at the compassion in the guys: "I didn't even know my mum's favourite colour," Robert said, "because I've never really listened to her. I asked her, and she broke down crying. Happy tears!"

Joy when we'd bump into a man in the corridor we hadn't seen for a while. "How are you doing?" I'd ask.

"I've stopped drinking miss," the guy would say, or "I'm going to the gym and eating well," or "I've never felt better." And often, "You've saved my life."

Or seeing the sparkle come back to someone's eyes.

"How's your week been?" I asked, during the check-in for our morning group. We were in the Healthcare group room. A quieter, more comfortable space without the distractions of the noisy wing. Fifteen of us sitting around, ready to share what had happened since our last meeting.

Spring morning sunshine lit the area with the feel of a friend's sitting room. Michael was an unkempt twenty-five year old man. A bag of bones. Face shallow, most of his teeth missing or rotten from years of drug use. He'd been in the "system" since a baby. Abused in care, he ran away at twelve and had been homeless since. He'd learnt how to use petty crime to feed himself, then his drug habit. If his sentence ended in winter months, or just before Christmas, he knew how to re-offend to get himself back in for warmth and a few hot meals. He could be out one morning and back in the next. To him, prison was home.

"Well miss," Michael said, "Last week I looked at dem sayings on the wall, and they touched me, miss. I like dem. When I got back to me pad, I decided to write to me nanna in Scotland. Her and me mum fell out years ago miss, cos of all the drugs an' that. Me mum lives in London. I never knew wot to say, but I wrote, and all these words I ain't heard of kept coming out of me 'ead. I just kept writing tings that I never knew I knew!"

The room was spellbound. Tough men wiped the corners of their eyes. Michael carried on. "Then I fort I'm gonna write to da police to see if I can get back all me stuff, miss, 'cos every time I gets arrested, they take me stuff, and if I had it all back that would give me a start wouldn't it miss?" A few weeks later, Michael turned up with new teeth (he'd applied to the prison dentist to sort himself out — "It'll make it easier for peeps to believe I wanna change, miss,"), a job in the Market Gardens[36] at the prison (one of the best jobs), and the news that his "nanna" had been so moved by his letter she had contacted his mum (her daughter) and arranged to go and visit her to see what they could do to help Michael.

Rewards like these kept coming. And kept us going.

And then there were the blows:

I'd won the contract at the prison because my application had come at a time when there'd been an underspend in the Northamptonshire council for 2015-2016. I found out that the same underspend was also available for the next year

2016-2017. "Brilliant," I thought. I went to see the substance misuse manager about it. He was very positive that Beyond Recovery would be renewed because, "You bring such value to our clients and to our team."

I spoke to Ian Fulton (the Council Commissioner) who said, "You are hands down the best service provider we have worked with, in terms of provision, reporting, impact and evidencing." And just to be sure, I met with Pete Middleton (Head of Reducing Reoffending) who said, "This is having more impact than I've ever seen, we should have it in all areas. Even the workshops agree that the men work better once they have done your programme; people become better at all things."

Everybody said that continuing with Beyond Recovery was a no brainer. We just needed the Drug Strategy Committee to ratify it.

The Drug Strategy Committee had a monthly meeting that was attended by the main Governor of the prison (the No1), the senior management team (SMT), the Head of Commissioning for the NHS,[37] the Head of Commissioning for local government, and third-party providers like Phoenix Futures, and me, Beyond Recovery. The March 2016 meeting was gathered to ratify spending for the "extra" services like ours. The deputy governor (the Dep) was sitting in for the No1 on that cold March day. The banter around the table was light-hearted. The expectation was that this was a simple decision, and we'd move on in the agenda. Comfortable and relaxed in the overheated boardroom situated at the front of the prison (and well away from any residents) the meeting droned on. I'd submitted our proposal for continuing the project for a further twelve months.

"We need new security lights," said the Dep. The assembled parties waited for his proposal on where the funds would be found to provide the new lights. "So instead of Beyond Recovery, I think we should use the funding to purchase the new lights."

Birds chirped in the trees beyond the car park, prison radios crackled on the belts of the officers in the room. My head spun.

"I'm not sure that'll work," said Ian Fulton, the Commissioner.

Ian went onto explain how the local council had spent many thousands of pounds refurbishing one of the prison wings to become a "recovery" wing and that the initiatives like Beyond Recovery were ensuring that this money would not be wasted. He laid out the case for why the programme should not be stopped when it was gaining such momentum.

I just sat there. Stunned into silence. Stunned with disbelief. Stunned at my own hubris. I had assumed everyone was right and that we were "in." I'd been wrong. Again.

The Dep was unmoved by Ian Fulton's plea but was forced to leave the decision until the following month due to a technical issue. I left the prison in a fog and phoned Paul Lock for some reassurance. "I can't believe what just happened," I said. I was sat in my car at the end of the prison car park, the high grey walls with their razor wire in front of me. The car windows were down to relieve the pressure in the car that matched the pressure in my head. The phone felt sticky, pressed against my hot tear-stained cheek. Paul laughed. A long raucous laugh.

"It's not funny," I said.

"It is," Paul responded. "This is your opportunity to

get creative. Did you listen to the people in the meeting? What do THEY want? It's not about just repeating what you did before, it's about listening to what they want now and offering that."

He was right. I had assumed we had a "thing" a "model" a "way", but we never have. There is always room for listening again to see what's changed. There is always the opportunity to be creative and fresh. There is always the space for innovation.

We went from having this amazing programme running well and changing lives to, "It's over Jacqueline, we need the money for other things."

After the call with Paul, I felt inspired and invigorated.

I went home, got the coffee on, and sat down with my notebook. I imagined every single person at that boardroom table. I recalled what they'd said and what they struggled with. I considered what solutions I could provide. I'd moved from a mindset of expectation to a mindset of service. Creative juices ran through me. Over the following couple of weeks, I developed a proposal that would meet the needs of every stakeholder in that room and the men I loved to work with. I no longer cared if we won the proposal or not, I was excited to be given the opportunity to present my innovative ideas.

Notes

35   Sai Weng lost his horse, Alan Watts https://youtu.be/sWd6fNVZ20o
36   The Market Gardens grow produce used in the prison kitchens. It is one of the most trusted jobs, only given to men who are 'low risk' due to their being tools such as metal spades.
37   The British National Health Service

Shifting Sands

"Ego is only what you think you are and what you
think of life, nothing more, nothing less."
~ Sydney Banks

The April Drug Strategy Committee at HMP Onley came
around quick. I'd prepared the updated proposal. I was
ready to give it my best shot. The usual crowd were there,
the Senior Management Team of the prison, the Heads of
Commissioning for NHS and local government and Phoenix
Futures. But this time the Head of Reducing Reoffending
was sitting in for the No1 Governor, and he was a big advocate of our work.

I'd created a proposal that would meet the needs of every
person that had been at the table at the previous meeting.
The proposal had:

- ◆ A course for drug dealers – to reduce the supply
  of drugs
- ◆ A course for people with addictions – to reduce
  demand for drugs

+ A course for people with complex needs[38] – to reduce self-harming
+ A course for gangsters – to reduce violence

I'd realised that it's no good just saying, "Yeah, we can do anything with one programme." The prison managers needed to see that I understood the complexities of the problems.

I was as pleased as punch. At this point, I didn't even mind if they still went ahead and bought security lights. The creative process of turning a negative situation into creative potential had given me more juice to see, "If I'm not doing this, I'll be doing something else."

I surveyed the room. Yes, I felt nervous but somehow the room felt different to me. More positive. More hopeful. More open.

ISore Media (the film crew) also had a pitch to present. They'd been invited to show some of the amazing films they'd made with the guys to kick the meeting off. "I can't get the film to play," the presenter said. An open window brought the smell of cigarette smoke into the room.

"Can you play my video?" I asked, referring to a film I'd commissioned iSore Media to create, a graduation[39] video showing some of the guys talking about their experience of our programme. The next minute, my video was playing on the large projector screen at the end of the room. Everyone fell silent, all eyes riveted on the twenty-minute film of Beyond Recovery's work. Guys with all sorts of backgrounds and a history of offending and addiction spoke:

Martin: "There was no learning to do, it was all within oneself."

Michael: "I knew God was within, but I didn't know how to access that power."

Craig: "I have been able to lift my level of consciousness. Hopefully."

I knew the film was powerful. I'd watched it many times and played it at several conferences; it still brought a tear to my eyes. But would it sway this tough audience? Would they be able to see past the guys' behaviour to the truth of what they'd found? Or would they just see manipulation?

The closing music stopped. There was a breath. "SLAP." The Head of Reducing Reoffending smacked his hand onto the wooden boardroom table. "Where do I sign?"

I exhaled; I hadn't even realised I'd held my breath.

He continued, "I worked with Craig when he first came in many years ago, and if you can turn him around, you can change anyone!"

I never had to pitch my ideas. I didn't need to. "This is it," I thought. "We're in!"

Our contract was renewed for a further twelve months. Another year to show the prison that the safety of the prison improves by improving the well-being of the guys.

The next twelve months saw the programme's popularity rocket amongst the guys and the staff. We had referrals from many of the departments: Offender Management Unit (OMU), Substance Misuse, Safer Custody, and even Education. I did a second research paper based on the three day "immersion" and in the same month was invited to talk to the prison next door to Onley, HMP Rye Hill – a category B prison for people with sexual convictions, known as "sex offenders," We even started workshops outside the prison walls for interested prison staff and officers.

"This is it," I thought. "There's no stopping us now!"

PRISON NOTES – APRIL 2016

We had a session with the peer mentors this week. The idea was to see what's fresh and see where they're stuck. I was so excited; I love working with Susan and it's always a gift to sit with these guys.

"I never really appreciated my family before," Wayne said.

Susan and I were sitting with eight of the guys in a circle on the soft plush chairs in the Healthcare group room. She'd just read a chapter from "The Missing Link" and the room was quiet as they reflected on the words of Sydney Banks. All ten of us sat still. Our hands rested in our laps or across the back of the blue chairs; sounds of birds tweeted through the barred windows. Wayne's face was lit up. He sat up straight in his chair, his long legs stretched out in front of him in faded blue jeans and Jordan Air trainers.

"I've always been the black sheep," he continued, "but now I can see bruv, I mean, my dad has always stuck by me. I never seen that before." The simple statement had a domino effect around the room. Everyone started to have a dad moment.

"You just made me realise my dad does love me," Andy said. He told us about how he had always judged his dad; he was absent and, "just threw money at us." He'd wanted his dad to have been better but, in that moment, he saw that his dad was just being the dad he thinks he should be and that in his reality, what he was doing WAS loving them. I looked over at Fats, who was sitting in the far corner by the tea table with a shocked look on his face.

"Tell me again what you just said about your dad," he said. His blue jeans and grey jumper hung loose on his body. Unkempt afro hair sprung out above his thin face, wet with tears.

"OK," Andy replied, and told the story again.

"Oh man, I can't believe how many years I've been fighting my dad," Fats said, doubled forward in his chair, head held in his large bony hands. We sat in silence. "I don't av to do dat any more bruv," he sobbed.

Every single person in that room told a dad story today. Every man and woman. Every age. Every colour. We all had Dad stories. Stories of misunderstanding. Stories of love. Stories of forgiveness.

People ask me from time to time what my vision had been. The answer: "To work with everyone who comes through that gate. And one day, to turn prisons into rehabilitation centres where people can get the help they need; families can get the assistance they need, and victims can get the support they need."

I assumed we would just keep getting more contracts in different prisons, providing we kept proving what we were doing, and people could see the lives that were being transformed.

I assumed the relationships we made with the various senior management colleagues would support this.

I assumed things would grow if I worked hard enough.

On all counts I was wrong. Again!

By September 2016 the Senior Management Team at HMP Onley, the "No1 Gov" and his Dep had moved[40] to another prison and a whole new set of senior people had come in to manage the prison. A new set of people with a new set of ideas. They had their own teams, and an immediate dislike for any initiatives put in place by the previous team.

Sigh.

Now I had a whole new group of people to impress. A whole new ball game. A whole new mountain to climb.

"It's OK," I thought. "We've got funds until April '17; loads of time to create new relationships." But that's not what happened. The new senior team had priorities, and too much on their minds to meet with me. I was frustrated to say the least. I wanted to yell at anyone who might listen. But nobody listened. I feared that all our good work would crumble. Then I'd have a great meeting with the executive director of prisons. "It's going to be OK," I told myself. "We can keep helping the guys, keep making ground, keep building this programme for new inmates. It's going to be OK." Then, just like that, the executive director moved into another role in another prison, in another country!

"Is it going to be OK?" Each time I wondered how I would carry on.

In the five years we were at HMP Onley, there were four changes of senior management. Four changes of No1 Governors. Four times, I built new relationships.

"Oh well," I thought, "Ian Fulton (the Commissioner

153

for Northamptonshire County Council, where HMP Onley is based) loves us. He will put in a good word." But, as life would have it, in Jan 2017 Northamptonshire County Council went into "special measures." They stripped back on spending. They stopped paying for "nice to have" services. They sold their shiny new premises. They had no more money.

And then. As if it weren't already hard enough. The commissioner, Ian Fulton. Our advocate. Our connector. Our friend. Retired.

"That's it," I thought. "I can't keep on going."

Notes

38 A person with complex needs will have a number of issues, such as addiction, mental health diagnosis and trauma backgrounds. Sometimes referred to as Dual Diagnosis. Many agencies cannot deal with all the issues, so the people keep getting batted around and not being helped.
39 When we finish each programme, we present the guys with a certificate and have a graduation party.
40 Governors are moved roughly every two years and they often take their teams with them.

Trying to Get a Man
Out of Prison

"We know what we are but know not what we
may be."

~ William Shakespeare

I've lived in the torment of trauma and suffered the consequences of my memories. I have bucket loads of empathy
for those who have suffered because of the actions of others.

And I've realised, over time, and with compassion for
myself, that I'm the one who keeps that adversity alive. I'm
not a victim now. It took me a long time to see that. The
answer was simple but hidden from me. When I started
working with people in recovery, I started to see that people
are never broken. The essence of who they are is never
harmed. The pain is kept alive with thought in the moment.
That's how the system works. Our minds have the power to
recreate events, to conjure up memories, to bring us to our
knees. We can go there, but we don't have to stay there.

I didn't show up to this work to fix my past, find forgiveness or inner peace. The work in the recovery field was

presented to me; the work in prison came to me. I never asked for it. I never searched for it. I never knew I wanted it.

But somehow it showed up, and I showed up. And when I saw how men whose lives had been spent in crime and violence and selfishness could transform into compassionate, caring, wise people, I knew there was something I could do to help society. I could not only change the lives of the people I was working with but could change the lives of everyone involved with those people, and of the people who may have been future victims.

And an interesting thing happened. As I saw past the behaviour and the sins of the people I worked with, I saw the parallel in my own life. When I realised that everyone has a bright potential within them, I saw it mirrored back at me. Because I could see the pureness of their souls, I found the pureness in mine.

In May 2016, I was invited to speak at 3PUK – a conference for people interested in the Three Principles paradigm to gather and hear speakers from around the world. It was the conference where I'd had my first insight; "I can do anything." Then here I was, three years later, at the Allianz Rugby Stadium in Hendon, London, being invited on stage to talk about the work I was doing in prison. It felt surreal.

When I'd been invited to present with a panel of the people I work with, my mouth dried up, and I heard a small voice say "OK." I was petrified. It was one thing standing up and speaking in front of a handful of people, but it felt like quite another to do it on a stage with several hundred people. And with other speakers who were so much more experienced than me. I tried to ignore my insecurity and figure out what I'd present.

I asked Anna Debenham to present with me, as she'd seen the work first-hand. And I wanted people with dramatic stories to maximise the impact on the audience.

I wanted someone who had been to prison, who knew what it was like to be locked up and yet still feel free, who could show that all human beings operate the same way and have the same pure essence of life that we all have.

I knew that some prisons have a scheme called ROTL (Release on Temporary License) which means a resident can have a pass to leave prison for the day. It's available for residents where it can benefit their chances of rehabilitation. It's not for people who are classed as a high risk to the public. Which is a good thing, right?

I knew a ROTL wouldn't be easy for the men we were working with as they were all "high risk", but I'd seen huge changes in a few of the guys, so I figured the prison might consider my request. I set up a meeting with the Head of Reducing Offending to see if I could get a ROTL for a couple of the guys. I wanted a guy we'd been working with for a while, David, but I'd brought a backup list just in case, with David's name at the end.

"Here you go, Sir," I said. The A4 piece of paper in front of him had my hit list of the guys I knew would do well on the stage. I sat in his pleasant sun-filled office above the Enhanced Wing, a wing that had been purpose-built to house prisoners who'd reached enhanced status through good behaviour, so could be trusted. Part of the top floor was a large, open-plan office for the Activities Hub — people who monitor and plan for all the activities in the prison — and the Head of Reducing Offending's office.

"Oh no," he said as he looked down the list with his

glasses perched on the end of his nose. He shook his bald head and pointed to each man on the list. "No." "Not him." "Definitely not him." "No way." Until he got to the final name, David. "Absolutely, definitely, not ever!" he exclaimed.

David was still classed as high-risk due to his previous propensity of smuggling phones and drugs into prison and for his violent behaviour towards other prisoners and staff. He'd changed a great deal since his first insight when he'd seen he'd been living in his negative thinking. He hadn't hurt anyone for many months. In fact, he was a big softie! He'd secured a good job painting the staff offices and was trusted. But his old reputation was still intact.

I was stumped. In a way, it was a compliment because it demonstrated that we worked with the toughest guys. I felt proud of my boys and how they had changed. I could see that we were making a huge difference. But that didn't help my plan of taking one of the guys to the conference. If I couldn't have any of our guys, how was I going to show the audience what transformations are possible when people realise they are the creator of their own experience?

I decided to give up the idea. A few days before the conference I was at the prison when I had a lightbulb moment. How about if David wrote a letter that I could take with me! I knocked at his cell door and opened the metal flap so he could see it was me. "Can you do me a favour?" I asked. I stood at the heavy steel door with its blue chipped paint on the landing of B wing. I spoke into the crack in the doorjamb to be heard.

"Of course," David said. I explained what I wanted and held my breath.

"OK," he said, followed by, "When do you need it?" The

landing was quiet as most men have a sleep during their lunch time "bang-up." An aroma of stewed vegetables, grease and sweat assaulted my nostrils.

"By 5:00pm today," I said. A tiny mouse scurried across the end of the landing.

"Jeez. It's a good job it's you MamaJ. Means I can't refuse!"

Saving the Lives of Future Victims

"I Choose Life."

~ David

The conference loomed and my debilitating fear of public speaking loomed with it. But when I wasn't thinking about the huge crowd or vexed about how I would look or sound, I was OK.

On the day of my presentation, I stood at the side of the stage. Aaron Turner, the host, introduced me as, "Someone who was out of her depth, but saw a need and answered it, and grew from there." I wished the earth would open and swallow me. My mouth shut like a clam. Sweaty hands held my notebook. My heart beat out of my chest like Roger Rabbit. I stared down at my pink shoes with the multi-coloured buttons.

"It's gonna be great." I whispered false bravado to my "panel" standing next to me. The audience laughed and clapped at Aaron's introduction and four of us walked up onto the stage and sat on the chairs that had been provided.

"Thank you," I said to the audience. One hand was in my lap on the smooth silk of my new dress, one hand held the microphone. My voice shook with emotion. The stadium was packed. People sat close together in a gigantic semi-circle that reached all the way into the adjoining rooms and the open glass doors at the back. I paused to let my mind settle. I reflected on my message: To talk about my passion for the people that need our help the most. To share my belief in the goodness of all human beings. To ignite the spark of oneness in the room. "I have a letter from prison for you," I said.

It seems unbelievable, but in no time at all I'd forgotten my nerves and was focused on rooting for my panel. Each one of them stood up and shared their story for fifteen minutes. When Sally proclaimed, "I'm Sally and I'm not an alcoholic!" at the end of her talk, the audience leapt to their feet in a standing ovation, tears streamed down their faces. The room thundered with the sounds of their claps. It was a true "drop the mic" moment.

I channelled my inner Madonna. I rocked the stage with my microphone headset. Instead of hiding behind the podium, I was in front of it. Leant on its tall black frame with my precious letter in front of me.

"I'll bleep out the swear words," I said. Seven-hundred people laughed. I took my time, often choked with emotion. David's story was brutal, humble, and vulnerable. It told of bad things and bad thoughts. It told of death, murder, and suicide. It told of violence, drugs, and suffering. It told of PTSD, anti-social personality disorder and anxiety. It told how men in prison fall through the education cracks and can't read and write. It told how they teach themselves, in their cells, on their own. The letter laid out the story of one man and his trauma and the story was grim. The air in the stadium hung still with a summer's breath. Tears spilled down the faces of the audience. Gasps of shock, and the giggles, rippled around the room. "I'll close with this final paragraph," I said.

> "What I need you to understand is that before this I wasn't a nice person. There is so much more I could tell you. So much heartache and pain. I've hurt a lot of people because I didn't care. I was a selfish, controlling, nasty, BLEEP. When things kicked into place, I suddenly had answers to questions I didn't know I had. I read Syd's [Banks] books. I can't put it into words, but I had this feeling. It's given me inner peace. It's taken my stress and anger and pain and depression away. Gone. I choose life."

The letter laid out that without the understanding of how we experience life, the men we work with would continue the lifestyles they'd had. They all knew that they would most likely have spent the rest of their lives in prison. And that even if they weren't in a physical prison, they would have been prisoners of their own angry thoughts. The letter concluded,

> "The course hasn't just saved my life, it saved the lives of my future victims. Because now I just want to help people and give something back [41]."

The audience leapt to their feet as one great thunderous crowd. They clapped, cried, and cheered. I glimpsed the impact the letter had had on them. At that moment, I vowed that I'd never listen to my fears about public speaking again. The message I have is way bigger than my own insecure thinking.

The way I see it is that the work we do in prisons, with the people who have committed heinous crimes, reminds them of who they were before their behaviour, before their misguided thinking led them to their crimes, before their contaminated version of life. By reminding them of their true nature that lies beneath all that, they wake up. And in that awakening their old behaviour no longer makes sense. They become compassionate and empathetic. They want to help others, not hurt them. And they start to think of ways of giving back to society, with an increased level of confidence and natural intelligence.

Notes

41   In 2019 David was invited by the conference organisers to be the keynote speaker. His talk is here https://youtu.be/5PKQ3wQxXi4

Could you Work with Sex Offenders?

"A journey of a thousand miles begins with a single step."

~ Confucius

"Could you work with Sex Offenders?" Ian Fulton[42] asked. The meeting with the substance misuse team from HMP Rye Hill was at a cafe in a garden centre in rural Northamptonshire. The clinks of cups and burps of steam in the coffee percolator mingled with low-level chatter from the other customers. The bright morning sunshine spread its warmth through the long glass windows. A gold earring glinted from the edge of one of the chairs. My insides stood still.

"I'm sure I could," I said.

Ian and the substance misuse team told me how they could see the Beyond programme working in their prison, with people who'd admitted their crimes and were ready for change. They could also see how the work could help the staff. We agreed to run a group once a quarter for the men and two team sessions for the staff.

Boom. Our next project. I was so excited. I wondered if it would be different working with people who had committed sexual offences. I mean, what they've done doesn't define them, right? But did I really believe that? My own childhood and the terrible stories we hear about these crimes clashed with my beliefs that no one was born evil. I figured I'd get to find out. I didn't see the opportunity as some sort of catharsis. It was just what had been put in front of me. I wasn't searching for anything there. It was searching for me.

Paul Lock agreed to be my co-facilitator. I felt more comfortable going in with a man. We set up a time to tour the prison and get ready for our new groups. Everything about the prison was different from what we had experienced before. Security was more intense, as it was a well-known "sex offenders" prison, where men come to serve their life sentences for heinous crimes after having served time in a maximum-security prison; others come to be rehabilitated from their violent behaviour, attitudes towards women, and issues with early childhood trauma and addiction.

I wasn't cleared to draw keys, which meant we were escorted wherever we went. All bags were searched and scanned. IDs were examined. In addition to the standard barred items (chewing gum, USB sticks and so on), there were restrictions on scarves (they can be used to attempt suicide or in a hostage situation), smartwatches, and car keys. Each time I entered the security reception, I'd be frisked and told off if I'd forgotten to put something in the locker. The next stage was to stand on the yellow footprints marked on the floor as an officer held the lead to a drug dog who sniffed my entire body, even standing on her hind paws to reach up to my chest. No-one smiled.

Once we were both ready, an air-locked door opened to allow us into a small corridor where we'd wait for another officer to open the door to the gatehouse. Then we sat and waited for our escort. My confidence seemed to have been left in the locker on the other side of the airlock.

As we sat waiting, we watched staff enter the building, shed their normal life, and don the garb of an officer in a high-security prison: large bunches of metal keys, walkie-talkie radios in black leather pouches, thick sharp fish knives, pointy wire cutters and long black tasers. All the accoutrements slipped into their places on tool belts wrapped around their waists. We sat in silence.

The double steel gate to the inside of the prison made an ear-splitting buzz every time it was opened. Then a bleep that increased in speed for every second it stayed open. This was to encourage staff to unlock the second gate, get out, and lock it again in as little time as possible.

Our escort, Joan, dressed in black trousers and a white blouse, collected us from the gatehouse and walked us through the steel doors and into the prison yard. "Good morning," she said. The inner perimeter of the prison was sealed off by double concrete walls on one side and tall iron fences on the other. Thick loops of razor wire decorated the tops of the fences. The heavy steel gates had the mandatory double locks plus a long clip to ensure the gate was in position and locked.

"Wow, a garden centre," I exclaimed. We stood just inside the steel gate of a thriving nursery. Long, thin Perspex tunnels lined one side of the walkway and flower beds on the other. In each tunnel were men dressed in grey tracksuits and yellow gardening gloves: potting new seeds;

turning over the soil; sorting a variety of vegetables; watering plants. There was a riot of colour, reds and blues and violets and yellows. Heady, perfumed smells filled the fresh morning air with the scent of heaven.

"The men are here for a long time, so they make it their home," Joan said.

She walked us to the Drug and Alcohol Treatment Unit (DAAT), where the substance misuse team had their offices and where our group room would be based. The unit was a set of Porta cabins based in a large expanse of organic gardens, surrounded by beehives. Each of the hives had its own swarm of bees that pulsated around the entrance to the hive; queen inside and worker bees going to and from the hive to the myriad of flower beds. We later found out that the hives and the organic gardens were special projects, set up as charities to help rehabilitate men with addiction issues.

There were more vegetables than a farmers' market! Vibrant marrows, tomatoes, potatoes, and beans grew in small beds, up sticks and under mesh blankets. A wooden trestle table and chairs stood in the middle of the gardens, with blue plastic tea-stained mugs on top. A serene pond with koi carp and a miniature stone bridge completed the picture. "I think we are going to enjoy working here!" I said.

Notes

42   The commissioner for Northampton County Council

MILES' Story

"I've been hiding the peacemaker inside."

~ Miles

There is an essence, beyond the behaviour, in every human being.

It's what I look for in the people I work with. It helps me see past my judgements of what's right and wrong. Past my abhorrence of what they've done. Past my heartbreak at the harm they've caused.

The knowledge that human potential and mental health lie within the consciousness of all human beings always manages to bring me back to love and understanding. It helps me find a way through the judgements to the root cause of the suffering: hurt people hurt people, and all people want is peace of mind.

My grounding in that knowledge was never tested more than after one of our groups at HMP Rye Hill.

"Wow," Paul said. It was Friday afternoon. We stood in the car park of the prison at the end of a three-day programme. The air tastes different beyond the thick grey walls and barbed wire. The sun is kinder. The birds sing louder. I saw a reflection of my own dazed mind on Paul's face, softened from insight. Our hearts beat in time, full of gratitude for the hours we'd spent behind those walls. The eight prisoners in the small Portakabin had brought gifts of humour and resilience, and stories of pain and suffering. I'd had my heart and mind bashed around like a tennis ball. Emotions swung from horror to delight, from pain to love. Back and forth from one minute to the next.

"I know," I replied.

Paul and I went for lunch. Words weren't necessary as we sat bathed in a depth of feeling that needed quiet. We parted with a final hug. "Safe travels home," I said. "I'll call you tomorrow."

I never ask what crimes have been committed. At first, it was to ensure I kept my mind clear of judgement. Treat everyone the same. Then it just became a thing.

Sometimes I got to find out the nature of the crime. A safety factor, for instance, if there is a danger to women. Or because the support worker had the opinion that I should know (it's the standard practice for other interventions). From time to time, I got to find out after I'd finished group, when I was doing a follow-up, or if some behaviour had been triggered.

This is the way it was with Miles.

Miles had stood out from the rest of the group. Sharp-witted and bright. Ready to engage. Asked loads of questions. He was a strip of wind with a fast scouser accent, in his late twenties. The whole group laughed at his antics. When he got embarrassed, he'd pull his red knitted hat over his face like a young child. He seemed to take care of everyone. He was the sort of lad you'd want to take home, give him a good bath, and feed him up.

Later that day, I removed my heavy work boots and curled up on the sofa in my kitchen, happy to feel the sunlight on my face through the dusty windows, grateful for warm socks and a steaming mug of coffee. My hands wrapped around the cup as I read the confidential email on Miles. Cold shards of dread pierced my fluffy reverie. A dense fog filled my mind. Mascara stained my face. "Are you OK?" Rob asked.

Shame welded my tongue to the roof of my mouth. The world shifted on its axis. I felt sick and dizzy and frightened all at once. "No," I said. Rob came to sit next to me, and I snapped the computer shut. "I need to lie down," I said. I lay on the sofa, and he wrapped me in my favourite blue blanket. I just stared at the kitchen table legs, afraid to close my eyes. Afraid to keep them open. Just afraid.

Miles had committed a crime so dark and horrible I can't even write about it here. I'd never even imagined something so terrible. I was ashamed I'd been so kind towards him. That I'd wanted to bring him home and look after him. I'd been stupid to believe there was goodness in everyone. How could there be? And how the hell could I make a difference with my quirky ideas? Questions whirred and spun, doubt flooded me, depression overwhelmed me.

I couldn't speak. I couldn't explain. I couldn't make any sense of it.

The whole premise of what I was sharing was that all humans are good at their essence. If that was in doubt, then I couldn't carry on. The thing must be true of everyone, no exceptions. Otherwise, it's a house of cards that would tumble down. I felt ashamed I'd even tried. The next day arrived. A dark cloud blanketed me, kept me sane while my world adjusted. Everything ached.

On the second evening, I texted Paul: "I don't know what to say." I said.

"I know." Paul's morse code of a nothing text told me he felt the same. He knew what I knew. He was living his own night of the long knives.

On the third day, I sat on the kitchen sofa in my usual spot. I felt like I'd been there for weeks. The wind gusted through the trees. Sunlight dappled onto the counter. The sound of a blackbird trilled into my heart. As the fog lifted, this is what occurred to me:

"Even the worst crime is still behaviour coming from a misunderstanding."

"Terrible deeds are done from an unhealthy mind."

"There is no line."

"All human beings are worthy. All are pure at their essence."

And finally.

"The work I do is more important, not less, when faced with things I don't understand."

I felt calm. And quiet. There was no elation at this insight. Just a deeper sense of my own humility.

That insight enabled me to carry on working at Rye Hill and showed me that no matter how bad the crime, the person's soul is not broken. It may be that they should pay for what they've done; their crimes may be unforgivable. It may be that they stay in prison for the rest of their lives. But it is still possible to uncover the health buried beneath that unhealthy mind and help them find peace. Hurt people hurt people. Our job is not to hurt more, but to heal.

A year later, I got the opportunity to sit with Miles again. I was supposed to have a follow-up group of four men, but for one reason or another, only Miles turned up. I'd wondered about him a few times and heard he'd been up and down. After our group, he did a special intensive programme that meant we couldn't see him. When I realised it was only the two of us for the next three hours, I felt a little tense, but I also saw it as an opportunity. I made us both a coffee and settled down to hear what was going on for him.

We sat in the warm Portakabin in the middle of the organic gardens and Miles told me his story. Born in Liverpool into a family entrenched in criminality, weapons, violence, and drugs. As young as five, he'd be taken to visit uncles in prison with mobile phones and drugs concealed in the cavities of his body. To him, prison was just another place some of his family lived. At twenty-one years old, he was in the chaos of a full-blown heroin addiction. He thieved for his habit and tried to find a way of belonging. He was rarely in charge of his own faculties and got involved in a gang of people committing horrendous crimes. He'd taken part. Was responsible for the fatality of a baby. Was arrested and sentenced for thirty years.

"You want me to carry on, miss?" Miles asked.

A long, slow breath escaped my mouth, my coffee stone cold. "Yes Miles," I said.

For the first ten years in prison, his life continued to be chaotic and uncontrollable. He was consumed by grief for the traumas he'd suffered as a child, and guilt for the trauma he'd caused others. Being sober didn't help. His days and nights were filled with horrific dreams. He had a bad case of PTSD. When I first met him in 2016, he'd made some headway into his addiction issues with the support of the drugs team, but he was still having to block his memories of his own past and his subsequent behaviour by self-medicating.

We both sat in silence for several minutes. The feeling was peaceful between us. I understood.

"Was there anything that stood out for you from our group?" I asked.

Miles leant backwards in his chair and stared out the Portakabin window at the bright blue sky, his red woollen cap pushed back on his head.

"I didn't really know what happened at first," he said, "but I just felt like there was hope. I felt the same feeling I got in church. At first, I couldn't believe that I deserved to be free from my tormented mind, so I kept getting involved in madness. And then in January I just decided to become drug free. It was random. I would still take it from whoever was selling and flush it down the toilet, but as time went by, I just stopped accepting it from people. And then the fella asks me to move it on for him, but I decided I didn't even want to do that."

We both gazed at the blue plastic cups on the little wooden table in front of us.

Miles continued, "I don't really know why, but I feel free. I still have twenty years to serve. And I accept that, but I feel freer than I've ever felt in my life. Another strange thing that has happened is I want to help others. I seem to have become a peacemaker. And then I realised that before, when I used to wade in and get involved, really, I was hiding the peacemaker inside by acting tough. I saved an old man the other day who was being bullied. I don't even know him."

Miles's pale face was lit with a soft glow.

"And get this," he said, looking at me with a cheeky smile. "Another guy walked into my pad the other day and told me he loved me! I would've kicked off even a few months ago and put him straight, but this time I just calmly sat down with him, and we had a good chat. I listened to him. Now he knows how I feel, and that I'm not interested in that sort of thing, and I know how he feels, and we have been honest, so now we can be good friends. I didn't even know that could happen."

The birds from the aviary just beyond the gardens chirped and chirruped.

"You know what, miss? I feel I can help other people and there is some good in me. I can make my sentence work by helping others and making all our time here easier and more peaceful. I never knew I had good in me. It seemed to me I was worthless. But now I feel a sense of connection and like there is a spirit inside of me; to me, it seems like God loves me and I feel great love when I listen to hymns and prayers. Something moves inside me."

I walked away from Miles that day feeling a little freer myself. His story gave me the hope that I can continue to uncover the Peacemaker hiding inside of me.

We Are More Than We Think

"I come to prison as nothing & I'm leaving a woman who has learned to love themself."
~ Beyond Recovery Participant

People often ask me how I kept on going through the ups and downs of the business. Through all the disappointments. Through the difficulties. They want to know how I got over my anxiety about public speaking, my feelings of rejection about not being heard, or my beliefs that "I didn't know what I was doing." I'd always believed myself to be stupid; a person who doesn't have big insights. The words came more regular than breakfast as a child: "You're so stupid," accompanied by a smack around the head. "You're stupid AND ugly." I heard it so often I believed it. For a long time.

As I grew up and had insights about what was possible, I overcame the things that seemed like flaws in me. I didn't think they had gone away, but I saw I could still make the best of my life. I was an optimist. I looked on the bright side. Did the best I could with the limitations I had. Smiled through the pain.

I pushed myself to what I felt were my limits. I held on tight, grit my teeth and made things happen. I was used to doing more than I thought I should be able to do. It's how I got my degree in Computer Science and Ergonomics when I was twenty-nine. I forced myself to study and work hard after work every night, putting myself through college in the evenings, sitting exams and interviews until I could get a place at Aston University.

It's how I got my master's degree in Networking Technologies and Management on a distance learning program with Sheffield Hallam University while working a full-time job and bringing up a teenage son as a single parent.

It's how I started a successful project management consultancy that I ran for five years.

I felt the fear and did it anyway. Bit back the angst. Swallowed the embarrassment. Drowned out the rejections. That's just how life is. Life is hard, and then you die. I said it was character-building to withstand the blows and never give up. I knew I was resilient, that I had tough skin, that I had grit. I remember one of my early jobs as a young woman when I told someone in a casual conversation about how my dad used to hold my hands to the fire when I was three because I was stubborn. The point was to demonstrate my stubbornness. But she was shocked. She just stood there with her mouth open. Not at the story but at the casual way I told it, as if it were OK; as if I could just shrug it off; as if I wasn't affected.

Dear Diary (June 1988),

I've never felt so alone. I went to work today with my black eye, else I would've lost my job. The other girls went out to lunch and when they came back, they told me if I didn't leave Tym, they wouldn't talk to me again. I can't believe they would do this to me. They don't understand. Last night Tym and I had a big row. Again. He was so mad at me. He threatened to lamp me if I didn't shut up. I didn't, and so he did. He'd stormed out of the car after we pulled up and just went up the metal stairs to our flat above the shops in Sparkhill. I sat there for a while, stewed on his nasty words, and then, fuming, I raced out of the car, up the metal staircase, across the rooftop and into the long narrow kitchen, shouting like a banshee. I ran into that kitchen, determined to stand up for myself, and I ran straight into his fist. The world spun and the next thing I remember, he was standing over me saying sorry. He kept apologising and trying to pick me up.

I felt all woozy and my face hurt, but I liked the attention. He was all soft and sweet and loving and when I got to the bathroom and looked in the mirror, I could see why. The whole of the right side of my face was a big black and blue mess. My eye was shut tight inside the huge bulging swelling of my cheek. It looked gross. He sat me on a stool and gave me a bag of frozen Birds Eye peas wrapped in my favourite pink fluffy towel. He says he'll never hurt me again. I really think he means it this time.

As I became more socially aware, it seemed that my ability to get over stuff and appear untouched by my past events was strange to people so I hid it, but I added it to the list of things that was strange about me.

It wasn't until I was sitting in the theatre for the first weekend of Michael Neill's Supercoach Academy back in 2012, that I realised that my capacity for withstanding the knocks is resilience. It registered that no matter how many things have been said to me, no matter how many things have happened to me, and no matter how many things have been done to me, I am not damaged. I'm not anything I'd believed about myself. I'm so much more.

The facilitator stood at the front of the room at that first seminar. He looked out at the audience of forty students and said, "You are loved." A dam burst inside me and poured out through my eyes. Who I *thought* I was melted into the fabric of the old worn theatre chairs. In my mind, I saw a little girl, a sweet little girl in the sunshine. One who skipped, laughed, and looked about with bright hazel eyes. Eyes of trust. I saw how pure and gentle she was. I knew she wasn't to blame for what was to happen. I saw how innocent she was. I saw how lovely she was. And I forgave myself. I embraced the little girl in my mind, and I knew that she was loved.

It all sounds very strange now, but I wanted to explain how I keep overcoming the ups and downs of this journey and why I can keep getting over my fears and insecurities. I learned about why it was possible to transcend our limiting beliefs. I know that every one of us is as innocent and as joyful as that little girl. I know that all we do is shroud our pureness in a wall of thought and we don't even know we are doing it. I know we are so much more than the things we think of ourselves. I know we are resilient, creative, resourceful beings who have the capacity and capability to do anything we want.

Every Moment is a Fresh Beginning

"We mostly see what we have learned to
expect to see."

~ Betty Edwards

I embraced my work in the prison with a passion that consumed me. Every evening I'd tell Rob stories of amazing people who were having insights and whose lives were changed. He wanted to know more.

"Let's go to Salt Spring Island, in British Columbia," I said. "Sydney Banks set up a school there before he died in 2009, for people who want to learn about the Three Principles. I hear it's gorgeous. And the school is 'taught' by those people who came to the prison a few months back."

I already knew we could stay with a couple who lived in Vancouver, because they'd flown in from Canada to see me speak at an event in Spain. (Even when I write that I feel like I'm having an out-of-body experience!) So, we planned a little holiday at the same time.

The slow ferry that moves from Tsawwassen in Canada

out to Salt Spring takes about an hour and a half. On the way it stops at several little oases where seals bask and creatures roam. The island itself is magical. A land without traffic lights, just courteous drivers. Soft brown deer roam along the paths, shy raccoons rustle about in the garden shrubs. Tiny wings of iridescent hummingbirds buzz close by as they dip their long thin snouts to drink nectar left out for them in bright coloured containers. My mind settled down from the one hundred miles an hour pace to an easy idle. Each day was a blissful blend of walking Indian trails, sipping hot lemon tea on the patio and picnics in our loft bedroom.

The Three Principles school was run by Elsie Spittle and Chip Chipman[43]. They'd have a Meet and Greet on the Thursday evening. At that event we got to meet the other participants and Chip and Elsie gave a little pep talk. "This time is for you," they said. "If you want to network, network with yourself." I took this to heart and allowed myself the luxury of not having to socialise or even talk about my work with others. I'd spent the last couple of years with work as my focus. Now was the opportunity to focus on myself.

The following day we arrived at the venue, an arts centre, in the middle of the town of Ganges, filled with light and air and a variety of paintings and sculptures from local artists. After fresh coffee and sweet baked pastries from a local caterer, we took our seats with the forty or so other participants in the bright conference room. Elsie and Chip sat facing us in armchairs at the front of the room. They looked peaceful and comfortable, with soft smiles on their ageing faces, and the sizzle of voices in the room settled to a hush. I sat next to Rob, thighs touching, his warm hand on my cool arm. I was excited for him to "see" something. I didn't think I was there for myself.

Elsie and Chip shared stories of Syd Banks and their own lives. They wove threads of universal truths about how human beings experience life and the power beyond that, through their sweet, gentle stories. My pulse slowed and my mind drifted like a soft summer breeze. The stir of an insight bubbled inside me. I reflected on how blessed I felt for the work I was doing in prison. I'd witnessed insight lighting people up from the inside like a candle that glowed brighter and brighter until it spilled out of their eyes. And I'd been grateful that somehow that ability was coming through me. As I sat in that gratitude, I realised something else, something I'd not known before. It's hard to explain, but it just came to me that the love I talked about, to the guys in prison, was indeed ME. That the source of all peace, the essence of human beings, the true nature that I pointed other people to was also me. I'd never even considered that before. I'd considered myself a conduit, but not *part* of what I was doing.

It seems strange to me that I'd already achieved so much and impacted so many people without knowing that fact, but I've come to see that as the nature of consciousness. We only ever know the reality that we are living in right now, but there are other levels of consciousness where we can see the same thing from a different perspective. After that insight, everything made sense to me. The communication in those prison groups is soul to soul, not what we say or teach, but where, inside, we are sharing from. I continued to get more insights during that weekend, the biggest being that we are all learning, all the time, through all that happens to us throughout our lives. The cliché "every day's a school day" is true, but I saw it at a deeper level this time, as opposed to understanding it from my intellect. I knew without a doubt that it's possible to keep seeing with more depth and more clarity for the rest of our lives. This makes me humble for what I don't know and grateful for what I do know.

PRISON NOTES – JUNE 2016

I love the way the men experiment with what we show them and keep allowing themselves to drop into a deeper state, to see more. They are so humble, they never think they've "got it," I was talking to Frankie the other day about what I've seen about addiction, how we all misinterpret feelings of relief to the drug or drink or gym or shopping or sex or even chocolate! When what's really going on is a mental shift. Our thoughts change, or pass, and we feel better, independent of the activity (drug, drink, chocolate, sex) but it LOOKS like it is the activity that makes us feel better.

He said it made sense but that he'd been struggling with his "using" thoughts. And although he'd been drug free for eight months for the first time in his life since the age of fifteen (he's now in his thirties) he'd gone through a very tough time in prison and was having cravings and urges. He battled himself with a torrent of thought. "I'll let everyone down. What about if I have something and can't stop? What will people think of me? Where will it lead?"

When he paused for breath I said, "It seems to me that your thoughts about not using (drugs) are causing more suffering than your thoughts about using them." I could see by the look on his face that this really landed.

He told me later, he knew deep down that a pill wouldn't make a difference, and that his good feeling wouldn't come from the pill, but would only come from a change in his own thinking, which would only happen when his mind cleared. But he'd been overthinking it so much he couldn't tell what was wisdom and what was not. So, he took it anyway. "But it did me good, you know," he said. "I got to see that the drug did NOTHING. I saw that I'm not an addict, and what was most weird was, I saw that I don't even like it!"

We experience the world depending on our level of awareness in any given moment. Because of that there are many ways to see what looks like reality. Each time I'm open to seeing something new about a situation I get fresh thinking, a deeper understanding or a whole new level of consciousness that changes everything I'm experiencing. Nothing is as it seems and "Everything is Possible."

Notes

43 One of the original teachers who came to Onley prison with his wife Jan back in Nov '15.

My Parents Were Innocent

"No-one can make you feel inferior without
your consent."
~ Eleanor Roosevelt

I'd given consent all my life for others to have that power. I
never knew I had a choice, until I made up my mind at forty
years old to live without the shadow of my father over me.

Insights appear in the strangest of places.

I mean, that's what I love about insight. It's got nothing
to do with where you are or who you're with, right? It's from
within in ... sight. So, it just pops up whenever. A story from
Rye Hill prison demonstrates this.

The day Paul Lock and I started our first group I'd been
more wary than I would have been in the prison next door,
despite my confidence that these men were just as wise
underneath their behaviour, just as whole, just as worthwhile. I was more guarded, less curious, and more closed.
They seemed different to me. They didn't jump around, play
each other up or shout across to each other as we walked

around the wings. They stood alone or sat at tables. We didn't hear the blare of rap and hip hop and dance music. Just the sound of a budgie or canary as we walked past the cell doors, where men with enhanced status could keep a bird for company.

During the group sessions the men were silent, sullen, and suspicious. A group of ten would sit around the edge of the Portakabin and wait. They expected to be judged, analysed, and measured. In other prisons, men would talk about their lives and their time in different prisons in vibrant, multicoloured language. These men didn't. They are taught not to discuss their crimes in case it indulges their fantasies. So, they stared, and they waited, and they expected to get very little from the group.

We surprised them. We sat with them and waited too. We didn't judge, analyse, or measure. We spoke when we were moved to. We asked them what they would like. We told them stories. And we waited some more.

"Can I do the group again miss?" one of the guys asked. Wild garlic from the organic garden beyond the open window drifted into the Portakabin. "I've not listened for the last three days because I was waiting for the catch. Now I know there isn't one I'd like to do it again 'cos it sounds interesting!" He wasn't the only man to do this over the two years we spent there. Men who have sexual convictions are subject to much psychological analysis. They were suspicious that when they relaxed we'd bring out a test. If we made a note in the group, they believed we were observing their actions. If we discussed something in whispers about what to do next, the room would hush, thinking we were discussing them. That is until after the third group in December 2016. A shift in me caused a shift in them.

PRISON NOTES – DECEMBER 2016

I found a new level of freedom today. In prison. It never fails to astonish me how much I see for myself when sitting with these guys. The man who impacted me is in the prison for sexual offences and has committed violent crimes against women. I'd kept my guard up. It was so warm inside the Portakabin, I was dozy. Paul sat to my left and we had ten men in a semi-circle. Today was our last day of the three-day programme and we had lots of long moments of quiet.

I felt Jordan shift in his seat to my right. I glanced at him, and he said, "I feel free." I was sitting on my hands. The worn fabric of the chair was scratchy on my fingertips. Warm sun filled the Portakabin with light. Sweet smells from the organic gardens infused the air. Birds chirped in the aviary.

"Wow," I said. At his words, a flush of wonder inside my body spread to my hands and face. My eyes pricked with tears. An explosion of fireworks flashed in my mind, followed by a deep sense of calm. His freedom had freed me. I didn't even understand why, I just knew what he meant and felt the same. He spotted the change and asked me what had happened.

I felt a sudden burst of gratitude towards Jordan, towards the men in the room, towards myself and towards my parents. My parents who've been dead for many years. In one big sudden moment I realised that they'd been doing the best they could. That their abuse and neglect had been them acting out their own trauma and pain. "My parents were innocent," I said to Jordan.

I've never seen this before. But because of Jordan's feeling of freedom, I saw I could have freedom. That I could let go of the pain I carried and move on.

After that I saw the men in Rye Hill with different eyes. I realised their psychological innocence. I knew that although their crimes or the harm they had done could not be forgiven, I could understand that they had acted out of their own trauma and pain. Their behaviour came from a mind clouded with hurt and torment and a desire to feel better. I know it's hard to accept this. I too have sat in judgement. I too feel the agonised mind melt of screwed up behaviour. I too feel the loss and sorrow.

But consider this for a moment. I'm ashamed of some of the things I've said and done when I've acted out of rage or hurt or insecurity. I'm disappointed in some of the things I've said and done that I know have hurt others, even people I've loved. I'm disgusted at some of my behaviour when I've been drunk and couldn't care less in that moment. And I would take all of it back, I would mend all of it, I would wipe all of it out. If I could. But I also know that from a healthy state of mind, from a grounded place of well-being, from a loving heart, I just wouldn't do those things in the first place. Or if I did, I would do way less harm and fix it more easily.

In the moment when I realised my parents' psychological innocence, I felt a freedom and a joy I'd never experienced. A deep sense of peace and gratitude for what they had done *for* me replaced years of resentment for what they had done *to* me. And it made me a nicer person. I no longer carried around a heap of insecurity, so I was kinder to other people. I no longer took everything so personal. I no longer had to protect myself. That freedom doesn't mean I condone their behaviour, it means I no longer carry the hurt with me.

The Visitors

"It was like sitting in a room full of philosophers."
~ Beyond Recovery Visitor

From the beginning of the Beyond Recovery prison project people have got in touch with me because they want to get involved in some way. Most often they want to volunteer to learn how to teach the understanding, or they want to gain confidence in doing so. Other people have heard about the successes and the transformations, and they want to see it for themselves.

I'm an open networker. I'm not territorial. I've invited people to come along and sit in our groups. I've shared our research in the hope it will help other people get their projects off the ground. I've shared the outline of our programme for people to springboard their own ideas. I've trained people and had many one-to-ones on Zoom and other platforms. I've consulted with people in Norway, Denmark, the Czech Republic, Spain, Mexico, Australia, New Zealand, and the USA to help them with getting work in the criminal justice systems of their own countries.

Over the years I've had many visitors sit in on groups,

or spend the day with me in prison, or sit in on one session. Some people come and sit in weekly on a ten-week program. The Beyond Recovery team all started with a period of observation. First, a visit to see if hanging out in prison is really for them, and if I like the way they are with our guys. If this goes well and they're still keen to volunteer, they come for a longer period of visits, for which they need to be vetted (a laborious process). Then there would be the potential to work with me as a volunteer (up until this point it is more of an overhead than a help to have the visitors).

I noticed two things:

1. By volunteering in the first instance, people bring a different energy to the work. They show up in a different way and are genuine in their desire to help. The guys love it. There's research[44] that points to the impact it has on people in prison when civilians are willing to give of their own time. It makes the residents feel as though people care. This in turn changes their perception of who they want to be in the world.

2. The visitors are always impacted by what they see in the men and in their own lives. Seeing people in prison have peace of mind does something to our own reality when we have so much more to be grateful for. Over the years we've had some very moving experiences with visitors. One of the most memorable for me was the visit by Steph and Kaye, two business ladies from Scotland who'd been on the same practitioner

training programme as me, and who'd become good friends.

Steph & Kaye

They came down from Scotland and stayed at a farmhouse near the prison. For a couple of days before the prison visit, they ran a group with some of the staff. I'd been impressed by how unfazed they seemed about going into prison for the first time. That was until they stood with me in the prison reception. "I felt like I was about to go on a really scary ride at Disney World," Kaye told me later. Seeing me collect my keys and radio made the girls wake up to the fact that they were in an actual prison and not being escorted by "the guards," As we walked through the grounds towards our group room, I gave them the tour of the facility.

"The men live in there," I said, pointing to the building next to the path we were walking on.

"What?" exclaimed Kaye. "They're in there right now?"

I laughed, but she was serious. All her insecurities about what it would be like to meet someone in prison had flashed into her mind. She was petrified.

Steph and I went off to stand at the gate to welcome the men coming off other wings, and Kaye stayed with Anna in the room where we were about to run our group. Kaye told us this story:

"Anna went out of the room to get the men in, so I was on my own. I just sat really really quiet. The first guy walked in, and he was huge and had scars and looked like a prisoner (to me) and he sat a few seats away from me and I just stared straight ahead looking out of the barred window.

He said, "You haven't been in prison before, have you?" And I was like, "No it's my first time." And he came and sat right next to me. Panic rose in my throat, and he said, "It's OK you'll feel better in a minute." In that moment I dropped out of my head into my heart and felt a deep connection to this guy. All the insecurity disappeared.

The next thing he said was, "I didn't know that I had mental health until I came on this programme. It's answered all my questions and I can't tell you how this has changed my life." He shared with me that he was doing seventeen years and that his sentence had been extended for violence and he had three more years and you could tell that however long he is going to be in prison, his experience of it will be completely different. That conversation changed everything for me."

The group was being facilitated by Anna and Lili so once all the guys were in the room, I left them to it. I interviewed[45] the visitors afterwards on video about their visit and both Steph and Kaye talked about how they found the men in group to be so kind, and funny. They noticed how settled the guys were and how they could feel them listening. One man was a bit more fidgety and halfway through the class he jolted back in his seat with a massive smile on his face. Anna picked up on it and asked him what was going on, and he said, "It's ALL Thought!" And just laughed.

"He saw that, on a level that was deeply profound for him," Kaye said. "What struck me was, here I was in a room full of people in prison and all I felt was love and connection. I felt privileged to spend that time with them. And to witness people seeing who they really are."

I asked Kaye if she had seen anything different for herself and she answered with tears in her eyes, "That we are all the same."

Steph told me about how she felt more noise and stress in her head than she had for a long time. Her experience of sitting in the room was like being somewhere where lots of different music was playing at very high volume and then it was just quiet. She could feel the men listening in a way she had not experienced when sharing with groups before. "There was a depth of feeling. It was like they were not trying to get it with their intellect; we were just in that depth together, and it was just so peaceful."

Steph was moved to tears when one of the guys said to her, "People is people init?" She realised it didn't matter that he was in prison, and she would be going home, both of them could experience the same in the moment.

Both ladies shared that prior to coming to the prison they didn't really have a deep understanding of "being of service," Afterwards, they saw where they could help others who are suffering. "When people are in trouble, and you can have that much impact in such a short space of time just by pointing to something so simple ..." Steph paused and then said, "This is how I know I can serve." And Kaye talked about how it had never occurred to her before to talk to people who were homeless or on the streets, and that she had even been a bit frightened of the idea. After her visit she went down to her local homeless shelter and offered to volunteer.

Notes

44   The impact of volunteers on stakeholders is described in this guide https://www.clinks.org/sites/default/files/2018-11/Valuing%20volunteers%20in%20prison.pdf

45   See a video of Steph & Kaye's visit here https://youtu.be/uQW5rB9fHNg and this from a visitor from Australia https://youtu.be/pQDC7Zm1vDw

Becoming A Speaker

"My life is not already set out for me. I can change anything."

~ Beyond Recovery Participant

Fear held me back. Until I realised fear was just thought.

I was invited back to speak at the conference where I'd read the letter from the guys. I still didn't love public speaking, but I'd seen the impact my message could have, and I was determined to push fear aside and allow the opportunity to open hearts and minds.

It was May 2017 and once again I'd tried to get a release on temporary licence for some of our guys who'd had life-changing realisations. Once again, I'd been unsuccessful. Once again, I'd need to rely on my wisdom to guide me. Once again, I trusted what would unfold.

The night before my talk I sat on the bed in my hotel room and said, "My talk is going to flop; the audience are expecting the guys and all they will get is me." I stood by the window and stared at the street below. My gut clenched with a fist.

"Oh!" I said. I'd had a sudden flash of inspiration. SD

at HMP Onley had been bowled over by the work we were doing with his clients and his team. Maybe he'd come and join me.

He said yes as soon as I told him what I needed. And the next day he got himself down to London to sit beside me on the stage at the Allianz Stadium in front of seven-hundred people.

I had my usual nerves but knew they'd pass as soon as I was talking about my favourite subject, the power of transformation. And then, as if to test my mettle, the strangest thing happened.

The host, Aaron Turner, had held a moment's silence in commemoration of the people affected by a bombing at a pop concert the evening before, in Manchester.

"And now I have the pleasure of introducing Jacqueline Hollows," he said. At the sound of my name, a third of the audience stood up and walked out of the room. Including many in the front row, the people who were my mentors. Ice-cold dread ran through my veins. "Why do they hate me?" Even Aaron looked startled. He glanced at me with a "What just happened?" look on his face. The people who'd stood up cleared the room while SD and I climbed the three short steps to the stage.

"I hope you're all here because you want to be and not because you feel sorry for me," I said. The audience laughed but the mass exodus had done nothing to calm my nerves. The words felt frozen on my tongue. My throat constricted and dried. I took a sip of water. I knew I needed to ignore what had just happened and speak. So that's what I did. After a few breaths, I'd settled. I could deal with my anxiety later.

"I'd like to tell you about Pip.

I was running a group with Paul Lock and this young man sat scowling at us. He was skinny, pale, and seemed very sad. The first thing he said was, "This class is rubbish, I ain't learning nowt." At the end of the first day, I asked how he was doing, and he said "confused." I talked to him a little about that and asked him if he could be OK with sitting with the confusion for a while because I've found it can be helpful to be confused. He looked at me as if I was a crazy person but agreed he would try to be OK with it.

At the end of the second day, as we walked through the prison grounds to escort the men back to their wings, Paul asked him how he was. Pip surprised us both with his answer. "The discussion opened some boxes I had kept locked away, some painful memories about my baby that was stillborn. Then I remembered some of the good memories that I'd been burying under the bad ones. I feel like now I can just enjoy those memories instead of fighting them."

On the final day, he turned up and said he'd slept all night for the first time in many months. "I have butterflies in my tummy, the good ones. I can't remember ever feeling like this before. I woke up and boom, 'I don't need anti-depressants, I'm not depressed!' His face was pink. He had a spring in his step. He beamed with gratitude. "It's unbelievable that this can happen. I didn't know it was possible. I now know that I don't need anything to be happy. I can just be happy. I AM happy!"

Pip has got six years left to serve in prison but believes he can be happy now instead of waiting to

be released. "I'm only twenty-four; I can have a different life." He looked at both of us with starry eyes, "It's
amazing how a few words can change your whole life!"

It makes me think about how our resiliency emerges
naturally when we stop fighting our painful memories.
And that's true for me too."

I got through my talk and between us, we did a good job.
So much so that I was invited to speak at many more events
over the coming years. Events based all over the world.
I'm grateful and honoured to say that I've spoken at con-
ferences[46] and events in Cape Town, Prague, Bucharest,
Los Angeles, Charlottesville, Salt Spring Island, Singapore,
Norway, and Spain.

Wow. When I write that sentence and I look back at
my life: littered with abuse, neglect, trauma, violence, self-
doubt, episodes of depression and suicidal thoughts; the
difference seems unbelievable. And let's not forget my
debilitating fear of public speaking. It is amazing to see how
life works. I could've sat at home thinking life was against
me and so what is the point of trying? Much like the guys in
prison could think the same thing – I'm here for ten, twenty
or thirty years so why bother to be different, happier, even
content? But I didn't and they don't. We were able to see
something new which resulted in opportunities and experiences beyond our wildest dreams.

For me, I now had this exciting whirlwind of travelling
and meeting people and making a difference in the world.
And even though I loved it, the one thing that kept me
humble was KNOWING that this wasn't where my well-being was coming from. My peace and happiness were and are

coming from within me. Knowing this means that regardless of what my life spans out to be, regardless of what my career is, and regardless of the ups and downs life throws at me, I can still find that gratefulness, that resilience, that humility, that peace.

Notes

46   One Solution https://onesolutionglobal.org/
     Understanding the Human Mind https://porozumenimysli.cz

Mind Spa

"This is like a spa for the Mind."
~ Retreat Participant

I'm always reminded of how I think something is going to be one way, and then it takes its own path. The journey is never linear and the more I lean into that, the more I just concentrate on what I know now, the more I embrace what is instead of what might be, the easier my life becomes.

For instance, back in 2015, when I'd started working at HMP Onley, part of the proposal was that I would also "train" the staff of the substance misuse service. I've always known that the most effective solution would be to work with the staff AND the residents. So with that in mind, I ran regular three-day programs for the staff. Some went better than others. It turned out to be an even bigger learning curve than working with the men. Some of the staff didn't want to be there, some argued, some just didn't seem to be in the room. But some liked it. Really liked it. SD loved it so much he went on to train as a facilitator himself so that he could influence the programmes that his team delivered.

By the time I'd started working at Rye Hill prison with

Paul Lock, I'd decided I didn't like working with professionals; that the only people I could work with were prison residents. They were my people. However, the idea of working with staff and residents alongside each other hadn't gone away, so I persevered. The Rye Hill drugs team were a tough crowd. We could see they would rather have been anywhere else. Paul and I tried our best and ran our sessions, but we didn't enjoy them. Well, that's a bit of a harsh view. We enjoyed the sessions, but we didn't think they did, except for one person who was impacted. Dani who was sweet and welcoming and made it all worthwhile. Once the first set of programmes finished, we stopped offering them to the Rye Hill staff. They didn't seem to miss them.

But we did keep working with the substance misuse staff at HMP Onley, and we came up with the idea of offering to meet with other professionals in the field, running the training as a three-day retreat. Now we just needed a nice venue. Neither of us were into the idea of a hotel conference room; we wanted somewhere with a bit more quirk.

One day I was driving past the turnoff to HMP Onley on the A45 and wondered, "What else is around here?" About a mile past the turnoff was another right-hand turn with a battered old sign saying, "Farm Shop," I'd passed this turn many times on my way from Daventry to Rugby. I love a good farm shop and was intrigued by this one, as the road just looked like a dirt track. It stretched as far as I could see. Just green on either side of me and blue sky ahead. The car rocked and crunched over the barely visible track. After half a mile, I started to doubt this was going anywhere, and a fear of trespassing rose like bile in my throat. The only options were to continue or to put the car into reverse and get out of there. I started to imagine how dark this road would be at night with no streetlamps for miles and spooked myself with imaginings of night creatures and worse. I locked the doors of the car, gripped the steering wheel, and kept on going.

Soon, much to my relief, farm buildings and sheds appeared ahead. It still seemed like it was a mistake, but at least I'd be able to turn around and drive back out. I took the final right hand swing and relaxed as the crunch of dirt and rock under my wheels turned into the smooth of tarmac. Civilisation! A couple of twists and turns past the huge sheds, I could see a carpark full of horse boxes and a few cars. Signs reading "Equestrian Vet" and "The Nose Bag Café" appeared. I pulled up beside a long, new pink brick building with a farm shop, double doors to a reception area, and a shop for equine clothing. A whole secret world of horsey things: horses, horse poo and horsey people!

Green fields stretched out, dotted with clusters of brown, white, and black horses chomping on the grass or flicking flies with their long tails. People of all ages and sizes wandered around in long leather boots and skin-tight jodhpurs, riding crops in hand. Black riding hats framed their faces. Girls with ponytails worn high on their heads, swishing from side to side, mimicked the horse's tails. I felt like I'd stepped into another world.

I meandered up the rickety metal stairs to the Nose Bag Café. The cosy bar/restaurant was well lit by floor to ceiling glass along both sides of the room. One side looked out over paddocks where junior polo riders were practicing their moves. Dining tables and chairs were laid out in front of that window. A glass wall on the other side of the room gave a view of the indoor ring where dressage horses and their riders jumped over mini obstacle courses. There was also a huge wood burner, surrounded by deep plush armchairs and sofas to sit on and watch the antics. As I settled in with a steaming cup of hot chocolate, I looked out the windows to the young people on their well-groomed horses. On the horizon, I could see a clutch of buildings nestled into the view. My breath took short when I twigged that the buildings were the three prisons: Onley, Rye Hill, and the young persons' institute. The juxtaposition of the two worlds seemed twisted. This was the perfect place to run our retreats for professionals.

We had twenty people turn up to the first event. We called it the Well-Being and Resilience event. Quite a few of those people were from the Phoenix Futures team and the others were from various social businesses, and the professionals included a few officers. During the first one we ran at the Equestrian Centre, one of the participants said, "This is like a spa for the mind!" The name stuck and we've been calling it the Mind Spa ever since.

Life's A Roller Coaster

"If you were able to fall a hundred times as a child and rise, you are able to fall a thousand times as a grownup and soar."

~ Matshona Dhliwayo

I have a clear vision.

In June 2017, Onley prison had a visit from the Deputy Director of Custody (DDC) Paul Baker. A tall, straight-faced man who seemed serious about his job. I happened to be in the offices at the back of the prison wing when he walked in and started talking to the Substance Misuse Manager. "Do you know why there's been such a significant reduction in prescription medications in the last twelve months?" he asked.

The hair on my neck stood on end. I could answer that. As they talked, my cheeks flushed and I knew I needed to speak up. At the next gap in the conversation, I said, "I'm Jacqueline from Beyond Recovery and I can tell you why prescription medications have reduced." Both looked at me. "When people start waking up to their own well-being, they stop needing external fixes whether that's legal or illegal."

Paul Baker asked me what I do. I told him about our groups and that, in fact, "We have a session just about to start. Would you like to sit in?" He said he would. I found Jacquie Moses, who was running the group, and let her know. She had a moment of panic.

"Sit in with me," she pleaded.

"You've got this," I said.

The group was awesome. Paul and his assistant were impressed. And I ended up going to a meeting at Petty France (Ministry of Justice HQ). It was so easy to get carried away with what it all meant. To see connections and meaning where there were none.

Within months, Paul Baker had moved to New Zealand, and that was the end of that chapter.

Round and round the merry-go-round I'd go. I'd experience great highs of hope. Another one, when a review from the health audit on the prison stated, "The prison must find a way of keeping Beyond Recovery." That had made it seem like a given; we were going to be noticed, to be funded, to be part of the service. But nothing ever came of any of it. I'd experience the lows of despair; each time a key person left, or a governor moved on, or a report lay unnoticed.

The prison system is an archaic lump tied up in all sorts of bureaucracy, which makes change almost impossible. Sometimes I'd feel like a pioneer, breaking new ground, smashing down barriers, opening doors. Sometimes I'd feel like the tiniest of tiny cogs in a huge, complicated, cranky machine. Sometimes I'd dash forward on my white horse, waving my colours, being the change I wanted to see. Sometimes I'd crash to my knees and weep with frustration, wondering how the hell I could carry on.

I met with people. I made phone calls. I demonstrated the effectiveness of our programme. I built relationships. And then it'd seem that every time I made some headway it all fell apart again. But every time, the thing that kept me going was the guys. Knowing I was making a difference, knowing I was shining a light, knowing that people were waking up to their own true nature. I told myself that was enough, and I was determined to keep going while I could.

PRISON NOTES – JULY 2017

I've been running some introduction sessions in the last few weeks so that the guys on the waiting list get the opportunity to sit in group for a couple of hours, ask questions, and see if they like the sound of our programme. I've loved it; the banter, the fact that no question can trump truth, the clarity that all their challenges are only coming from one place! This week a guy called Kevin came along. "How do you do, miss?" he said. His muscles strained at his tight white t-shirt, his dark skin glistened with oil; a scent of soap and aftershave wafted into my consciousness. He was very well-spoken, bright, and engaging, and he'd come to see what all the fuss about our groups was about.

"Nice to have you here," I said.

Kevin joined in the conversation with great enthusiasm and was making everyone laugh. The only thing was, he kept giving the other guys lots of advice and "techniques" because he'd been studying NLP. I'm committed to keeping the conversation clean of advice, to allow space for people's own wisdom to emerge.

"Are you up for seeing something new?" I asked Kevin.

"Yes, of course, Jacqueline," he answered.

"Well, you might want to forget NLP[47] while you are in class. Leave it at the door, you can always pick it up when you leave."

He agreed and put his name down for the next group, but I could tell he wasn't very happy.

Six weeks after that diary entry I sat in on the group Kevin was in and asked him how he was getting on. He told the group the following story: "After Jacqueline said, 'forget NLP' I was angry. I went back to my cell and thought 'Nah man, I'll forget Beyond Recovery!' 'Cept, when it came to the start of the group, I decided to give it a go bruv. At that time, I was smoking and drugging, so I weren't getting much out of the group. Jacqueline had given me *The Enlightened Gardener* (by Sydney Banks) which I'd thrown on the top of my shelf, I was too busy smoking and drugging to even pick it up.

"Then, in group one day, someone tells me they read it and it blew their mind! I thought 'Wow, that little book on my bookshelf.' That night I picked it up and I read *The Enlightened Gardener* followed by *The Missing Link*. I read them man, all the way through, and through again. I couldn't stop reading. When I was done, I gathered up all the drugs, all my burn[48] and all my pornography and threw it all away, I didn't even want to give it away, I threw it away. I don't want all that stuff contaminating my mind or anyone else's mind. I'm not interested in that anymore. I don't even look at the female screws with badness anymore. People have started noticing I'm different. I feel different. I have a clear vision."

Notes

47 NLP – Neuro-linguistic programming is a way of changing someone's thoughts and behaviours to help achieve desired outcomes for them.
48 Burn – Prison slang for tobacco.

Mind Behind Bars

"I always thought the public hated me, judged me,
so I judged them. I now see we are all the same,
we are all one."

~ Beyond Recovery Participant

I stood in my shower with hot water cleaning the prison grime off my body and my achy feet. The steam filled the bathroom with sweet smells of eucalyptus and lavender. I rested my head on a towel. Another day of gratitude and grind.

"Oh!" I said. Instead of the sleepy comforted feeling I was looking for, I was alive with enthusiasm. An idea bloomed inside my mind. "Let's run a Three Principles conference in prison!" As soon as it landed, it felt like one of those flowers in the desert that spring open as soon as rain drops on them.

There was a hell of a lot to get sorted to make it possible: logistics, security clearance, booking rooms, agreeing on refreshments, creating brochures, sorting the visitor rules and searches. And of course, preparing the guys to present on stage (for the first time in their lives) in front of unknown visitors! But the team were into it and so we just kept over-coming challenge after challenge.

At the end of July, we had a final green light to go ahead with the date of 23rd August 2017. Less than a month away! It was all hands to the pump to get ready. We all pitched in to prepare as best we could. We had weekly meetings so the speakers (the prisoners) could bond. All the men were risk assessed by the prison for suitability, so we lost a couple due to infractions on their records in the last three months. The Governor told me, "If they get anything on their files, they'll be excluded." I kept my fingers crossed that our remaining speakers would behave in the run up to the event.

It was remarkable. We'd been so busy organising the seminar that I hadn't even had time to stop and think about what an incredible thing we were doing, until one Thursday afternoon, when I met with two of the guys who were peer mentors. I'd asked them to put together a brochure and nothing had yet happened, so, I asked them what they needed to make this happen. They looked at each other with that "Are you going to tell her?" look. I asked what was up, "Well," Angel said. "We've never been to a seminar; we don't know what we need to do." We were sitting on the low chairs in my office in the prison. Both men were wearing their blue Beyond Recovery branded Polo shirts and smart jeans. Embarrassment caused them to squirm on their seats.

"Of course!" I said. The next day I brought in several conference brochures to show them what sort of thing goes on. It was another one of those moments of remembering that their worlds had been very different from mine.

Two weeks to go with everything full steam ahead, I realised we'd better get some visitors. I took some time out from the prison logistics and sat in my garden, with a spreadsheet of possible visitors on my laptop on the picnic table in front of me, my daughter-in-law Lollie on the other end of my phone. Lollie's brilliant at getting past gatekeepers and getting people to agree to help, and she was up for the challenge of filling the chapel at HMP Onley with people who could make a difference to the guys' lives. We worked as a team and after a week, we'd contacted around one hundred and fifty people. We got a healthy list of twenty-seven who said "Yes."

"It's happening," Angel said. We stood side by side at the back of the sunlit chapel at the end of the long corridor of prison wings. The oak wood beams and skylights made the room light and airy. The chapel felt sacred, with its large wooden cross of Jesus hanging behind the altar and holy books on bookcases around the side of the room. I could feel the heat of Angel's skin on his arm next to mine. The nervous energy connected us; two people standing at the opening of an event we'd created together. No one would've known one was a prisoner and one wasn't.

"Yes," I said. It was hard to tell the difference between the team and the guys, all of us dressed in Beyond Recovery Polo shirts. If you looked again, you'd have noticed the team had black belts with silver chains and key pouches, but the equality we felt showed in the body language and easy camaraderie. We waited for the guests, the members of the public who were going to be filling the seats laid out in rows in front of the altar, which had been turned into a stage. The guests were searched before they were allowed to walk through the prison, so we knew they would be a bit jittery when they came.

"I'll stand at the door and greet them," Angel said. "Frankie, you show them to the refreshments table, and Enzo, you help them find their seats."

The guys had it. They'd practiced for weeks and asked lots of questions from us, and now it was over to them. As each guest walked in, Angel shook their hand and guided them to Frankie, who took them to the long trestle tables covered in white tablecloths with tea and coffee and biscuits laid out for them. I greeted each guest and ticked them off our visitors list.

Once the guys had got everyone settled down, I took to the stage and gave a welcome speech. I could see some of the guys dotted around with different people in the audience. You couldn't tell who was a visitor and who was an inmate. We'd planned for just four of the more grounded guys to be on stage, the rest to sit with the guests and answer any questions. It was such a wonderful sight. All the excited faces of the guests and of the guys sitting together. Barriers breaking down as people got to see the humanity of each other. Hankies being lifted to damp eyes moved by compassion.

And then they were on. They followed the agenda and introduced each talk. Frankie told his story of recovery from a lifelong habit of addiction and crime. He spoke passionately about how he'd always been searching, through drugs and relationships, for love and happiness, only to discover he had really been hiding. He had suppressed the real Frankie, and through uncovering the real him, he'd discovered friendships, happiness, and joy, and beaten a twelve-year heroin habit.

Then, four of the guys took their turn onstage, sitting with a coffee table in front of them. They demonstrated what happens in our groups by having a discussion between themselves about how their relationships with partners and children had changed. About how jealousy and insecurity were no longer a problem, and how grateful they were to have their children back in their lives.

Just before the lunch break, Mouse read a rousing poem of what it was like to experience freedom in prison, which had the visitors clapping and crying all at the same time.

The guys went back to their cells during the lunch break. We'd asked for them to join the buffet lunch delivered by the onsite café, "The Lock Inn," but that had been a step too far for prison security. Over sandwiches and coffee, the team mingled and chatted to the guests. All of them were bowled over. People who'd come because of my relationship with them but who'd been nervous were gushing with praise for the work we do and for the incredible transformations they were seeing.

The heat of the day and the many bodies in the chapel had the guests wanting a bit of fresh air. A few decided they would put up with having to be searched on the way out and on the way back in again and asked to be escorted out to have cigarette breaks. Then I had the great idea of taking the others around the parade ground of the prison. It was only when I'd counted eleven guests out of the door and arranged for one of the team to walk behind them as I was in front, that I realised I needed to call it in to the comms team. They'd be looking on the cameras and seeing this big group of people moving around without permission! I stopped mid-sentence and snatched up my radio, "Hello JO, Quebec 29, permission to escort the chapel guests around the parade ground, Quebec 29 over." The radio crackled.

"Permission granted Quebec 29, JO standing by."

After the lunchtime lockdown, the officer assigned as our security escorted the guys back to the chapel. Once they were all in and the doors locked, we settled down to the afternoon's agenda.

Angel told his story of trauma and anger and crime against others – his honesty and detail shocked the room. They'd experienced him that morning as one of the kindest, most nurturing hosts – ensuring all the performers got their turn, ensuring all the guests were looked after. He told them he'd been diagnosed with anti-personality disorder because of his lack of victim empathy, yet now he not only felt compassion for his victims, he felt compassion for those who'd harmed him as a child. The guests laughed when he said, "I can't even watch *Britain's Got Talent* without crying now."

Enzo told his story of being "a crackhead" and how he'd blamed his ex-wife for everything that ever happened, most of all for him giving up his dream of singing ten years ago. During one of our groups, he'd realised, "It wasn't her, it was me." The forgiveness that came with that also came with the ability to stop taking drugs. He told us he never thinks about drugs and asked permission to sing to the guests. Every hair on every neck stood on end as he belted out a couple of verses of Puccini's *Nessun Dorma*. His face glowed as he finished, and the whole of the room leapt to their feet in a standing ovation.

The final slot of the day was given over to all twelve guys on the stage to answer the questions the guests had. During the day, the visitors had been encouraged to write their questions on a card and hand them in. One of the guys read out random questions and each was answered by whoever wanted to answer it. It was delightful to hear the different answers, from the heart and in the moment. Then the question was shouted by one of the guests, "How can we help you?"

The answers from the guys humbled me:

"More Sydney Banks books."

"Funding in the prison for Beyond Recovery programmes."

"Help us set up Three Principles workshops when we get out."

"More events like this."

At the end of the day, I took the stage to hand out certificates and to thank the audience. I knew we'd gone some way towards showing that people in prison are just people. Just like me, just like everyone. The guests left buzzing and bright eyed, and the guys left wide eyed and in a bubble of happiness.

After the event, the team and some of the visitors were invited back to our home for celebration snacks. It was a stunning summer's day, especially appreciated after being cooped up in the hot chapel. I was aware of the juxtaposition of the freedom of our guests sitting on chairs and benches on our patio, amongst pots of summer flowers, and the guys who would be locked behind their doors right now. Isn't that punishment enough?

All the visitors were moved and impacted. I heard snatches of conversations; "It's incredible how anything is possible when you get out of your own way," and, "That was more impactful than all the trainings I've been on. I could've saved myself thousands of pounds." Everyone agreed. "This was the best Three Principles event I have ever been to."

Several years later, when most of the men who hosted the seminar had been released, they would tell me how the day was pivotal in their development. How their minds had expanded to what is possible beyond what they thought of themselves. How they'd always been sure that the public hated them, that they were lost causes, and to see members of the public being impacted and having insights of their own made them feel good and want to do good, to be good. It made them feel part of something bigger. How it had been one of the happiest days of their lives.

The Big Bang

"There is only one way to avoid criticism: do nothing, say nothing, and be nothing."

~ Aristotle

"As I listened to your letter from prison at the 3PUK conference, tears streamed down my face. After all the business training I'd had, it was the moment I realised 'This, is where it really makes a difference.' I knew I wanted to help." This is an extract from a note by Gary Burton.

Whenever I present at a conference or seminar, people will contact me afterwards to see how they can help. One of the people was Gary Burton, a very successful businessman with a big heart, and a strong Essex accent. He looked like a cuddly bear. He called my mobile one evening when I was at a B&B in a little village called Long Buckby, in Northamptonshire.

"Hiya Jacqueline, it's Gary Burton here." The farmland outside my window was filled with fluffy white sheep with little black faces. They grazed on lush green grass that seemed to go on for miles. Beyond that were fields of yellow rapeseed. The open windows filled my small, neat bedroom with waves of late afternoon heat and the smell of a nearby lavender bush. A bee buzzed its busy mission in the summer air. The smell of scones from the kitchen below added to this idyllic scene. "I'd like to volunteer for you," Gary said.

Many people have offered to volunteer over the years, kind-hearted people who would like the work experience and I'm always grateful for the interest. I've never forgotten what it was like to be doing this alone, but often the time it takes to get them vetted and key trained, to induct them in the prison, and then to train them, adds more of a demand than help, and I've turned people away. Gary had been trying to get hold of me for a couple of months. He was on sabbatical from a successful business and had experienced a personal transformation. He was keen to help in any way he could.

I felt inspired by his enthusiasm, so we set a date for him to sit in on a group as a visitor and see how he felt. He was delighted. He's been with me ever since. He spent six months as a volunteer, very hands-on, doing anything that needed doing whilst developing his own skills for facilitating. He was humble and heartfelt. I remember one time when he and I stayed late in the prison to photocopy a ton of research questionnaires for the next few groups. Gary struggled with the photocopier.

"I tell you what," I said, "I'll photocopy, you staple. I guess your PA[49] used to do all this stuff for you?" Gary sat behind a desk in the prison office with piles of questionnaires to be sorted and stapled.

"Well, the thing is, it's worse than that," he said. "My PA had a PA!"

I teased him a lot for this in the years that followed, but

in that moment, I had more respect than ever for this big kind man. There he was, the CEO of a huge multi-million-pound organisation, washing plastic cups after group and spending his evening stapling questionnaires.

Gary[50] went on to be a big part of BR, acting as a sounding board for me for business and inspiring me with his fresh ideas. By late 2016, Rob and I had rented a beautiful home near the prison to reduce the travelling after a long day of teaching and project management. Gary had a five-hour drive to get home to Norwich, so he would often stay with us and became one of our closest friends.

Over the years, Gary and I have had lots of "brainstorming" sessions to see how the business could move forward. One Friday morning in September 2017, we sat at my long oak kitchen table, a laptop in front of me and a notepad by my side. We had to figure out the best way of maximising the impact in the prison, eeking out the small budget we'd been awarded, and getting the attention of the new No1 Governor. Earlier that year, I'd bid for and been awarded the final underspend from Northampton County Council (NCC) of £29,000. This was it. There was no more money after this. Not from this source, anyway. I wanted to make it count.

We had a waiting list of ninety men who wanted to do the groups. There are over seven hundred and fifty people at HMP Onley at any given time and we could only work with up to fifteen in a group. By now I had a team of eight facilitators and volunteers, but we struggled to get rooms at the prison, so there was always a juggle of dates and resources.

"I've got a question," Gary said. My shoulders were hunched against the cold day, inside my big blue Beyond

Recovery hoody. I cradled a cup of hot tomato soup. "Instead of spacing things out, why don't we just flood the prison with a group every week? We'll be able to service the waiting list, and at some juncture, there must be a tipping point!"

WOW. It was a bolt out of the blue! Instead of doing what we've been doing for the last eighteen months, why don't we try something new? The air was electric with inspired excitement as the two of us mapped out what that would look like.

"Yes," I responded. The warmth of inspired ideas had flushed my cheeks. A tiny white feather lay on the table next to my notepad. "Let's do it!"

I've noticed that everything that has its own energy just seems to fall into place as soon as you think it. This was no different. The plan came together, and from October to December 2017, we ran a three-day group for three weeks each month; twelve groups in total. The work was shared among five facilitators and four volunteers, reaching one hundred and twenty prison residents. Gary describes it as, "four months that changed my life forever."

As you can imagine, this plan needed a lot of management. I stepped away from running the groups and got more into the role of project manager. This also meant I could give the other volunteers more opportunities to facilitate. Susan, Lili and Jacquie were fantastic at working alongside less experienced facilitators and bringing them along, all the while having an impact on the men in the groups. The regular groups gave us space for trying things out and then tweaking our program the following week for anything that had not worked. It also gave us plenty of data for our second research paper that was published in 2018. It was a crazy busy time, going into prison week in and week out, but we had a lot of fun, a lot of laughs, a lot of tears, and a sprinkle of drama.

Like in one of Gary's first groups.

Remember that big green button which is a panic alarm that we can press if we are in trouble, the one that Will pressed when I first had my meeting in Onley and all the officers came running? Well, I've always prided myself on the fact that in the eighteen months I've been working in prison we've never had a "bell press," The guys will often comment on it because pressing the bell is a regular occurrence in other groups! As the saying goes, "Pride comes before a fall." Today I went into prison to support a group Gary and Susan were running. It was to give Gary some teaching experience. While I was waiting for them to come out of the group room with their big bag of purple cups ready to be washed, there was a huge commotion outside. Everyone ran to the windows to see a man on the roof on top of E wing.

The guy seemed to be in good humour, teasing the officers below who tried to persuade him to come down. Soon the attack dogs were brought in to bark and make a big fuss. I guess it was to scare the man off the roof, but if that was me, I'd want to stay up there! It's a huge deal when someone gets on the roof. The whole prison stops all activities until the situation is dealt with. Men will sometimes use the roof as a way of getting into trouble so they can be shipped out of the prison to avoid some beef they have with another inmate.

I headed to the kitchen to help wash up and as I got onto the corridor; I saw the team. Gary looked exhausted. "How'd it go?" I asked. Gary's pink round face was grey. His blue eyes had bags under them, as if he'd been in that room for three days instead of three hours.

"Not well," he said. He plodded towards me, a bag of dirty cups in one hand and his clipboard in the other. We piled into the kitchen and washed up. Between them, they explained how noisy the group had been, how it had been hard to settle them down and so on. The first day is often difficult, so I wasn't concerned. I was compassionate to the team while they got over their morning. I knew that after lunch, they'd have a fresher view.

Just as we left for lunch, one of the girls from the substance misuse team came through. "We've found out who was on the roof," she said. "It was JJ. Isn't he one of your guys?" The grey on Gary's face dissolved to powder white as he realised that the man had left group and instead of going back to his wing, he had staged a roof protest! It wasn't Gary's fault. The guy was in debt and had been scared that he was going to get beaten up back on his wing.

"If you forget your problem while you're in here, you may have more clarity," Gary had said. Going on the roof was the thing that came to him, because if he went on the roof, he would get punished by being put in the Care and Support Unit. In there, nobody could get to him. He's safe. Problem solved!

Notes

49   Personal Assistant.
50   In 2019 Gary Burton became a director of Beyond Recovery.

ANGEL 2018

"Oi, you big lump, stop making so much clatter!" the officer shouted. Angel sat on the scratchy grey blanket covering the wafer-thin mattress of the excuse they called a bed in the segregation unit. Faded afternoon sunlight filtered through the barred window, highlighting dirt ground into the corners of the stark six foot by four foot cell. No other furniture, apart from a grubby toilet with a cracked seat, and a tin sink. A piece of grey gum was stuck beneath the sink bowl. Angel's hands, smattered with blood, held his head between his knees as anger drained and shame tore through his body. His ribs and thighs ached from the tussle with the screws. His ears tuned into the rats that scuttled just beyond the wall.

"I've fucked up," Angel said to himself. "I've self-sabotaged just when everything was looking rosy."

Earlier that day Angel had been nicked for a stash of phones the officers found in his cell. He knew he'd been stupid, but he'd wanted to make a few quid to send home to his mum to buy his little girl the doll's house she wanted from Harrod's for her birthday. His sister had been on at him all month. He only got twenty minutes a day on the stupid phones on the wings and she just gave him non-stop earache about what a shit father he was and how everyone else was picking up the pieces.

He'd cracked and done what he knew how to do, talked to a few people, made a few phone calls, found a bent screw and before he knew it, he was back in business. The paper[51] to be made from a phone stash was decent enough and it weren't drugs, so he'd justified it all to himself as being harmless.

Trouble was, it wasn't as easy to lie these days. A couple of the support staff who'd been proud of his change had noticed a difference in his behaviour and started watching him, even reported him on the incident reporting system. Doesn't take long for intelligence to build up and staff to get suspicious. Worse part about it was that some people expected him to fail; now he'd proved them right. Next thing he knew he was being dragged out of bed in his underpants by four officers and having his pad strip searched. He hated it. They had no respect for his gear. They'd chuck it all out the pad onto the shitty floor and turn everything upside down. They knew what they were doing though, and soon found the stash in a plastic Tupperware box with a blue lid, behind the toilet.

"Be careful with that, it cost me a mint," Angel shouted from his place outside the cell door, as the officers scooped his stuff into black plastic sacks and escorted him down "the block."

Several hours later, in the quiet of the night, Angel sat there with his head still in his hands. The moon peeked through the bars of the cold dark cell; Angel stared at the shadows on the wall. Then, "flash," A lightbulb moment! He snorted with laughter as a fresh idea occurred to him. His skin warmed with the flush of well-being. His eyes rolled at his own craziness as his mind freed itself from the misery of blame.

All his life people had labelled him, stupid, dyslexic, disordered, PTSD, criminal, selfish. All his life he had labelled others, idiot, pathetic, gangster, whore, pretty, ugly. All his life he'd believed the only way to prove himself was through being the toughest and having the best: designer clothes, fast cars, pretty women. Laughter rumbled in the pit of his stomach and roared like a tsunami up his body, crashed into his chest and spurted out of his mouth. His teeth chattered with the humour of what he'd realised. He leapt up off his creaky metal bed and then crashed down onto his bruised knees. He held his hands in the prayer position and gazed up through the barred window at the moon smiling down on him.

"Thank you," he whispered. Calm now as the insight rolled a wave of peace over his tortured mind. "Thank you." He reached for the pen and pad he'd brought with him in the small bag of personal belongings they'd allowed him to keep, and started to write.

Notes

51   Paper – slang for money

Making Headway

"Now I have more understanding of how my
mind & thoughts work."

~ Beyond Recovery Participant

Prison governors are busy people. That might seem obvious
but it's worth just having out there that the role of running
a prison is not one to be envied. Especially if you care about
the residents. So, I wasn't surprised that none of the governors I'd invited to the Mind Behind Bars Seminar at HMP
Onley could commit to attending.

One of the invitees was the Governor of HMP Leicester,
NP. I'd been impressed by the TEDx[52] event he'd hosted at
his prison earlier in the year. It turned out that NP couldn't
attend our event, but he was interested in what we were
doing. I discovered he'd be at a TEDx gathering at the Space
Station in Leicester, so I booked tickets to go along and
tweeted him. "Looking forward to meeting you in Space."
On the night of the event, I wondered how I could manage
to bump into him. I didn't need to worry.

He saw me as soon as I walked in and headed straight
over. With a bow of his head and the smallest of smiles, he

said, "You wanted to see me; what do you want?" His large frame dimmed the light in the room. A stern, impatient face was softened by huge, kind brown eyes. All those breakfast meetings where I stumbled through my sixty-second pitches flashed through my mind!

"Here's my brochure. I want you to come and see my boys at Onley and see if you like what we do."

"OK," he said. "You're on." My face lit with the biggest smile. I couldn't believe it would be so easy.

The day for the governor's visit came a couple of months later, but all did not go as planned. First, HMP Onley was on lockdown all morning, meaning that none of the guys were being unlocked and all normal regime movements had been cancelled. We were assured that the afternoon's activities would take place, but it couldn't be guaranteed. I was on a knife edge all day. Would they be unlocked in time?

The prison was still in lockdown when NP arrived, so I fetched him from the gatehouse and escorted him back to our office. I spent the next hour and a half talking to him about various aspects of the programme, how it all started, how we were evidencing it and answering a myriad of other questions he had. Because the afternoon regime was running late, I was thinking of ways to keep him there, and crossing my fingers and toes, we would get to run the group. Without any prompts, different members of the prison staff who had been on our programmes popped into the office and told him how their own lives had changed because of our groups. NP was impressed, but said he wanted to hear it from the men themselves.

"I want you to know, whatever I think of this, I have no money," he said.

I had no time to think. The bell rang to signify that the men could be moved, but that it would be quick. I hustled NP into the classroom on J Wing. He sat on one of the blue fabric chairs and waited. As each guy walked in, they introduced themselves and shook hands with the Governor. Then they'd walk around the room to hug anyone else who'd arrived, before taking a seat themselves. NP told me later he'd never seen such companionship in a room full of prisoners and he'd been touched by how welcoming they were to him.

NP introduced himself, "I'm Governor NP from HMP Leicester." Bright autumn sunshine cast a glow in the shabby room. The guys had worn their best clothing. The bond and the love between the guys was palpable. It felt like we were about to have high tea in a cosy cafe!

"Welcome, Gov," Derrick said.

"I've only got fifteen minutes, guys," NP said. "Jacqueline's told me what a great programme this is, but I want to know what you think of it."

"I'll start," Kieran said. Everyone sat in perfect stillness as Kieran talked fast with his broad Irish accent. He leant forward in his chair; hands clasped in front of him, the deep scar from his eye to his jawbone jagged and raw.

"I loved fighting man, it's the only way I could feel anything. I spent twelve months in the Seg and lived for the moment the door was cracked, so I could jump the screws."

Governor Phil's face was straight. If he was feeling anything, he was not showing it.

"And then three months ago I met this lot." Kieran waved his arm in my direction and our eyes locked in a moment. Tears of gratitude sprang to his eyes. "I've made friends. I didn't even know that was possible. I taught meself to read. I've always been alone. I know how to look after me. But in this group, I've found out the most important thing ever-sometimes you just have to say one word to someone to help them through their day. A little kindness goes a long way."

There was a moment's breath, then all the guys clapped and patted Kieran on the back. And one by one the guys talked about how the Beyond Recovery programme is not about what they should do and how they should be, but about them, about realising for themselves who they are underneath their badness, and what they are capable of. They mentioned gang members that they have recommended to the programme who have come back being kinder and happier; they mentioned how life has got sweeter and simpler for them. They mentioned how they don't have the stresses and worries they used to have. Their final suggestion, that the officers would benefit from the programme to make them happier, had Governor NP laughing out loud.

NP told the guys how impressed he was to witness the warmth and love in their greetings and that even more than that, he'd noticed that when one man speaks, the others listen and there aren't ten others trying to jump in. He told them he has never seen prisoners listening and supporting each other the way these men do. At the end of the session, he said, "Right guys, I'm going but I have one last question for you. Most of my prisoners have a six-week turnaround as they are on remand[53]. Do you think this would work on such a short timescale?"

"It's simple," Derrick said. "First you tell the men they

are not broken. That's what made the biggest difference to us. Everyone else tells us we need fixing." Derrick continued, "And remember that even just a little change is worth it. People find their well-being in their own time. At least give them the chance to be pointed towards it."

"OK guys," NP said as he stood up, his six-foot four frame towered above us all. "I've been telling Jacqueline that I want this in Leicester, but I have no money. Now I've met you, I feel so inspired and moved by you all I think, F**k the money! Money can be found." The guys leapt to their feet and cheered as NP and I left the room.

One the way back to the gate we talked with excitement about the possibilities, and NP told me to contact him to arrange to see his prison in Leicester.

It all seemed so positive and real.

But... Yes, here is that BUT again. Not long after my visit to his prison in Leicester, where we'd looked at group rooms and discussed a way of getting funded, Governor NP got promoted and moved on to lead the team at HMP Nottingham. This meant that not only could we not work in HMP Leicester (remember how the new Governors always want to bring their own things in) but that NP was super busy in his new prison because it was in "special measures" meaning they had a lot of work to do to make the prison safe.

I was gutted. I felt like the universe dogged every step I took. Once again, I wondered if I should just give up. Was it all worth it?

Notes

52   TED is a non-profit devoted to spreading ideas, usually in the form of short, powerful talks (eighteen minutes or less). A TEDx event is a local gathering where live TED-like talks and performances are shared with the community. The difference between TED and TEDx events is that the former takes more of a global approach while the latter typically focuses on a local community that concentrates on local voices. Officially, the 'x' in TEDx stands for 'independently organized TED event' - but it's more of a TED multiplied.

53   On remand – in custody pending trial.

DERRICK's Story

"If I made up something in my past that I thought
was true, what else did I make up?"

~ Derrick Mason

I have met many "characters" during my time working in
prisons. Men who you can't forget. Gentle giants. People
who can hold a room. Funny, loud, inspirational people.
And sometimes in amongst those characters is a gentle, quiet
soul. A man of substance.

The BR Apprenticeship Programme was created so that
prison residents who really stood out could be trained as
facilitators. I've experienced these guys teaching and the
way they share is purer than anyone I've met on an outside
training course. The programme ran for ten months and was
a deep dive into how to teach or share the Three Principles
understanding.

Many of the guys wanted to do the programme. In
prison it is one of the things that men can aim for, to be a
Peer Mentor. It's a badge of honour to some. It's a way of
helping your parole to others. Of all the different schemes
for Peer Mentors, I like to think that ours was different. I

wanted the guys to have as good a training as someone would get on the outside, with organisations like One Thought or the Three Principles School. I wanted to teach them in a way that was consistent with the spirit and the direction of the teachings of Sydney Banks. I wanted them to be grounded and to be confident that they are the source of the material, that they need to just share from their own wisdom, that they are everything they ever needed.

So, I was careful with my selection. I chose people who had attended several of our groups; who had experienced a definite transformation; and who had scored well on the well-being tests.

The ten-month long programme included a day a month for the apprentices' own learning; attendance at all groups for the prison population in between; and then co-facilitating groups with one of the core team. I ran the first programme in 2016, and out of the eight men in the group, we qualified two. Angel was one of them.

In our second programme, we qualified Derrick. I saw Derrick as a quiet, confident guy with a big heart. He was introduced to us by one of the other guys, who'd persuaded him to come to group. Derrick said we were too simplistic. He told us that he'd go back to his pad and think about what we'd said in group, to see if it was true. One night, he stared out of the barred window in his cell and remembered how he'd blamed his mum for all his problems for the whole of his life. In that moment, for the first time, he considered that she'd been doing the best she could. In Derrick's words:

"I saw that my mum had done the best she could, and feelings of resentment for her disappeared and I felt

pure love, compassion, and affection for her that I
didn't know I was capable of. It hit me – all these years
I'd blamed my mum, and I saw it was me. I wondered,
if I can question that, what else can I see different? I'd
blamed her for all my insecurities and now I saw it as
my own thoughts and my not being present. I started
seeing my partner different, after all these years. I could
think about my relationship with her in a different way,
too. I realised I had the power to change anything. I can
be up in my head if I want. I have always analysed and
lived in my head all the time, but I saw I had the choice
to do whatever I want."

This realisation kept Derrick coming to groups, and we saw
him blossom as his dark thoughts fell away and new fresh
ideas about how to live occurred to him. A few months later,
I decided to recruit Derrick as part of our team to work in
prison on our behalf.

PRISON NOTES – DECEMBER 2017

We ran a peer group with the guys in Onley today to
give them the results of who would be our Beyond
Recovery Champion. "I only have one space," I said.
We sat in the group room on K wing, with our latest
graduates from the Apprentice Programme. Everyone
assumed it would be Ken I would choose for the role.
They knew the job would come with the much coveted
"red band" meaning that the recipient would be trusted
to move around the prison without escort. Everyone
in the room wanted the job because they could say

they work for Beyond Recovery, they would see vulnerable prison residents, and they would be allowed to promote our groups.

The guys were lit. They love these meetings and the feeling that gets generated when we're all together. The guys all started jostling Ken and saying things like, "We all know it's you mate, well done."

Before it went too far, I blurted out, "It's Derrick."

There was a gasp of surprise from each of the guys. Derrick's blush tinged his dark skin with pink and his big brown eyes widened. Ken, a well-built, fair-haired guy with an east London accent, leapt from his chair to shake Derrick's hand. "Well done mate, well done."

Ken told me later he'd been disappointed, but at the same time really pleased for Derrick.

"Wow, that's a shock," Derrick said. He stood to shake my hand, his tall slim frame swamped by his baggy jeans and loose jumper. His eyes brimmed with gratitude.

Derrick worked for us as a Beyond Recovery Champion for a few months and he became an asset, but we lost him when he got his move to an open prison in London. I was disappointed, although I knew that it was positive for him. I hoped he'd get in touch when he was released, and I wrote to him, but I didn't hear back. So, I just prayed he was doing well.

What can a Volcano Teach Us?

"It's within all of us. That ability to change. That ability to be our true self. That ability to live in love and feel love."

~ Christine Heath

All we have to do is have a nice life and want other people to have a nice life.

I was invited back to speak at the 3PUK conference in May 2018 with "one of my guys." A teacher called Christine Heath would be the host of the session. "Yes please," I said. I knew I could ignore my insecure thoughts and that I'd be glad I'd done it after the event (a bit like I never want to go to the gym, but I'm always happy after I've been!). I popped the date in my diary and got on with life.

It was only when I sat on the front row that I started to tremble. "Oh my giddy aunts," I said. "We're opening the conference!" The huge auditorium at the Allianz Rugby Ground was warm from the heat of June and the bodies that were crammed into the space. Each side of the stage was

237

flanked with large monitors to project the speeches to those in the audience too far away to see.

"Please welcome Jacqueline Hollows," the host said.

I talked about how any of us can do amazing things. That when we listen to ourselves, we notice those sparks. That when we are impacted in ways that make us act differently or see the world differently, things come to us. There is no effort. I shared that Beyond Recovery was started from such a spark.

"When Jacqueline is talking, it reminds me of the volcano, Kilauea on Hawaii, that's happening right now," Christine said. "The lava came up from the core of the earth and had nowhere to go, so it went off to the side. And then it went underneath the ground for a couple of miles. All of a sudden it came up with an eruption, blowing red hot earth two hundred feet in the air. And then another one happened. And then another one. And now we're up to about seventeen. First of all, when each eruption happened, it looked like it wasn't flowing, and then within a little bit of time, the lava starts flowing."

She continued, "Even though Jacqueline wasn't sure what she had found, something inside her got touched. She was able to see things in different ways. She was drawn to help people, then pretty soon she was drawn into the prison, then pretty soon she was doing a programme, and this year she is going to be speaking in Singapore about the results of that programme. And it's going out far beyond her into the world.

"That feeling of a spark of an idea can't be stopped, like a volcano can't be stopped. It finds a way of erupting. It finds a way of flowing. It finds a way of creating."

Christine continued, "At that place where we all connect, that's where we wake up from, that's where the lava comes from. As it comes through us, it starts to touch other people, and they have little eruptions. They start to see things different. And pretty soon they touch other people, and it stretches out all over the world. That's the power that feeling has. It guides. It cleans up your life. People change without effort."

"It's within all of us. That ability to change. That ability to be our true self. That ability to live in love and feel love. It doesn't matter what's different about you. It doesn't matter what you've been through. It doesn't matter what you've done to other people. It doesn't matter what they've done to you. You have the ability to live in your innate health, in a clear, happy mind. You have the ability to just get quiet and listen. You have the ability to listen to your wisdom."

"Each step. Each moment. Each impact. It's all part of the flow of the lava. It can look chaotic. It can look destructive. It can look difficult. But when you follow the flow, the good that's built in gets a chance to breathe. When you take each step, you get to create the dreams you didn't know you had instead of the ones you think you should have."

Enough, Enough Now

"When your mind is heavy with thought,
your judgment can be clouded."
~Beyond Recovery Participant

Life is gritty. It is dirty and gritty and smelly and dark. It can be warm and fluffy. Rainbows and butterflies. But it's often gritty. And neither is good nor bad. It's just life. Like weather is neither good nor bad, it's just weather. The impact of weather, what we think about it, how we feel about it, and how we feel about how it enhances or interferes with our plans, that's what makes it good or bad. The weather itself is just weather. But, and it's a big but, it doesn't feel like that when I'm in the thick of it. When I suffer. When I'm broke. When I cling on and think I can't possibly carry on.

The ups and downs of the last few years started to take their toll on me again. The highs of standing ovations were in combat with the lows of not making any headway in the criminal justice system. It didn't seem to matter how many transformations there were, how many research papers I'd written, how many times prison staff said our programme saves lives. I just didn't seem to be getting anywhere. And I was working hard. Every week I would juggle several projects, motivate the team, think of ways we could support the guys. I would write research material, run groups, write bids.

Every week I would be exhausted. I forgot what weekends were like. I forgot what having time to myself in the evenings was like. I forgot what I was like when I wasn't being the boss of Beyond Recovery.

Rob saw all this and insisted I take time out.

He booked us a vacation on Salt Spring Island to visit our friends and relax. I had plenty of time to chill out, take walks, and visit with people we love. But I just couldn't stop my mind from moving. Here and there, like a roadrunner, it went. There was so much going on in the business that I couldn't switch off. I would get up at 4:00am to watch the glorious sunrise, then tackle emails, jump onto video calls with different people in the team and do my part to ensure things would tick along in my absence. We'd all been trained well. I knew they could handle it all, but I was a snowball falling downhill, unable to slow down.

I guess at the time it felt like a break, but I'd only slowed down to about fifty miles an hour from eighty. At the end of the vacation, I booked some time with a mentor of mine, Elsie Spittle, who had been a friend of Syd Banks and who had a very special way of helping people to still their minds, to listen to the inner silence.

Dear Diary (June 2018),

I embarrassed myself today. I can't believe I was such an idiot. I'd sat with Elsie yesterday in her cute cottage eating salmon that her husband, Ken, had caught from his recent fishing trip. And we just chatted. I did wonder what everyone was going on about how she gets you to still your mind, because it seemed to me she didn't do much. I had a lovely time, but that was about it.

So, when I went back today, I told her about how I was going to change the world with Beyond Recovery, explaining the projects I had on the go, and I just didn't shut up. I went on and on and on. I was even getting bored of my own voice. I could hear myself rattling on, but I couldn't stop. And then I noticed her face. She looked pale, her eyes had glazed over, and she looked like she was going to cry.

"Is this making sense?" I asked her. The ticking of the grandfather clock sounded loud in the absence of my torrent of words. Her comfy sofa invited me to nestle into its deep cushions.

"I think you need to lie down!" Elsie said. "I know I do." She lay down on the sofa opposite me, resting her white hair on one end of the sofa and her little stockinged feet on the other.

I was stung. Tears sprung to my eyes and shame coursed through my body. I'd broken Elsie. I did what I was told and lay down on the sofa. The warm sweet air filled my lungs. I stared at the white fluffy clouds in the blue sky outside her window. The clouds melted my shame, and the sweet air rocked me to a gentle sleep.

Elsie told me later she'd never said that to anyone before, but it felt right to her and that when you speak from the heart, even when it hurts, it comes with a blanket of love, so the blow is cushioned, and the person knows it's true. After I'd rested for about an hour, I felt Elsie by my side. "Shall we go for a drive?" she asked. I felt very still. No longer ashamed, just peaceful. All thought had left my head with the clouds. I felt a deep stillness within me.

We drove around the island. Elsie pointed out places where Syd had talked, where he had lived, where he had fished. After a while she popped a Syd Banks' talk into the CD player. We listened to his Scottish lilt as we drove down the lush green lanes of the beautiful island. At the end of our drive, Elsie dropped me off at my Airbnb. "The silence is your friend," she said.

"Wow," I said. It was 4:00am the next day and I stood on the patio of the tiny apartment to bask in the sunrise. The world was aglow with reds and oranges. A soft breeze kissed my face. The patio, a small rectangle of stones, seemed like the gateway to a view of the Gods: my horizon was a bay between two islands.

The early morning sun nestled atop the hills and stained the water with its blood. To the right, the mountains in the USA were visible in their morning misty shroud, not yet ready to show their faces. The patio balanced on a steep incline leading down to a beach, full of lush green vege-tation that housed a myriad of wildlife, birds, insects, deer and raccoons. Huge trees draped their branches and leaves across the vision like a pair of living curtains. A humming-bird feeder buzzed with the little incredible creatures in their effervescent bodies.

I held the pen I'd used to birth a poem. I stood still in my pyjamas; a light blue shawl wrapped around my shoulders. I felt still. Still as anything that has ever been still. My mind had crumbled into a steady throb of nothingness. I heard every sound. I felt every brush of the air on my face. I could taste aliveness. The sun crept its way skyward, its colours diluted with the atmosphere. A hummingbird hovered right in front of my face, as if he saw me, as if we shared something, as if we were one. "Yes," I whispered.

A couple of days later, I made my long and winding way home. It took twenty-four hours from the time I left the little apartment until the time I arrived on my doorstep in the UK. Before we took off, I cancelled a lunch with my friend at the airport, as I wanted to stay in the stillness for as long as possible. To allow what I had experienced to permeate my soul. I thought I'd learned what I needed; I thought things would be different; I thought I'd never overwork again.

All that felt manageable until I hit the tarmac at Gatwick airport! Phone on before the airplane doors were open. And then, without missing a heartbeat, I stepped into work mode. The bleep bleep of texts and missed calls being received and answered. Collect my luggage. Check my email. Go go go. Navigate the escalator. Find the driver. Phone my assistant. Work work work. Fix problems. Deal with questions. Sort issues. Find solutions. Think think think. Check things, answer things, be busy, be important. Juggle juggle juggle. That's what you do, right? When you've been away, when you've stopped to take a breath, when you've been lazy. You have to make up for it, right?

That was Tuesday and I don't think I stopped for the

next three days. I was a Duracell Bunny[54] with a loaded battery. Things to do, people to see. Push, push, push. Friday morning arrived, an important day. I'd planned a focus group at HMP Onley with a dozen of the men, to talk to a couple of potential investors. It was a big morning. It was a beautiful, heartfelt, impactful morning. And even though the meeting couldn't have gone better, my chest was tight; I was moving too fast. Breathe, I said to myself. Just slow down and breathe.

The thing was, I just didn't feel I deserved to stop. I mean, I'd just been away; I'd had those lovely moments of stillness. "Get over yourself," I said. On the same day as the investors visited the prison, I had an interview in London, eighty miles away. I was fortunate to get a lift from one of the team, but that meant I chatted all the way down instead of taking a nap. Once I was dropped off, I found my way to the venue across town. Each step seemed like a mission. Inch by inch, I made my way to the interview, my head getting fuzzier and fuzzier. My eyes misted with the need to sleep. My feet ached from walking around the prison all day.

The interview was seven minutes long. (Yes, I did just take three hours to get to this venue for an interview that was seven minutes long). A deliberate, short, seven minutes. I did a five-minute presentation which was followed by two minutes of questions from the panel. Rapid-fire questions. The next question out before the last answer had spilled from my mouth. Like a firing squad. Up against the wall. "What is …" FIRE. "How do you …" FIRE. "Can you …" FIRE.

"I hope to see you again," the interviewer said. Oh, it

was over. My mind whirled. I know that I shook hands and smiled and said the things I was supposed to say. I know that somehow, I walked out of the room, through the office and turned left through the door to the stairs. I know I started to walk down the stairs. And then the tears came. Floods of them.

"Buzzz" went the door as I let myself out onto the street. Sunlight glared with happy brightness. It bounced off the tall glass buildings that surrounded me like stern sentries that guarded the city. The heat of the late summer sun stifled the air, hot and unbreathable. Buildings stared unseeing at my crumpled face. Four huge, thigh high stone slabs lay unimpressed with the turmoil in my mind. Water spilled over their edges in a constant flow. Workers rushed around in their bright coloured summer clothing – reds and yellows and oranges and browns. I wore my branded polo shirt, grey trousers and cute pink, flat shoes. I'd been going for a summer professional look, my hair caught up in a knot in an attempt to keep my neck cool. And I sobbed, "I was rubbish," I said to no one. "Just rubbish."

I leaned against one of the shiny buildings, as if it could hide me. I wanted to merge into its still, uncaring façade. Tears streamed down my face. I just felt so so sad. A deep, dreadful well of sadness.

"It's not that." I knew it wasn't that I had been rubbish, it was something else, but what? I didn't know. All I wanted to do was go home, but even that seemed impossible. The tube and a train and a drive at the other end seemed just too much. Way, way too much.

I called Rob. Sobs racked my voice. He was kind and sweet. "Just get to the tube," he said. Yes, I could do that.

I could get to the tube. It took me a while to remember how to get a ticket. Even my PIN number for my debit card eluded me.

I felt overwhelmed. I didn't dare think about why I was overwhelmed. That didn't make sense to me. I'd just been on holiday. What was wrong with me? I didn't think I should be overwhelmed by that. But it would do for now. I had a reason. It made me feel a tad better. Enough to get myself home. I still don't know how I got home, but I did. I took each step at a time. A route I had done thousands of times now seemed scary and difficult. I couldn't bear to be with all the people, the rush, the noise. I couldn't speak to anyone. I stayed in my own miserable bubble and got myself home.

I survived. Just. Not recovered. Not felt better. Just survived. For the next two weeks, my brain was full of fog. I cried all the time and at everything. The sadness became a sort of despair. I cancelled everything in my diary. I imagined I would always feel like this. My mind had gone.

I'd had a breakdown. My mind just crashed. It wasn't just coming back to work after a vacation. It wasn't just rushing around in the summer heat. It wasn't just the last week. It was the last three years. It was not stopping for anything. It was all the pushing, pioneering, trying. It was all the rejections. It was all the sleepless nights. It was all the worry about money. It was burn out.

I'd followed my insights. I'd followed my wisdom. I'd followed my intuition. But I hadn't followed the voice that told me to slow down. To take time out. To stop. Until I'd been with Elsie. Until she'd shown me that my mind was racing. Until I'd recognised that I had the ability to press the pause button.

And then, as if I'd not learnt anything, I went from all still and gentle to ramming the accelerator on and racing at a hundred miles an hour again.

I could've been gentler with myself. I could have slowed things down and reviewed the priorities. I could have slept when I needed to sleep. But I didn't. I raced and ran and laughed with pride as I took on jet lag. But who won? I didn't know this at the time, but my mind said, "Enough." It showed me "Enough," by stopping me in my tracks. It was all I could do to get out of bed in the morning and get dressed. It took several weeks to start to function again and a further few months to recover any sort of normalcy.

During the time of my breakdown many people offered advice. So much advice. The list was endless: go to the doctor; it's the menopause; you're working too hard; speak to this person or that person; take this blood test or these supplements. And so on. It was all well-meaning. It was all an attempt to help. But even though I couldn't think, even though I believed I'd never be well again, even though it was a dark, dreadful, horrid experience, I knew that in time I'd know what to do. I knew I didn't need to search for a reason. I didn't need to find a solution. I didn't need to take any well-meaning advice. I just needed to be as I was and follow my own intuition.

And my intuition was simple, uncomplicated, mundane even. It said, sleep, or eat, or go for a walk, or cry. And I did what it said. Everyday things that I "felt" like doing. Look, I won't say that knowing I didn't need advice, and I knew to listen to my intuition felt good. It didn't. It was nasty. But I was OK being in the nasty. I gave myself permission for that. At least I was feeling something and not just the numbness of exhaustion. I just knew I didn't need to scramble about trying to fix it. And little by little, day by day, the fog began to lift. I'd wake up and feel I could take a shower that day. I would cry less, my head felt less fuzzy.

The first thing I did as my world started to return to normality was to give a presentation at the University of Birmingham. I was nervous, and the presentation was a bit flat without my usual sparkle, but as only five people[55] turned up, I guess it didn't matter. At least I'd ventured out and tested the waters of myself in the world again.

I wondered if I should stop running Beyond Recovery. If it was time. I could still run groups with the guys as a volunteer. I didn't need to run a business. I didn't need to keep battling on in a system that didn't want me. I didn't need to face all the uphill. I'll slow down. I'll do something else.

Notes

54 The Duracell Bunny is an anthropomorphic pink rabbit powered by Duracell batteries. Its used to imply a person who seems to have limitless energy and endurance.

55 Of the five people, one was Rob, two were the other presenters and one was a volunteer, which meant there was only one person in the audience!

Act III

Each One Teach One

2019 – 2020

ANGEL 2020

That night in the Block in 2018, I wrote my heart out. I didn't even know what was coming out of the pen. I just wrote until my wrist just about dropped off, and then some. The pen even snapped, and I scrabbled around in my kit bag and found an old pencil so I could carry on. It poured out of me. I found answers to questions I didn't even know I had. I found forgiveness for people I believed I'd never forgive. I found compassion that made me heart ache big time. It was like God was speaking directly to me and flushing all the bad out of my head onto the paper. Emptying my broken spirit of all the pain I'd given others and been given. Squeezing the pus out of the wounds I'd been picking at the whole of my life.

It was a long night. Tears flooded as fast as the pen wrote. Sobs racked my ribs worse than being in the ring. My whole life flashed in front of me, each distressing event released out of me. Eventually, I got back to the moment behind the sofa. I saw my mum's black-rimmed eyes and drained face. I saw my dad's eyes glinted with fear, not with steel. I saw my own little scared face, the piss down my legs and my shaking white hands. I realised that I was just a baby. That everything I'd done since was out of misunderstanding that moment. That it could've played out different.

I'd always thought I had to be the way I was. That things panned out the way they did because everyone else was to blame. That I was forced to live the life I'd lived. As I wrote, I heard a voice saying "You can start fresh" over and over. Each word that went down on the page was a full stop on the shit life that I'd had and that I'd led. Each sentence purged me of the need to keep a hold of the hurt.

I'm not proud of my past. I don't expect forgiveness. All I can say is that I realised I'd been living in a complete misunderstanding of the way life works. I thought the shit that went on in my head was real. I thought when someone hurt me, I had to hurt back twice as hard. I thought I was broken.

That night showed me I was just lost.

That maybe I can't ever make up for what I've done, but I can do my best to live my best life now. I've devoted my life to helping others. Since I got released in 2019, I've helped people on the streets by talking to them, giving them love, telling them about how Thought works, and sometimes buying them a burger or a coffee. I've formed a group for people with PTSD and started showing people what it's like to live in mental-health instead of concentrating on mental-illness. I've got a girlfriend and a cat, and I love my simple life.

I do still get mad sometimes or think that people

have done bad to me, but I don't dwell on it, and I don't stay in that low mood for long. I just put it down to experience and try to be a better man.

I choose life.

Bouncing Back

"Humility isn't thinking less of yourself,
it's thinking of yourself less."

~ C S Lewis

Is it courage to keep going in the face of adversity? Why even try when the barriers are so high and the odds so low? Why not pack up and go home? Why keep on? What's wrong with me?

These things went around and round in my foggy head as I navigated through my depression back to health. Toward the end of my breakdown, as the fog cleared and I started to function again, I had an insight. It was one of those moments when something unexpected popped into my head; where nothing has changed but all the world looks different. I'm always amazed when this happens.

I was sitting up in bed, my fluffy, cream coloured quilt wrapped around me against the early morning chill. I gazed out the window across the fields and felt this thought arrive. I felt it before I heard it. And then I heard it ricochet between my ears.

"You're about to see something big."

It's a funny thing to think. After that there was just space in my mind, and a sort of "hmmm, interesting," My hands snuggled around the cup of hot, fresh lemon and ginger tea they held. The room was full of bright yellow morning light. A symphony of birdsong and the heady smell of pink blossom and white peonies wafted through the open windows. I felt as if the green of the trees coursed through my veins. A dizzy bliss surrounded me. There was no difference between me and the air or the fields or the birds or the blossom, or the sky itself.

It seemed in that moment that everything I was aware of, including myself, was all part of one Consciousness. "Wow," I said, "Wow." In that moment, it occurred to me from deep within my mind that every single living creature is part of the universal essence of life. I just felt a complete oneness with the whole of nature. In that moment, there was no good, no bad, no hurt, no pain, no right way, no wrong way. Just this: every single moment of every single day is a simple expression of Consciousness. Because of that, we are all connected at a very deep, fundamental level.

The place that I experienced, that experienced me, was beyond personality, beyond the human mind, beyond any- thing I'd ever felt before. I knew in that moment that all the material of my life experiences had their place in the grand scheme of things. All of it. Like I said earlier, life is gritty. It can be dirty and gritty and smelly and dark. And yet, in that moment, I could feel a profound truth that transcended all my preferences of like and dislike. It went deeper than something I thought, or a nifty saying on my wall. It felt true from within the depths of my soul.

I felt a deep peace come over me and, just like that, my

depression dropped away. I knew I could do whatever I wanted because it's not the doing that matters. I knew that I couldn't be broken because nobody can. I knew that no matter what experience I have, I don't need to be afraid. I saw it was time to reassess, to prioritise, to learn, but not to give up. I realised that everything is a manifestation of the source of life and that we can't get it wrong.

The world looked very different to me from this new perspective.

I got up, got dressed, and asked myself, "OK, what now?" I made a tentative approach to my desk and started to go through work emails. I did one thing at a time, as my brain's gears ground back to life. After a while, I felt over-whelmed. It felt like a ping-pong ball bounced between my ears. So, I stopped. It's simple, now I've realised it. The breakdown had helped me recognise when I needed to stop. I'd gained a sensitivity to the warning signs. I learned to see when the pause switch needed to be pressed. Back in the day, before the start of this journey, when I partied hard, it was the same. I'd not known that there was an "off" switch.

Other people used to say to me that they knew when the next drink would be one too many; that never happened to me. Other people knew they'd "had enough"; I could never tell for myself. Other people could have a glass of wine and put the rest in the fridge, but not me. I would push on through the night, past the time when it was sensible to stop, past the point of no return, past caring. When I stopped drinking, I'd had the same attitude about other things in my life, like chocolate or cake or coffee. It was an innocent lack of awareness of when I'd had enough. Now I could see that working was just one more thing that I hadn't known when to stop.

The gift of the breakdown was to alert me to the feeling of overdoing it. Not in a, "I'm scared to overdo it in case I breakdown" sort of a way. In a way of being able to notice what happens inside my head when it's time to take a rest, to stop pushing. Now, when I noticed my head was full, I stopped, made a cup of tea and went outside to get some air. As I pottered around my garden and dead headed the flowers, I'd feel all the mental noise clear. In that moment of clarity, I'd know what I needed to do next.

The breakdown taught me that I needed more space. I needed to listen to my body. I needed time out to relax. I'd experienced first-hand what overwork, overwhelm and overthinking do to our systems. I saw that each moment is precious in itself, and all I need to do is be present to that. When I do that, my mind is even more productive than it was before. I saw that magic comes from the space, not from the doing.

HMP Nottingham

"You must be the change you wish to see in the world."
~ Mahatma Ghandi

It seems to me life is like a huge jigsaw puzzle. Sometimes I can see which piece goes where and they slot in with ease. Or I have a piece missing but don't even realise it until it's found under the rug near the table.

I love it when all the pieces fit together. I have patience to recognise that other people have bits of the jigsaw too and that while they are working on their part, I may need to wait until I can slot my last pieces into place.

For instance, take the journey I had getting to start running groups at HMP Nottingham.

It was 2017 when Gov NP sat with our guys at HMP Onley and said, "We'll find the f***ing money. I want this in Leicester." And then there was a long circuitous journey which could make a play in its own right, involving: NP becoming the Governor at Nottingham; the Prison Minister Rory Stewart and the Ten Prison Project; and a business angel I met at the 3PUK conference named David Kowitz, who was on a mission to reform prisons.

And so it was, that in February 2019 we started working on Delta wing at HMP Nottingham, as part of Rory Stewart's Ten Prison Project. We started with a two-day orientation for the whole of the Beyond Recovery team (there were six of us by now), which included prison security training, induction of the wing, and a talk on how the prison regime works at Nottingham. Pauline, our SPOC (single point of contact) had sourced a room to run our groups and an office, shared with the wing staff, to store equipment needed for group (refreshments, an urn, flip chart paper and pens, CD player for playing Syd Banks' recordings).

"Do you think anyone will speak to us?" Paul said. The grubby old prison wing had four landings with metal staircases at one end to reach the other levels. The chipped dirty blue walls clashed with the dark brown of the cell doors. The lower landing had started its upgrade to a more therapeutic wing with brand new blue two-seater sofas scattered around the edges, and a new pool table in the middle. Paul and I sat on one of the sofas amid the suspicious eyes of blank faced men, determined not to engage, dressed in grey sweatpants and tops.

"Are we safe?" I asked.

Some of the men had pulled a couple of sofas together into the centre so they could sit and chat shit. We wandered over to them and asked how they were. Most got up and moved away, but curiosity got the better of a young man with a deep welt down the side of his face. "Wot do you do miss?" He asked. Perfect icebreaker. Paul and I told him about our groups and before long, we were joined by other men. Some of them even asked for their names to be added to our referral list. I was pleased with that outcome. It can take a while before the residents trust new people. I knew I needed to get comfortable with being there; I was going to be around every week for the next few months.

PRISON NOTES – MARCH 2019

We did the first Notts group this week. There's a thorny pleasure to starting work in a new prison. Knowing I have an elixir the residents all want, but they don't know it. Waiting to see the tiny sparks of hope fanned alive. I know they think we're crazy, talking about peace of mind, and the miracle of life, and how our world is created inside out. It's not a conversation a group of men in prison are used to having. Some of them might have read self-help books and attended many courses, but still, they're not used to unconditional love.

You can tell that by the way they come into the room, chatting about how the system has f***ed them over, how this man needs to be beaten up, how they used to enjoy this drug or that lifestyle. And then there we are, all smiles and warm handshakes. Encouraging space and silence and meaningful conversation.

It's a weird juxtaposition, but I love it. I know it's strange to say, but I love that uncomfortable feeling; a mix of being a bit scared, a bit insecure, a bit daunted, a bit out of my depth. I love it because I just go with it. It doesn't stop me doing what I'm doing, and the reward. Wow! The reward... it's incredible! To see men have insights that stop them from being big scary hairy things and turn them into gentle giants, that has got to be the best thing in the world. To start with people

grunting at me and then having them fall over themselves to make me a cup of tea or turn a fan on to cool
me down because they've found their gentle selves
inside is the sweetest feeling in the world.

Our first group in HMP Nottingham, was daunting despite
the preparations. On the first day, a chap called Iain sat next
to the table with the hot water urn so he could have a never-
ending supply of coffee. I'd switched the urn off until the
next break because it would bubble away just when we were
having a quiet moment. The third time he flicked the switch
to on, I said, "NO. Iain. It's too noisy!"

The long wide room used to be a cafe with big industrial
hot-water pipes running around the walls. They pumped
out a heat you could cut with a knife, raising the pressure in
the room. The café fixtures had been removed, leaving white
spots of plaster where things used to hang on the grubby
blue walls. A tiny red paperclip lay on the dark blue carpet.
The cables of a large flat-screen TV on the wall opposite the
window dangled like dead snakes.

Iain didn't like being told what to do. A loud, rambunc-
tious Irish man in his fifties, he wore a grey vest top to
display his pale flesh covered in tattoos and a mass of dark
hair on his chest. "I was only making a drink," he said. His
bitter frown deepened. I could smell his resentment. He'd
already complained about being "five years over tariff"[56] on
his IPP[57] sentence. He'd been in prison eleven years and had
done every course and "heard it all before," He interrupted
at every opportunity with, "I know what you're going to
say." He couldn't hear a thing for two days.

I've never given up on anyone, no matter how irritated

I get. I might get frustrated, but I know that everyone is only acting out of their own state of mind and when that shifts, they shift. The final day of that three-day programme proved this once again. Even the room felt different when we entered first thing in the morning. When the men came and took their seats, I could feel the space. I could hear the breath. I could sense a shift. The room felt soft, worlds apart from the energy we'd experienced only two days ago. Each man shared small insights they'd had. Each man listened. Each man showed gentle respect. I noticed Iain didn't interrupt with his loud, cocky jokes. I asked him to share where he was at.

"Well miss, I was talking to me wife 'tother day, and I told her I've seen I spend all me time being bitter and angry an' that, about being over tariff. But daft thing is I'm the one hurting meself! The crazy part about it is that the time has already gone! I can't do nothing about it, so I need to move on and live for now. If my attitude were different, then I think the people around me would be different. I could go to parole and instead of being bitter and getting angry with them about what has already happened, I could go with hope and inspiration in my heart. My wife said she's been telling me that for years, but I told her 'This programme is about self-realisation' and until you realise it yourself, you don't realise it at all."

Boom.

I was more than thrilled. My heart soared like a robin in spring. Tears filled my eyes at the simplicity and depth of his insight. An insight that will change everything for him. I was high with happiness. Paul and I went for dinner that evening, but we were speechless; we just kept staring at each other, eyes filled with gratitude and amazement. We'd smile and shake our heads at the wonder of watching thought in action. Every time someone has an insight like that it feels like a blessing, like we get to witness someone waking up for the first time out of their own suffering. And of course, just one person having an insight like that, especially someone with such a big personality, creates a ripple effect on the whole group, and on the wing itself. And Iain wasn't the only one. We had incredible moments of insights and shifts in perspective from other men in the group and continued to build on these over the next six months.

Notes

56   Tariff is the length of the prison sentence.
57   IPP stands for Indeterminate Public Protection. The term is no longer used as it creates a feeling of hopelessness. Residents will often give up, thinking they will never be released; therefore, their state of mind and behaviour deteriorates.

The Butterfly Effect

"My gut is never wrong. I just need to listen to it
more often."

~ Beyond Recovery Participant

You never know how a thing is going to turn out until it's
done. You never know the chain of events you start when
you take that first step. You never know how many people
you will touch.

I guess we're not supposed to know how things will turn
out. That's not the point. The point is to take the step without
knowing. The point is to do what can be done right now and
leave the rest to unfold. The point is not to worry about the
things outside of my control and take care of the things I can.
We are all doing the best we can in any given moment.

I used to have a habit of second guessing myself. I'd take
a step and imagine what the result might be. If I applied for
a grant or some funding, I'd imagine what would happen
when we got it. I'd spend it before I even knew I was getting
it. I'd plan for what we'd do, map it all out, spend all this
time and energy forecasting the future, which might not
even happen!

I don't do that anymore. I go as far as I can go and then let it be. Wait for the next piece to fall into place. This works well but there is always a little hope that skulks around the corners of my mind, a little bit of imagination busy planning a future. So, I love it when I realise that I really don't know. When the idea is far beyond my current view. The truth is, the ripple effects go far beyond our tiny imaginations. We can't foresee the twists and turns of the path ahead. At any given point I might know my personal "Why" for doing something, but I can never know the bigger "Why," The Universal "Why,"

For instance, consider the insight I had in the park where I'd fallen in love with people with addictions, where I KNEW I wanted to work with them. I couldn't have known that would lead me to prison. Or that prison would lead me to publishing research papers. Or that I'd be building a team, working in prisons around the UK, running a workshop in South Africa, or writing a book! I couldn't know one of my greatest joys would be developing the peer mentors into leaders and pioneers. As Steve Jobs[58] once said, "You can only join the dots looking backwards."

Dear Diary (March 2017),

Wow, I feel like I'm in a dream. I'd given a talk at the One Solution conference in Cape Town and this lady came up afterwards. She's a teacher at the prison called Drakenstein. She wanted to know if I'd come and talk to her boys at the prison. Amazing! Of course, I said yes. So, on our day off, while everyone else was doing touristy things, Rob and I went to the prison that Nelson Mandela was released from. It was surreal. A local lady, Gill, offered to attend with us so that she could drive us there.

On the day of the visit, I was very sick; I'd caught the tummy bug that had been going around, so I spent a lot of time bent double and feeling faint. The guards welcomed us and showed us around the medium security part of the prison and then we were taken to the classroom where I was meant to give a talk. I stood at the front, weak and dizzy. Rows of young black men, with tattoos of numbers on their arms and necks, stared at me with curiosity and waited.

"I've come from England to find out. Where do you feel most in flow? And where do you feel most stuck?" In no time, they were chatting away about how football made them feel in flow and schoolwork made them feel stuck.

"Here's a strange one," I said. "I'm standing here, a white woman from England, and yet I feel close to you. There's something that connects us, that makes us the same. What do you think that is?"

They shouted out answers like "our blood" and "our hearts,"

I kept saying, "What else?"

The room quieted and one young man said, "Our spirit".

Well, that did it. For the next thirty minutes, we had the most amazing conversation I could've ever imagined. Twenty-five South African lads in prison and me. We talked about the Oneness of life and the illusion of separateness. I forgot I was ill. I felt present and in the moment. One guy had his head in his hands at the back of the room. Gill, seated next to him, asked if he was OK.

"Yes miss," he said. Tears streamed down his face. "I didn't know it was so simple. I wouldn't be here if I'd heard this before. I killed someone, miss." She asked him what he'd heard. "We make up what we think of other people. We act bad toward them because we think they're different from us. We hurt them and when we hurt them, we're really hurting ourselves because there isn't no difference."

One of the best days of my life. We left the prison on cloud nine and took photos of us standing by the Mandela statue in his Long Walk to Freedom stance.

Sometimes there is no next step. It's just the experience in the moment that is the purpose. For a while after the SA trip, the teacher and I corresponded about me training some of the staff to deliver workshops to the guys. That never came off, but what the experience did for me was, it showed beyond any doubt that there is a universal language that speaks to everyone. And that being present with people, no matter who they are, opens that channel of communication. Sometimes I take a step with no idea of where that will lead, and years down the line, that step has rippled out way beyond the moment I was in. Take the 3PUK conference as an example. Back in May 2016, when I'd unlocked the heavy gates in HMP Onley on the two's landing of J Wing, that led me to ask the guys to write a letter to be read at the conference. All I'd had was a moment of inspiration to ask for a letter. That was all I knew. Nothing more, nothing less.

I didn't know that would be a catalyst for a bigger ripple.

I didn't know that the letter would be so powerful. I didn't know people would be so impacted. I didn't know that years later, the letter would still be talked about. I didn't know it would lead to Gary Burton becoming a director. I didn't know it would lead to some of the guys we have worked with becoming sought-after speakers around the world. I didn't know I'd end up on a writing programme of someone in the audience who hadn't even created her writing programmes at that point!

I didn't know that in 2019, two years after reading that letter out, I would sit facing the stage at the same conference while Rabbi Shaul Rosenblatt[59] read out that letter again, then invited one of the guys we'd worked with onto stage to tell his story in his own words. I mean, seriously, how could I have known that asking a guy in prison for a letter would still be creating an impact years after it happened, that people I've never even heard of would find their lives changed? I think I'd be overwhelmed if I tried to think of what the ripple effects could be instead of just doing what occurs from that soft space of insight. But I do see that it shows a glimpse of what is available for everyone when we just take each step and do the best we can in that moment.

We are always walking into the unknown. We make up that we know how it will unfold. It's a thing we do. But we never really know. The most daunting step is to start, but then life will out. It has to. It's nature. Life finds a way.

Derrick Mason was another one of those unknowns. After he'd got the champion job with me at HMP Onley, he was transferred to another prison and then released, and I didn't hear from him.

You know that feeling when you think of someone, and they call? I was walking through London back to my hotel after doing a day's training for new facilitators, when Derrick popped into my mind. The next morning, I woke up early, and over breakfast, checked my Facebook messages. I love the intense rich smell of morning coffee and pastries in cafes. I sipped my delicious brew and smiled a little smile. "OK," I said. There was a message from Derrick asking me to get in touch. He said he'd been doing well. He'd been working as a painter and decorator, and he was "getting on with it."

"Want to come to a conference?" I asked him. The 2019 3PUK conference was coming up, and we'd be running a series of workshops. Derrick was delighted.

When he turned up at the conference, he got a surprise. "Sit up front with the guys," I told him. A couple of the guys were already sitting on the chairs at the front of the room, microphones setup in front of them. Cameras were poised, waiting for the audience to trickle through. Derrick had just arrived.

"OK," he said. He shared his story with the audience and saw the impact of his words. I watched from the front, proud of my guys.

The microphone for the audience was going around the room for people to ask questions. "I don't know what you did, and I don't know what this is," Derrick's partner said, "but since Derrick met you in Onley, he changed. His phone calls were different. His attitude was different. His words were different. And all I knew was I wanted this in my home. I've had three kids with him, and he was never there. He went away [to prison] each time. Now he's there. He's present, and he's with us."

No need to search for meaning. No need to figure it out. No need to hope for what it might be. Each moment is enough. I wake up each day and do what I need to do. I let life take care of the rest.

Notes

58   Steven Paul Jobs (24th February 1955 – 5th October 2011) was an American business magnate and investor. He was the co-founder, chairman, and CEO of Apple. His Stanford commencement address https://youtu.be/UF8uR6Z6KLc

59   Rabbi Shaul Rosenblatt – one of the organisers of the 3PUK conference.

The Download

"Our eyes are the windows to the soul, and only when our eyes are free of yesterday's scratches will we see today with any clarity."

~Sydney Banks

There was a time when suicide seemed like a viable option.

When the resolution seemed clear: remove me from the picture, and everything will be better. It was a measure of my own self-worth. Of how little I thought I brought to the world.

Dear Diary (August 1994),

I nearly did it today. I wanted to. I really did, but I bottled it at the last moment. I dragged my tired body to our neighbour's house. It felt like I was stepping through treacle. Over and over, I kept thinking, "Once again, I've f***ed up. Once again, I've failed. Once again, I've hurt someone, and my life's a disaster. I disgust myself." I wanted to end it all. I'm sure everyone would be better off without me. Darren was with the neighbour, Bobby,

---

having a guitar lesson. I walked into the open door of the little cottage at the end of the mews. Bobby and Darren sat in his living room, both holding guitars. Darren's seemed so big in his little hands, his blond hair falling into his eyes as he bent his angelic head to look at the strings. Bobby was teaching him "Bridge Over Troubled Water". He carried on when I walked into the room and stood in the doorway.

I didn't know what to say. I'd had some vague notion of saying goodbye or something cliché like that. I can't even be original when I'm going to check out. But I said nothing. It was all too much. Darren's pink cheeks flushed from the happiness of finding music making itself out of the ends of his little fingers. I turned away as tears scorched my cheeks. "I'm going for a walk," I mouthed to Bobby. He nodded and Darren looked up, smiling and proud that Mum had come to see him play.

The joy of seeing my boy playing guitar disappeared with each step down the stony path to the river until the roar of the water shoved them aside and my inadequacies flooded me. I knew where to do it, the bridge a couple of miles in front. It was dark and slippery on the towpath and its hard-stone walls plummeted to the river below. The pills in my pocket rattled when I tripped on a stone. I reached my chosen spot and perched on the edge. I waited. A gold guitar plectrum was nestled between two stones. Thoughts of my badness crashed in my mind. Water rushed under the bridge. A flash of the scene I'd just left of

> the guitar in Darren's hands lit up the dark. Then I saw
> a future with Darren's big blue eyes turned dark; his
> goofy smile wiped out; doubt tarnishing his life. And
> I knew I couldn't do it. I'd never want him to have the
> insecurities I had.

Darren was eight at the time of that journal entry. I had suicidal thoughts after that, but I no longer saw it as a call to action. So, like all thoughts, when we don't focus on them, they faded. It's not like I didn't ever think about suicide again, but after that, it was never with conviction, and in time even those thoughts just no longer occurred to me.

Now, when I have one of my "Is this the end?" moments, it's no longer followed by such dark solutions. These days it's more like, "Hmmm, what will I do next?" The journey of Beyond Recovery has been one of overcoming challenges, punctuated with moments of euphoric joy. The doom and gloom of the next challenge followed by the next breakthrough. Just when I'd think I was on the road to sustainability, I'd find myself in another cul-de-sac.

In September 2019, I came to one of those moments again. I'd finished the six-month project with HMP Nottingham, and I didn't know what was going to be next. I was aware that to scale, to be able to impact more people, and to grow, I'd need to create some financial stability. I'd enrolled in a course that helps entrepreneurs do just that, the School for Social Entrepreneurs (SSE[60]) in London. I was due to spend a day learning with the SSE, and as I walked toward the venue near the More London[61] area, I noticed the way the sun glinted off the stone water features. I had a flashback to the previous year when I'd had a breakdown in that very spot. The wide pedestrian area had been designed as a place to reflect, to take a moment in a busy life. The trees wore autumn colours of reds and browns. Birds chirped above the noise of traffic. Blue sky peeped through white fleecy clouds.

"OK," I said. "What am I meant to do?" I leaned against the wall of one of the skyscraper buildings and smiled at the life around me. Nothing happened. I laughed upwards and said, "Ha! Nothing to say then?" I shook my head at the absurdity of "asking the universe" and giggled at myself. A woman in a button-down grey suit and black stiletto heels flashed me a smile.

I decided to sit and enjoy a moment in a café before the course started. Coffee in hand and notepad on the little bistro table, I wrote whatever came to mind. Within half an hour, almost by accident, I had a three-page business plan on what I needed to concentrate on over the next six months. Plus, how to do it; what we should be doing after those six months. I was surprised at what I'd written, surprised at the ease of writing it and surprised that I had such clarity. Again, I was shown how life happens when we stop trying so hard to make it happen.

It appears the universe answered after all.

Notes

60   A training organisation for non-profit leaders. https://www.the-sse.org/
61   More London, part of an area known as London Bridge City, is a development on the south bank of the River Thames, immediately southwest of Tower Bridge in London. https://en.wikipedia.org/wiki/More_London

A Grown-Up Business

"We make a living by what we get, but we
make a life by what we give."
~ Winston Churchill

Three things were clear to me from the business plan I put together in that little café. First, I needed to secure some work to keep the business afloat. Second, I needed to step back from daily tasks and focus on longer term opportunities. And third, I couldn't do it alone; I needed to work out who was with me and who wasn't.

I've seen so often, that "the energy flows where the attention goes." What I mean by that is, as soon as I started focussing on business growth, I got ideas about how to make that happen. All sorts of ideas occurred to me that I hadn't seen before.

The work we'd been doing at Nottingham prison had helped reduce some of the issues, such as violence and drug use. The Head of Drug Strategy was so impressed; she put us forward to pitch to a new Violence Reduction Unit, set up by the Police and Crime Commissioner in Nottinghamshire County, focussed on youth violence: The

Notts VRU. They liked what we had done, and they needed new solutions to deal with the issue of youth knife crime. I submitted the tender application, and within a few weeks, we were awarded the contract, with the backing of the 3PRC (Three Principles Research & Consultancy) team in Charlottesville, who created a research protocol to measure the impact.

PRISON NOTES – DECEMBER 2018

WOW, Ron McVety has backed me through the 3PRC to evaluate our work at Notts prison. I'm already proud to be a co-author of three research papers[62] evidencing the impact we had at Onley and Rye Hill. Of course, I know what we do works because we see people change and their lives change, but prisons and funders need to see hard evidence. The evaluation was way more of a job than I'd considered it would be back in 2015 when I started. But we got there with two papers and another one about to be published. I'm glad we did it.

One paper is in the "International Journal of Offender Therapy and Comparative Criminology" another one is in the "Journal of Offender Rehabilitation", and the third is in the "Journal for Violence against Women." It thrills me to have contributed to the body of research evidencing human potential. I'm grateful that we kept on going. Grateful that the team helped and stuck with it, and grateful for my co-authors and everyone behind the scenes. It feels amazing. And now comes the cherry on the cake. Jeanne Catherine and the research team will do all the hard work and make our research protocols even more stringent. I'm so grateful for all these wonderful people that believe in what I do.

A further six-month project was perfect. This would take us to March 2020 and give me the opportunity I needed to develop other opportunities and take the business forward. I wanted to give Derrick the development he needed. So, I put together a tight team that could deliver the whole programme. I would step back and support them without being tied up in the day to day.

Then, wouldn't you know it, our wonderful administrator broke her foot and could no longer drive, let alone walk around the prison all day, so I ended up being more hands on that I wanted to be. I stuck to my mission though, and for the next six months, when I wasn't in the prison, I worked on new opportunities, relationships, and products. I wanted to grow our traded income so that we weren't reliant on funding or contracts. I developed a healthy funding strategy and created space to grow the business, all the time keeping my eye on my own work life balance to ensure I had time out for family and rest. It may seem like I was doing a lot, and I was, but I'd learned to recognise where I needed to step back, or let something go, or curb my own ability to create ideas.

One of the things I missed during this new phase was facilitating the groups, so I would often think back to the start of my work in Nottingham.

PRISON NOTES – MARCH 2019

Jacquie and I ran the second group in Notts this week. We had six new guys and three of the men from last week. I love it when they get so affected, they want more. Raymond was one of them. "Is this OK miss?" he asked.

Despite the blustery winds howling outside, the group room was overheated and muggy. Rivulets of sweat ran down my back. Our chairs were set in a circle with a small flip chart between the two of us. The water urn and refreshments were messy from the guys getting their first drink. A used tea bag sat on the blue carpet in a wet brown stain. Raymond had remembered how hot the room was and had brought in a small fan which he'd plugged in to face himself and then switched the rotator on so that the cool air reached our facilitator chairs next to him. "Yes, thank you," I said.

This week, the men were kinder, more considerate to us and to each other. They were compassionate. They were teaching each other. Men who'd already had insights helped the other men to see when they were "overthinking" or "projecting." They used words that made sense to them, to what they had seen. They were moved by Syd's CDs and often refer to his words. They've really started to see what's possible. I bloody love my job.

We don't teach the men we work with to be kind, or to curb their language. We don't teach them how to get over things or have better relationships. We don't teach them to maintain their recovery, or how not to be angry. We don't teach them to be creative or how to develop compassion and gratitude. But they learn all these things. Because these things are innate in every single human being. And given half the chance, these qualities rise to the surface naturally, without effort, without even knowing what they are.

Notes

62   Research papers are listed in the appendices.

Kindness Changes Everything

"Kindness is like a magic potion. It can only do good."
~Beyond Recovery Participant

"I'd love to sprinkle some fairy dust in Onley," I said, a mug of hot chocolate warming my hands. "The guys love a pre-Christmas group. Who's up for it?" The team sat round the lunch table in 'Nott a Costa' HMP Nottingham's staff restaurant, after a morning of group. I felt a mix of exhaustion and gratitude. We'd been at Nottingham prison for six months, but we still had this sweet feeling for the groups at HMP Onley. "Me!" Lili said.

"Let's do it!" the rest of the team said.

Christmas is a hard time of year for the guys and for their families: suicides go up, self-harming increases, and there are more "nickings" for brewing hooch or stashing mobiles. It's a hard time of year for many: feelings of loneliness, issues with homelessness, people who have lost loved ones. People in prison experience all these feelings plus the impotence of being locked up.

The BR team has done Christmas groups in Onley since 2016. We always think of them as the easy groups. We usually get a list of men we've already worked with, so they know the score, and there is none of the awkwardness or resistance of new guys. They're always happy for a pleasant distraction. We bring a lightness. A joy. A heartful of love. The Christmas groups felt less like formal teaching, and more like visiting family to share the Christmas spirit, as some of my notes from the different groups, describe:

PRISON NOTES – DECEMBER 2016

We had such fun this week in prison. Fun and tears and full hearts. It really shouldn't be this wonderful! Paul Lock offered to do some filming of the guys for posterity, so we got them all in the room on K Wing where we could nab one at a time in the little office next to it and interview them. Jacquie M sat with the guys in the room to keep them occupied. Norman, who turns up every week to blag coffee from me, sniffed out the cake. I managed to get him to agree to be interviewed. He told us he couldn't sleep because something weighed heavy on his mind. "OK," I said, "Anything else?"

He looked blank. "You don't understand miss, I have this terrible thing on my mind. I can't tell you about it, but it's so bad, it's so very bad." I assured him that it was OK, we could help with it, whatever it was. His face pictured doubt and a little bit of curiosity.

The next day, he came back full of excitement. "You won't believe what's happened, miss," he said. "I thought you guys were a bit mad, miss. I never told you anything, yet you kept saying you could help me. I thought youse are the ones that need therapy!" His blue eyes twinkled.

"Anyway, I watched myself some TV. Some old crap about a mum who'd forgiven a man who'd murdered her son. Me eyes were glued to the screen. It was like a thunderbolt hit me straight on me head." The small ladybird tattoo on his neck looked like it was dancing with his story. "Oh my Lord," he continued, "I sat bolt upright as I suddenly realised if she could forgive someone who murdered her son, then I can forgive the scum that raped my sister.

"I've never even thought that's possible, miss. Me mum and me sister keeps telling me to let it go but I couldn't. It just went round and round in me head. Then when I heard that mum forgive, I realised I can forgive. It's weird, but that night I slept and slept and slept like I've never slept before!"

PRISON NOTES – DECEMBER 2017

Wow, unbelievable. Susan and I ran a focus group today for the substance misuse team at HMP Dartmoor. They're interested in commissioning us to run groups at their prison. We had eight of the lads we've been working with, and I made sure they were a mix of guys who'd really been impacted and newer ones who were only just seeing something. I've never done a "focus group" before, so was not really sure what to expect. I trusted the guys to say whatever they felt and knew it would be OK, but I was blown away. Just overwhelmed by what I heard in that room. I asked the guys to be honest and ignore the fact that we were in the room, and then I sat back. To all our surprise, the guys talked of love and connection and overcoming addiction. They talked of hope they'd never experienced before. They told the Dartmoor crew that everyone needs to learn what we've taught them. I bit my cheeks to hold back my tears. Regardless of what happens with Dartmoor, Susan and I left feeling the love and knowing the impact we've had on these guys. The best Christmas present ever.

PRISON NOTES – DECEMBER 2018

We ran a "Christmas Special" for the peer mentors this week. It's been a special year and this lot were a special group. I think these are guys we're never going to forget. Leon, Chris, Dan, and Derrick. We've never laughed so much. It was like being at a family gathering. I'd put together a care package with drawing books and pencils and a soft towel for each of them. We laughed out loud as I asked each of them to close their eyes so I could put each care package into their open hands. They were nervous and fidgety. Leon boomed in his loud voice, "Never ask a man in prison to close his eyes in a room full of inmates!" But God bless them, they went along with it. Hope stole their fear. I'd brought some Christmas treats, including a brioche in the shape of a Christmas tree to "tear and share" and they loved it. We forgot we were in a stinky room on K Wing. We talked of hope and resilience and giving gratitude to our families. As the alarm sounded for group to end, we spontaneously joined arms in a big circle and danced around singing "We wish you a Merry Christmas," I'll never forget this Christmas.

Those prison notes demonstrate why I'd had no reason to assume that a 2019 Christmas Special would be any different, right? Except I forgot one thing: this year, instead of the group being for people we have already worked with; it would be a group made up of new people, residents who Safer Custody[63] had asked us to work with. A list of men who'd been labelled as violent. The ones who'd struggled to change their behaviour or caused some damage to themselves or others. Men who walked off their wings with shanks down their pants. Men who smashed up their cells on a regular basis. Men who had no desire to change.

Not such an easy group after all!

Once I'd spoken to the team and we'd got our heads around the fact that this group wasn't going to be so easy after all, we visited every guy on the list to narrow it down to the ones who had at least half an interest in being there. I love those wing visits to see the guys. It helps to create a feeling of trust; they turn up to the group knowing a bit more of what to expect, and the ones who can't come or aren't interested get taken off the list. Plus, it gave an opportunity for the two trainee facilitators, Dave, and Carola, to meet the guys and get comfortable.

Even after all that effort, it's always an unknown; who will show up, how many, and what states of mind they'll be in. I relish that moment before the start of a new group. It's a hinterland between nervousness and excitement. A pause. A breath between one state of being: busy, planning, sorting, thinking, managing, walking; to another state of being: clear-headed, present, spacious, open. The edge of running a group in prison, that first session, is an exquisite taste of anticipation. It's looking into an abyss. I know that I don't know what will happen next. I embrace the myriad of feelings that come with that. It's a slide into a warm bath of emotions. I sit very still while they wash over me, wash me, wash everything away. My busy mind finds a tap to let the thoughts run out so that I don't even see them. I can hear the comms people over the radio, issuing the commands to "unlock," "get in position," "report manned gates"; I can respond to comments made by the team; I can feel the breeze from the open window. But the stillness supersedes it all.

And then. They're in! The rowdiness of checking each guy into the room and getting them settled. The nerves. The quiet. The eyes on me. The start.

The men looked tough. We had some of our previous graduates in the room, which helped, but some of the other guys had scowls the size of a tornado.

Toby stood out to me. A thirty-something gangster from Ghana. Tough, well-built, gold teeth and eyes that told me he wasn't happy to be there. I did my thing. Started group. Created a calm, safe space. The guys asked questions, and there was a bit of banter but nothing too hard. During the break, I sat next to Toby.

"Is it always this hostile?" he asked. My mind whirled. Hostile? I hadn't noticed!

The radio announced, "All prisoners to return to their wings," and there was no time to ask Toby what he meant.

The next day, I noticed that Toby was marked as Keep

on Wing, which means he wouldn't be allowed to come to the group. We knew he was one of the dangerous ones, but I was determined to give him a chance. We went to see Safer Custody.

"It makes no sense to keep him back. In fact, it could cause more harm than good. He's done one session with us; it only seems right to give him a chance to hear something new," I said.

Less than an hour later, I stood outside the Healthcare group room. As I ticked each man off our list, along comes Toby. "Ahright miss?" He asked.

My long, black, matrix-style coat flapped about in the wind. My cold hands held the blue clipboard with the list of names for our group. "Yes, Toby!" I said. "I'm so happy you're here. We fought for you this morning." The scowl slipped off his face as surprise took over.

"What do you mean?" he inquired. I told him what happened. I could see him soften like melted ice cream.

We didn't hear a peep from him all morning. During break, I sat next to him. "What's occurring?" I asked. Sounds of the kettle being boiled and chatter from the guys filled the room. There was a dark tea stain on the carpet by my booted feet.

"Nobody has ever been so kind to me, miss," Toby said, his large hands clasped on his lap. "Nobody wants me in their group. I know why. I know I'm a pain," he continued. His soft voice caught in his throat. "Nobody's ever fought for me, nobody's ever been this kind." We sat in silence for the rest of the break. I nodded to him when it was time for me to return to my seat.

On the final day, Toby turned up a face full of smiles.

He looked half the size without the clenched shoulders and fraught look. He lapped up every word we said. During the afternoon break, I sat next to him. "How you doing?" I asked. I could feel the fabric on the soft blue chair beneath my hands.

"Well miss, I've realised that I ain't ever listened to no one!" Toby said. "It's the first time ever, I feel like other people had something interesting to say. I've even got caught by the police because I wouldn't listen to others." He grimaced as he stole a cheeky look at me. "But when Lili was talking, I could feel her love, her truth. My heart felt like it understood what she was saying. And I ain't gotta clue what that means!" Toby's smile was broad, his eyes sparkled. I could feel the softness in his body. "I hate groups, miss; I don't even know how I ended up on this one, but I want to be involved in everything you do."

There are all sorts of theories and studies about what works to rehabilitate people. And what doesn't? Theories about how people change and why they don't and theories about complex psychological tools for measuring shifts in consciousness. Yet I think there is a simplicity that is overlooked. In the hundreds of people I've worked with, I've found two things to be effective on everyone: kindness and listening. Two magical tools that we can all access. I believe the world would change if we all took a moment each day to be kind to each other. If we all stopped and listened to each other. If we all were kinder and listened to ourselves.

I checked in with Shaun in the Safer Custody office at the end of the three-day programme. "Did anyone have a significant change?" he asked. The overhead lights glared bright white light into the room.

"Toby," I said. The air in the room expanded as the whole team breathed a sigh of relief.

"If he's changed, we'll all be grateful. And we'll all be safer," Shaun said.

In early January 2020, I dropped by to check on how Toby was doing. "He's changed beyond belief," Shaun said. "He is kind and helpful to staff. He's been counselling inmates. He's now got a job in the prison. He is a different person! Oh, and he wants to do as many groups as possible."

After all that worry about it being a hard group, it turned out to be the best Christmas group ever.

Notes

63 Safer Custody is a department in prisons dedicated to looking after the safety of the prison, staff, and residents.

A Miracle Intervention

"I fully concur with the participant's description of
this intervention as a 'miracle'".
~ Paddy Tipping, ex Chair of Nottingham's
Violence Reduction Unit

I see miracles all the time. It sounds dramatic, but it's true.
Men reconnect with their children after years of no contact.
Addicts become drug-free after a lifetime of suffering.
Women drop years of insecurity and blossom into warm
human beings. A visitor to our groups said, "It truly was a
miracle. I saw transformations before my eyes in the three
days I was in that room, in people whom I didn't think could
possibly change."

Out of transformation comes gratitude, love, being of
service. People from disparate backgrounds discover tastes
for reading, classical music, opera, and theatre. They become
free and compassionate, and loving.

"You won't believe what just happened," Derrick said.
I'd walked into the group room at HMP Nottingham, as
the Beyond Recovery team was finishing up. The residents
spilled out onto the yard. Sunshine filtered past the thick

grey bars on the window. Motivational posters covered the walls.

"Tell me, Derrick," I said.

He explained that two of the men in the room had been from rival gangs. We hadn't known that. It had somehow slipped through the security checks. They'd dominated the room. One of them, Jordan, a mixed-race guy in his twenties, a mouth full of gold teeth and tiny locs threaded into his hair, had been in a previous group with us.

Derrick shared how Jordan had opened the group with a story about how his friend had died in his arms, and that he didn't want to see any more killing or dying.

"To start with, I was just gonna kick back and enjoy the coffee," Jordan had said. "Then it come to me that I have a choice in how I take things. Like if someone annoys me, I have a choice about how I take it. I never understood that before. It was mind blowing to me." He went on to say that he realised that seeing there were choices meant he could use those choices for good.

While Jordan was waxing lyrical about choices, another man, Des, was getting wound up. Des, a well-built dark-skinned man with short natural hair, aged nineteen, had been involved in the crime Jordan was talking about. That was why he was in prison. Des's mind raced while Jordan talked. All he could think of was how it'd kick off as soon as Jordan realised who he was. He kept very still, his big hands folded in his lap, coiled like a spring and ready for action.

While Derrick told this story, his face shone with wonder, his brown skin warm against the bright blue of his Beyond Recovery polo shirt. He continued, "At the end of the session, Des walked over to me and Jordan. I could tell

Jordan was wary. Des asked Jordan if he knew who he was."
Derrick's brown eyes were wide. I could hear a bird singing
in the yard. "So, Jordan tells the geezer 'I think I've worked
it out, mate.'"

"The fellas just stood looking into each other's eyes,"
Derrick continued. "I held my breath man. It was a mad
ting. I could feeeeel the tension. I thought it was gonna kick
off, so I just stood real still. Then Des asked Jordan, 'What
we going to do about it?'"

Derrick continued, "I wasn't aware of anything else in
the room; I didn't even see you come in, MamaJ."

A cool breeze carried the smell of coffee and biscuits in
the air.

"After what seemed like forever, Jordan just piped up
'We could let it stop here.'"

The sound of an alarm in the distance pierced the air.

"It seemed like another eternity, then they just shook
hands. They shook hands. I couldn't believe what I was
seeing." Derrick's eyes sparkled. "It's unheard-of Jacqueline,
men shaking hands like that, it just doesn't happen. They
gotta deal with their people and everything. The unwritten
rule is 'do or die,' you know," Derrick explained.

"Last thing Jordan said was, 'We can be real with dat.'
Then the officer called 'Freeflooooow' and we all shook
hands and they left. It was amazing man, beautiful." Derrick
stopped talking and looked at my awestruck face.

We were buzzing. I couldn't believe it either. I've seen
many wonderful changes in understanding: forgiveness;
acceptance; compassion. But I've never seen "real time" gang
members make their peace because they've had a shift in
consciousness.

The next day, both guys turned up. Both wary, like lions circling a boundary, each waiting to see where the other was at. "I was surprised at myself," Jordan said. "I never imagined I'd be in the same room as this guy and not hurt him."

As the group sessions continued over the next two days, both men saw more about what was possible from this new place of understanding. In an interview after the group, Jordan said, "That last session taught me forgiveness. I was in the room with the same guy who killed my friend, but I didn't recognise him. Then when he spoke to me, I started to understand him as a person. I saw his remorse. I understood him as a human being, as one like me, not labelled as a 'rival.'"

Our researcher went to see Des and get his side of the story. "How did the group make you feel?" she asked.

"A miracle. This was a miracle. A heavy weight on my shoulder was lifted. It was like a closure. I realised that the very moment I can see 'the human' in someone, I automatically think, 'If I fight, I fight with myself.'" Des sat opposite the researcher in the tiny office at the end of the prison wing. "The group allowed me to be myself and to open up about my feelings without being judged. I felt I could be real, to be the person I am behind closed doors."

The two guys suggested that the best thing to do would be to build a glass wall with all the rival gangs on either side, teach them understanding, and then break the wall down so they could all hug.

PRISON NOTES – DECEMBER 2019

The press office for the PCC rang today. Turns out they are doing a piece on our work on the Knife Crime project because the chair of the VRU, Paddy Tipping, had sent them the case studies from the rival gang members who shook hands. I was worried I'd said the wrong things. But when I saw the draft, I cried with gratitude and relief. Paddy Tipping quotes: "Although still in its infancy, this Violence Reduction prison mentorship project is having dramatic results and changing the way these young men view the world and other people. What was once considered impossible or even too risky—such as encouraging rival groups to meet and share their experiences — has been achieved and this gives me so much hope for the future safety of our county. I fully concur with the participant's description of this intervention as a 'miracle.'"

It's About Freedom

"All my life I have been running, when I finally
stopped & faced what I was running from...
Guess what it was? Myself!"
~ Beyond Recovery Participant

It was many years after my dad died that I realised what had happened. In a surreal moment in his hospital bathroom that dark March night in 2009, I'd found my true nature. I didn't know that's what it was. I'd just felt my heart expand when I saw through my judgemental thinking of me, of him, of our history. That moment shaped the next few years, and the Beyond Recovery journey. It was a portal to a deeper connection with the true essence of life. And it carried me on my walk to freedom. I'd never connected the two things, the freedom I experienced and the journey of transformation that followed. But when I found this old diary entry, the relevance clicked into place.

Dear Diary (March 2009),

It's over. He's gone. I've tried my best these past four months. I've tried to be a good daughter. I've tried to forgive. It's been hard. One of the girlfriends called me last weekend and told me Dad was on his last legs. I drove straight up to Derby. "You're not looking so good, Dad," I said. I stood in the doorway of his bedroom in his little terraced house and looked at his broken body on the bed. Pale, skinny, where was the scary man he used to be? The double bed swallowed his bony body. Crumpled sweaty sheets, abandoned hopes. Air perfumed with rotting flesh. "The paramedics are on their way," I said. I switched on my internal project manager and started to sort shit out.

The weekend passed in a blur of hospitals, doctors, paperwork, visitors, and ghosts from Christmas past. Family crawled out of the woodwork; someone tried to contact my sister. Girlfriends wiped his mouth and declared their love. An ex-wife turned up to stake her claim. I was patient. I answered all their questions. I fetched and carried. And I kept my beady eye on his progress. A paused breath, in this whirlwind of activity, was when the doctors asked me to sign the "do not resuscitate" forms. This man I didn't know had his life in my hands. This man who had tormented me was now to be killed by me. This man I did not love hung his breath on my ability to be strong. I didn't want to do it. I didn't think it was right. I didn't know enough.

I signed the forms.

He just lay there.

They moved him to a ward on his own. The bed undulated.

He just lay there.

They strapped him up to tubes to keep him pain free.

He just lay there.

They told me I could go home.

He just lay there.

I read aloud from a book I'd found at his bedside table.

He just lay there.

I took his hand in mine and read him to die.

He just lay there.

"Kick one of the patients out of bed and get some sleep," Darren, my son, texted me. I read it out loud.

Dad laughed.

"What?" I told Darren he'd laughed, and he texted back, "He won't laugh when he finds out it's him you are going to kick out of bed!"

I told Dad.

He laughed again!

"You can hear me, can't you, you old bugger?" I said.

He just lay there.

The sound of his raspy breath from his open mouth synchronised with the sound of the undulating bed. A harmony of dying. His face shallow and grey, his hair white, his body as frail as a frail thing. He lay in that single hospital bed with the cot sides up like a child. There was a dim light coming from the overhead flu-orescents, turned to night mode. The bedside table empty of flowers or gifts or framed pictures. The door to the adjoining bathroom was ajar for quick functional visits. I'd been in that hospital for seventy-two hours. My unwashed hair and smudged make-up told the story of a woman at the end of her vigil. I sat with my left hand in his right hand and the book on the bed. "Well, I'm going to keep reading until you go," I said.

He just lay there.

Sadness drenched my body. It weighed down my limbs and pulled at the corners of my mouth. It filled my eyes with its watery doom. It dimmed my heart. Sadness for the life not lived, things not said, the father not had. Sadness for the child not loved, the misguided man, the wasted chance. "I'm sorry," I said.

He said nothing, but in a slow and deliberate move-ment, he raised his right hand, the one with mine in it, and lay it on his chest. "Me Too," the air coming out of his mouth said.

The light in my heart dried all the sad away. A whoosh of peace coursed through my veins. That was it, but that was enough. I read. He lay there.

A few hours later, before the sun rose, before the visitors arrived, before the hospital bustled to life, I decided to wash up a little and clean my teeth. I looked at the girl in the mirror. I was surprised at what I saw. The most beautiful face gazed back at me with

> a kindness that filled her eyes. Gentle and light, she seemed to stare right into my soul and fill it with love. "Who are you?" I whispered. She just kept loving me with her serene gaze.

That moment when I'd looked into the mirror after spending seventy-two hours in the hospital, taking care of things but not taking care of myself. That moment when, instead of seeing a tired girl with bags under her eyes, lank hair, and no make-up, I saw someone beautiful. I saw someone kind. I saw someone loved. I didn't know what that was or who that was.

Later, when I had time to process, I realised that in that moment of connection between us, there was a simple forgiveness. And in that space, a peace had swept through me that cleared my mind of all thought; all judgement; all pain; all ego. Freedom from holding onto what was wrong and who was right. I didn't know it at the time, but freedom dropped the scales from my eyes and allowed me to see my essence. The essence we all have beyond the pain of our imagination. The essence that cannot be broken.

It's only now, in 2020, during the COVID Pandemic, while writing about the incredible journey of Beyond Recovery, that I realise just how much that experience of freedom impacted my journey. I'm not sure I could've done what I've done without that realisation. By getting a glimpse of the true nature of my soul in that mirror, I got a glimpse of the true nature of all souls. I didn't know it then, but it was the surreal experience of forgiveness towards my dad and myself that opened my heart to seeing the essence in people regardless of their circumstances.

I had no clue where it would lead me, or even that it was significant, but looking back I can see how the new path opened for me in that moment. After my dad died, I ended up with the responsibility of clearing out his house. There was a lot of angst with various family members and ex-wives, but one thing that stands out to me now is a random paper I found in his desk drawer.

"What's this?" I wondered. Dad's little home office was the back bedroom of his terraced house. The bedroom window looked out over his long narrow garden, filled with stone statues of naked nymphs and dark green ivy. The garden was flanked by the turret of a 12th century church on one side and a tall, graceful birch tree on the other. The light from the blue cloudless sky filled all corners of the room. "Looks interesting," I said. I held a printed copy of a newsletter about a training program called Supercoach, run by Michael Neill. I'd never heard of this guy or the training program, but my interest was piqued. I liked the energy I felt in his words. The next door was open. I followed that path through that door and ended up on Supercoach. I kept following that path. The path that led me to uncover the true nature of people in prison.

The Key Maker

"There is a good voice within me that knows
right from wrong."

~ Beyond Recovery Participant

Everyone wants to change the world. Reach more people, end poverty, eliminate stigma, feed the world. I'm guilty of that dream too. My mind imagines a world where we rehabilitate, integrate, and treat our fellow human beings in the way we'd want our children to be treated. I imagine a world where there are no prisons. Where there is no stigma. Where there are no "others."

But it all starts with one. Each time someone wakes up to their potential; each time I see a face brighten with an internal light; each time someone stops me and says, "You've saved my life", I remember one person is enough, more than enough. It is all that is ever needed.

Each One Teach One is a phrase created by enslaved African people. These people were denied education. So when an enslaved person learned to read, it became their duty to teach someone else. Just one other person. And that person would teach another. Like the butterfly effect that ripples out across time to many but always starts with one.

Many of the men and women we meet in prison can't read or write. Some of them have never been to school, coming from travelling communities or "road families[64]" or dropped out because they'd been labelled naughty. Sometimes they teach themselves; then they get drawn to teach one of their neighbours. Each person who wakes up can wake another. Change has happened throughout history by one person standing up for others (Princess Diana), one person helping another person (Florence Nightingale), one voice speaking out (Greta Thunberg), and one person standing against unfairness (Rosa Parks).

From the beginning of the Beyond Recovery journey, the dream was always to have the guys, the people with the lived experiences, be the teachers. From my first group in prison, I saw how the guys were the ones who would be the leaders to solve the issues in society. And now I'm witnessing that dream come true. Even when it was difficult, I didn't give up on it. I knew that one day it would be the guys I have trained in prison who would be the ones leading the programmes, the business, and the communities.

I grew my team from people who had trained as practitioners but had little experience in delivery of programmes. I gathered a small team of people who had big hearts, some grounding in the Three Principles and a desire to help. I always used to say, "The only thing you need, is to love the guys, the rest can be picked up." Anna, Susan, Lili, Paul, Jacquie, Gary, Al, Pete, Dave, and many others, all came and learned on the job with me. And we were impactful because we did our best, we showed up, we listened. But even then,

I saw the impact it had on a group when "one of their own" sat in. Someone who had been through group before, who had some insight to share, who had walked in their shoes. After the first group, I started inviting people back to help with the next group, to be peer mentors. I had T-shirts designed for them. It also did wonders for their confidence and helped them to embed their learning and go deeper with their insights.

PRISON NOTES – JUNE 2015

Craig made me laugh today. "There are men in this room I would be scared to put together," he said. I was running a group in the classroom off K Wing at Onley prison. The sounds of clanging and crashing from the noisy wing kept interrupting my flow. Raised voices bantered back and forth, metal crashed against metal, stereos blasted out a cacophony of drill, and RnB. Our little room was one of three offices at the end of the landing, tucked away in the corner. A long thin room that could hold up to twenty people at a push. I smiled at Craig, his tall frame leaned forward, his face earnest. "But Jacqueline sees the good in everyone, somehow she sees past what I'm seeing," he said.

Everyone wanted to be a peer mentor. All the men think they are qualified, so I developed a way of filtering who could come back and wear the T-shirt. In the early days, I was more interested in getting numbers. Meaning that I needed to have at least ten new people in each class so I could build the evidence[65] of the programme. I also had a theory that there would be a tipping point where the number of men impacted would start helping the other guys in the prison and it would be enough of a ripple effect to impact an exponential number of residents. When this started happening in HMP Onley I knew we were onto a good thing. I remember the deep feeling of satisfaction when Zach, one of our Peer Mentors said, "Thank you for helping us to help ourselves."

A natural progression from Peer Mentors, was to train the guys as facilitators. Hence the Apprentice Programme was born. A ten-month programme that would train Peer Mentors to become facilitators, providing them with opportunities for grounding their own understanding and opportunities for sharing in groups. Of course, we still had all the difficulties of men being transferred to other prisons halfway through or falling off the path in some way and having to be excluded from group, but the programme was a huge success. And we wanted to be able to support the guys on release, so I setup something called Academy meetings in London, so we could meet once a month and just check in on how they were doing, where they struggled, and reflect on their own solutions.

These groups led to Derrick becoming part of the team on the Knife Crime project in Nottingham and some of the other guys getting involved.

PRISON NOTES – MARCH 2020

My heart is full, my body is tired, but my heart is so very grateful. I know I'm truly blessed to be doing this work. Yesterday morning when I was waiting outside the pickup point at the hotel, I watched the team walk up the road from the train station. The team and the BR men had all travelled up from London together. As I watched this cloud of Beyond Recovery Polo shirts storming up the road, my heart swelled. "The Beyond Recovery Massive!" I shouted.

The noises from the train station on my left and the main road behind me, full of traffic, dimmed. I could hear laughter and light-heartedness as the team joked and jostled with the boys. Wilson struts with a boxer's stance, even smothered in his khaki parka with pockets filled with music and cables. His smooth brown skin and big brown eyes poked out of the furry hood of the parka jacket. A wide grin spread across his face when he saw me standing there. Chris was wrapped up against the cold wind, with an oversized coat and a thick grey woollen scarf wrapped around his short black locs. I could see his big smile and gold teeth before I could even recognise his face. And then there was Derrick. Walking with confidence amongst his peers, the man, the teacher, the leader. My heart skipped a beat. "Look at you lot!" I said. Hugs and loud greetings followed before they all stored their luggage at the hotel and pile into the cars to take us to HMP Nottingham.

The guys were brilliant. I'd been a bit worried about having three of them help run the group. I'd been concerned they'd speak too much or overshadow the young men who were learning. But they were brilliant. Absobloodylutely brilliant. They listened. They shared. They were compassionate. They were insightful. They learned. Everything you would expect from a team of amazing teachers. I felt like a Jedi knight. I wanted to waft my hand across the team and say, "My work here is done." After group, I walked with them onto Delta Wing to collect the paper for our flip chart. Chris and Wilson went through each gate ahead of me and I locked each one behind us. "You two look like criminals," said one of the residents of Delta Wing.

"Not anymore, my man," Wilson said, his smile as broad as his shoulders.

Not anymore.

That last group at Nottingham was a dream come true. Little was I to know it would be the very last group we'd run in prison for a long time. It seems fate lined the stars up just in time. "Wagamama's?" the taxi driver asked. The six-seater white taxi took us on our ten-minute journey from the hotel to the restaurant through the early evening traffic. After a long couple of days in prison, it was nice to be going out to bond over the wonderful session we'd had. Streetlights and car lights flashed through the windows and lit up our smiles as we sped along, cosy in the back of the cab. Two rows facing each other, six of us squished into the tight seats. The rich sound of laughter reverberated with the wheels of the speeding cab. "Chris was worried," Wilson said, telling us of how Chris had been concerned he didn't have the same experience as the rest of us. "But I told him, 'All the Avengers have their own special superpowers, all unique, and you have yours.'" Lili squeezed my hand. I was glad the dark cab hid the tears that sprung to my eyes. This day had been a dream come true. Training the guys to lead the teaching was the last piece of the jigsaw. It couldn't get any better than this.

Can you see how it grows and blossoms? It's not the result of battle plans and world domination. It's not the result of social media strategies and templates and platforms. It's not the result of a five-year plan. It's the result of one step at a time, one moment, one idea, one person. It's the result of putting one foot in front of the other. It's the result of taking a step into the unknown, again and again and again. It's the result of trusting and following the ideas that come. It's the result of picking myself up when things look bad. It's the result of bringing everyone else along with me.

But it all starts with a step, a moment, an idea. And another, and another, and another. And anyone can take a step. Just that step. Just that one step in front of us.

Notes

64   Families where fathers and uncles are all embedded into the criminal lifestyle.
65   The research needed at least 60 people to have gone through the program.

The Breath-taking View at the Edge of the World

"The intuitive mind is a sacred gift, and the rational mind is a faithful servant."
~ Albert Einstein

Mountain climbers take pictures at the tops of mountains. There is a moment. A moment of pure bliss, of gratitude, of deep satisfaction. A moment where nothing else exists.

The pictures show smiles and happy hearts because they've reached the pinnacle, the top, the end of the climb. They're not thinking about the trek down or their aches, or how they struggled to get there.

Nobody takes pictures during the relentless climb. Nobody wants to record the pain and anguish of taking it to the next level. Nobody wants to remember the blisters on top of blisters, the aches and pains in every joint, the dehydration, the tears, the fears, the sweat and blood, the hunger, and the sleep deprivation. We just want to remember the view from the top. The breath-taking view at the edge of the world. Because when you see that view, it's all worth it. The view from the top makes us forget the rest.

But there is a path to get there, and it's rocky, and it makes you want to give up and question your own sanity and it takes guts and courage. And sometimes you reach the top only to find that it's not the end. And sometimes you get lost. And sometimes the weather shifts from bright sunshine to a raging blizzard that is so bad you can't keep your eyes open from the sting. And you can't take off your heavy gloves to eat because of the danger of frostbite. And you can't talk to anyone because the wind is too noisy for you to be heard. And all you want to do is cry, and make it all go away.

Dear Diary (June 2012),

We did it! Our little band of intrepid explorers made it. We'd started as six strangers who met at a business network thing called BOB. I remember the morning when Els asked, "Does anyone fancy doing the National Three Peaks Challenge?" Her sunshine hair bobbed as she looked around the table with her big blue eyes. The challenge was to climb the three largest mountains in the UK: Ben Nevis in Scotland, Scafell Pike in the Lake District and Snowden in Wales, all within twenty-four hours.

"I'm in," I said.

We'd started the journey together: me, Martin,

Cookie, Jacky, Els, Pete and Becky. For six months we trained, walked and climbed loads of mountains. We'd got to know each other and bonded. I'd got blisters and aches in places I didn't even know I had, but nothing, NOTHING could have really prepared us for the actual Three Peaks Challenge.

Less than forty-two hours ago, we'd been fresh and excited and full of confident smiles at the base of Ben Nevis in Scotland, with all the other teams looking to complete the challenge. We'd driven up the day before and spent the night in a dorm together. Too excited to sleep. As we stood at the bottom of Ben Nevis, we waved off Becky, who was tasked with preparing the meals we'd need to eat in our minibus while she drove us between the mountains so we could sleep and not lose any time.

The view on The Ben staggered me. The morning mists, snow halfway up even in June, deer and wildlife all around. It took us just over five hours to climb up and back down again. It was hard, but I loved it and the team loved it. We'd had a good laugh and a good old singsong. The sting was knowing another climb was waiting for us when we reached Scafell Pike. We were a bit jaded by then but pulled ourselves together, changed our sweaty socks and tops in the van, grabbed some bumpy sleep, and then knuckled down when we arrived at the foot of Scafell Pike and got it done. I didn't enjoy that climb; it was hard and shaly, and the weather was horrible. It was just a task to get completed. One of the worst bits was feeling my stomach do gambols when we saw a man with a broken leg, bone jutting out of the side of his trousers, waiting to be airlifted off the mountain. It reminded me; the mountain takes no prisoners.

On the way to Snowdon, our bus got slowed down due to runners carrying the Olympic Torch. The streets were lined with cheering people. Becky woke me up. I glanced at the torch, grunted something, and went back to sleep. Too exhausted to even register the enormity of the moment.

We started the final climb at 4:00am this morning. No smiles. No songs. No happy voices. We sniped and bitched at each other. But we dug in and got the climb done, and, somehow, we made it.

And then. The summit. The view. The breath-taking view at the top of the mountain. "Champagne?" Martin offered. He'd carried a bottle of Veuve Clique and some plastic glasses in his backpack, nestled among energy gels, ibuprofen, and water bottles. The morning mist hung like an eerie shroud around the lush green mountains and valleys. A large round ball of fire adorned the sky and paved a streak of red glory towards the dial on the summit. The edges of the trees looked singed by the sun's fire. Dense mist hovered over the huge lake below us. Deer and birds and rabbits were woken up by the sun's bright life force and began their foraging for food. Trees and shrubs showed off their muted colours of reds and browns and mossy greens. The pain had been worth it. My knees felt crunchy, my back strained, and my clothes were stuck to my body with sweat, but I felt as soft as the mist and as alive as the fierce sun. My dry throat and burning toes were nothing compared to the feeling of having conquered the world. "Hip hip hooray!" The rest of the team lifted their glasses and opened their arms to me.

March 2020 – As I sit here and do the final edits on this book I've been writing for over three years, a labour of love describing my labour of love, I'm reflecting on the journey and the view at the top of my mountain. The journey into the criminal justice system; the journey into the world of a non-profit business; the journey of me and the wonderful people I met along the way. As I sit here, I'm not thinking about the climb. I'm sitting with gratitude on the edge of my world. The view is breath-taking from here, but I wanted you to know about the climb; I wanted you to know about the steps that lead to the edge of the world; I wanted you to know that it is OK to fear, to worry, to feel you will never make it.

Like Joseph Campbell's "Hero's Journey," the summit comes again and again and again during our lives, as we negotiate the countless Separations, Initiations, and Returns. We Return to start with a new Separation, a new climb. There is not one top of the world, one edge, one peak, there is just the one we are taking at any given moment. Just as there is no end or limitation to the potential of the human mind. Of my mind. Of your mind.

Epilogue

When Normal Stopped Being Normal

"We always live in uncertain times. It's just a bit
more obvious right now."
~ Rabbi Shaul Rosenblatt

This book was finished when I wrote about the breath-taking
view at the top of the world. I felt that end was suitable
enough to be able to give a flavour of hope, knowing that
Beyond Recovery and the people we serve in prison would
continue growing from strength to strength. I felt that
the reader could be inspired and would have found some
ways of tapping into their own wisdom and inner voice; of
finding the courage to take the next step; of stepping into the
unknown with at least a little faith that things work out, even
if there is a roller coaster ride along the journey.

And then, in March 2020, the world was rocked by
COVID-19. And everything stopped.

The issues with the virus, the increased deaths, and the
wild spread of the disease had been going on in different
countries since December 2019 but wasn't declared a pandemic by the World Health Organisation until March 2020.

For some people, including me, there was a feeling that "it would just blow over," or "it's just the flu", or "it won't affect my life,"

I was wrong.

I don't watch the news, it's too negative, and so the Coronavirus and its impact on society was only in the periphery of my vision.

I knew people were dying, but I figured people die from the flu every year, right? And I knew some countries were taking special measures, but it all seemed over the top to me. I knew people were panic buying (toilet rolls of all things), but I imagined it would soon stop.

I was too busy, too cocky, too ignorant.

I carried on regardless. A bit like those posters we see: "Don't Panic and Carry On." I'm British, right? I got on with what I needed to do and wondered when the madness would stop. I had a thriving business to run. I had people who needed me. I had to keep going.

Tuesday 10th March – I'd managed to persuade Governor NP at Nottingham to squeeze in a meeting with me before he went on his holidays. A great meeting where we discussed the next contract. He revealed that the Violence Reduction Unit had told him they wanted us in Nottingham and their feeder prison HMP Ranby. The VRU were also suggesting that each of the respective Governors fund half of the project for their own prison. "I want you here, but I've got no money," NP said. We sat in his huge, light-filled office at the comfortable end of the prison. I could feel the oak veneer of the table beneath my fingers. "You know I'm supportive of you," he said. His large hands were placed on the table in front of him, and his big brown eyes held my gaze. I could feel my toes sweating in my woollen socks and Levi work boots. "How much were you thinking?" he asked.

"Five thousand pounds," I replied.

"OK," he said.

OK! I was overjoyed. We'd gone from no money to a quarter of what I needed to raise in minutes. Back at my desk, I'd logged onto the antiquated prison computer to type up the notes Governor NP needed when his dark shadow loomed over me. I smiled, and he held up two hands. "Ten?" I asked.

The air in the large admin office was stuffy from hot radiators.

"Yes, I can give you ten thousand!" he said, nodding his big, bear-like head.

It felt good. It felt amazing. It felt like I'd cracked it.

That evening I had a conference call with the organisers of the Recovery from Addiction conference in Minnesota, where I was due to be speaking in May. They were still planning to go ahead with the conference "unless the universities close," At the end of the call, I made a request that we all do what we can to help people with their fear. "We all have a duty, given what we know, to put stuff out there at this time of panic," I said.

Wednesday 11th March – I was surprised to be able to get a space at the station car park. The roads were so much clearer. "More people must be staying at home." I was booked on an early train to London for three meetings: one with Derrick to discuss his role with Beyond Recovery; one with the Virtual Reality[66] expert, Nina and our business angel David

Kowitz (DK); one with the film company ACME to explore a documentary.

It was spooky standing on an empty platform at what should have been a busy time of day. It felt like I was in the middle of a dystopian movie. The feeling got stronger when I received a text from Nina, "Can we do our meeting online due to Coronavirus?" I answered that we could and wondered if I was doing the right thing, travelling to London. A chill ran down my spine when the next text was from DK. He wasn't sure if he could make it because a friend was being tested for the virus. The train pulled into the station, and I decided to go anyway.

On the train, there were plenty of seats, even the ones with tables. Business as usual for me; laptop out as soon as I was seated. "OK," I said. The comfortable train sped its way to London. Fluffy white clouds of new-born lambs dotted the lush green fields. Streaks of yellow painted the pale blue sky. The MacBook open on the table in front of me was bursting with words and numbers being crafted together in the orchestra of a pitch.

"We are arriving at Euston," the train guard said, and I closed my laptop with a satisfied sigh. Another job done.

I'd been so engrossed in my work I'd forgotten I was in the middle of a horror story where all the people had disappeared, but soon remembered when I saw the empty tube station. The relief at not having to elbow my way onto the tube to Aldgate was tainted by the creeping feeling that I shouldn't be out of doors. But once I'd found the café where Derrick was waiting for me, I forgot my disquiet.

We bought coffee and lunch and discussed Derrick's future with Beyond Recovery. We got excited by all the things we would do and how we would change the world. We said we'd do a month's trial before making it an employed position. We loaded up the MacBook to conduct the meeting about VR with Nina and did the best we could to hear her in the noisy café. After that meeting, we moved on to the quirky little studio that was the base for ACME Films. DK turned up, and we discussed various ideas with the producer and the director. They were going to be pitching to BBC3 in a week. I felt very lucky to be sitting there discussing a documentary in which we would feature.

Later that day, I made my way home and forgot all about the dystopian nature of my journey, too full of hope and possibility of what the future would bring, to think about the world coming to an end.

Thursday 12th March – Sonia and I were walking through the long carpark next to the high grey stone walls topped with barbed wire on our way into HMP Onley to run our Thursday afternoon group. We discussed how we should be respectful of the fear surrounding us about COVID-19, but there was no need for us to join it. We talked about how we knew how to listen to wisdom. We were naïve. While the team ran the group, I slipped away to go and work in the coffee shop at the Equestrian Centre down the road. I had a couple of hours to get the board report finished, and a great place to do it. Sitting on one of the large comfy sofas, I had a view through the plate-glass windows of the paddock where horses were jumping in a competition. Again, it all felt like business as usual, and I was getting plenty of work done. I re-joined the group for the closing comments and to do the debrief.

"Thanks, miss, my head's so much clearer now; I catch myself ruminating, and I just stop it!" one of the guys said.

From there, I went on to prepare for the prison staff programme I had started running on Thursday nights. I could just about manage to squeeze a couple more hours of energy into teaching the lovely small group of officers and support staff on our Mind Management training, but once done, I was delighted to be finished and looking forward to a day working from home on Friday.

Friday 13th March – The team meeting is not until 9:00am, so I have time for an extra cuppa in bed and a catch-up of the week with Rob. "I'm getting a top-up," I said and popped my bare feet out onto the striped rug by the side of my bed. A silver star sticker was on the carpet next to my big pink fluffy slippers.

"Car service in one hour," my phone flashed. What! Well, that put an end to the easy morning. Next, I was up and throwing on clothes, packing my laptop away and rushing off to Daventry to get my car serviced. I'd do my team meeting from a cafe.

Sunday 15th March – I received a voice text from one of the team. "I'm ill. I'm not sure that it is the virus, but I have a temperature and a cough." A series of things occurred to me in a flash:

"I was with her on Thursday."

"She could have spread it to the team."

"I could be incubating this virus."

"We could endanger the men."

At that moment, it all got very real.

Monday 16th March – I didn't know that there'd been a shift. A click. A waking up.

I didn't know my awareness had suddenly expanded in the moment after that phone call. I didn't know that this was the *After*. That I had woken up into a new world, a new level of consciousness, a new way of thinking about the pandemic.

I just knew what to do next. Reassure the team they didn't have to travel regardless of the things we had on. "I'm cancelling all non-essential travel," I said. My iMac displayed the faces of the Beyond team in little boxes on the screen. All their faces looked bright. I could see they agreed; they were relieved. It felt motivational and warm. We were in this together. Whatever happened, we were united. "Anyone who wants to travel can, but where possible, I would like to reduce social mixing."

After the meeting, I sent cancellation emails to those I could and started to think about logistics, hotels, and train tickets. I felt a sense of calm confidence, as if I were in a daydream. I was strangely unconcerned about my travels and plans for the business being thrown wide open. Throughout the day, I watched the events in my colourful, busy diary disappear in a puff of cyber smoke, one by one. As it turned out, I was only a little ahead of the curve. By the end of the day, even the main events, and the important conferences I was meant to attend, all got cancelled.

Wednesday 18th March – I woke up with a strong desire to go to HMP Onley and hand deliver a letter to each of the guys in our group, so they'd know we were thinking of them and hadn't abandoned them. I decided the safest thing would be to visit at lunchtime when they are behind their doors to minimise the risk of infection. I went to see Safer Custody first, who were very pleased to see me, and then I made my way to each wing. The corridors and wings felt eerie at lunchtime, with no men walking through them, no shouting, no bravado. Just long lengths of grey corridors and locked gates.

I was in the main corridor about to unlock the gate to Bravo Wing when I heard "Jacqueline!" It was Troy, a young man who had opened up in group for the first time the week before, telling us of his self-isolation, his desire for suicide, and his desperation at wanting a different life but not knowing how to get it. He'd been emotional at the end of the group but had felt relieved. Free.

"Hello," I said. "What's happening?"

"I'm going to hospital for my swollen hand," Troy said. Two uniformed officers stood across the corridor by the gate to H wing in their black and white uniforms, radios silent, faces patient. Troy had come and stood next to me. No longer allowed to shake hands in this strange new world, we looked into each other's eyes for a long moment of connection. His, bright blue and wide. Mine, filled with joy at seeing him. He looked even younger than usual with his blonde hair cropped short and his oversized, baggy sweatshirt. Hope swelled between us.

"You take care," I said. "I will put your letter in your cell." Another sliding door moment. Being on the corridor at that exact moment at that exact time for our worlds to touch. I'm always amazed at how that works.

Monday 23rd March – Prime Minister Boris Johnson gave the following announcement:

> "The coronavirus is the biggest threat this country has faced for decades—and this country is not alone.
>
> All over the world, we are seeing the devastating impact of this invisible killer.
>
> From this evening, I must give the British people a very simple instruction:
>
> **YOU MUST STAY AT HOME**
>
> No Prime Minister wants to enact measures like this."

Rob and I sat together on our sofa in the kitchen, watching the announcement on his MacBook. I could feel the rough fabric of his jeans beneath my hand. My mind was blank as I tried to absorb the enormity of the news. Locked Down. Not allowed to travel freely. Not allowed to mix with family. Not allowed to go to work.

"That feels weird," Rob said. And it was. We didn't really know what to do with ourselves. How to process the strangeness of the situation.

There was stuff to do. Cancellations and refunds and that sort of thing. But nothing could be re-arranged because we didn't know when we would be able to move around freely again. It wasn't like, cancel something this week and put it in for a couple of weeks' time. Nothing was going to be normal for a while. We didn't even know what normal was anymore. Or how long "a while" would be! The once busy calendar, which had to be juggled and jiggled to fit people in, was now wide open. No one knew what was going to happen. Or when. I realised that all the opportunities I'd created since September, all the potential work that had been on the table, all the interest we'd received...

Was

All

Gone.

It was weird. But instead of feeling devastated, I felt peace. I felt like the world had a gift. A wide-open space. A time for stepping back. A time to hunker down, re-evaluate, reflect. A time to just be when there was nothing else to do.

Notes

66   Virtual reality is a simulated experience that can be similar to or completely different from the real world. Applications of virtual reality can include entertainment and educational purposes.

Afterword – What's Next?

"Everything that is, and everything that will be,
will cease to be."

~ An old Irish proverb

No matter how devastating an event may be; no matter how difficult life seems; no matter how unexpected the cause of our distress; there's always a next.

Life goes on, and so do we. It seemed like the world stopped during the COVID-19 pandemic. Lives were lost, and families torn apart. I couldn't imagine a 'next'. I talked about 'just being' and seeing what would come. I often said, "Oh well, if I never work in prison again, then I've done my bit." I trusted that 'something' would come.

But there's a difference. A difference between what we think might happen and the actual flow of life. There's a difference between saying something is over and believing it is true.

The fact is COVID-19 crushed the business of Beyond Recovery. Like many others. For us, the death blow was

325

immediate. Funds stopped. Contracts were torn up. And, worst of all, prison residents got banged up for twenty-three hours a day. Access to the guys and girls we'd worked with was barred. New times, new needs. The well-being of people in prison wasn't one of them.

I fought it for two years. We pivoted by creating distance learning programs and we completed our training curriculum. I even visited some of the more vulnerable residents for a few months while I was allowed. The world of Beyond Recovery wasn't just a business to me; it was my lifeblood.

But, in prisons, the lockdown went on. Years after the rest of us could go about our business, past the time when masks were no longer the norm, beyond the virus and more, prisons kept their residents isolated and locked up.

It's not in the scope of this book to comment on the politics or the rights and wrongs of the prison system. I'm merely focussed on the situation as I saw it and how it affected Beyond Recovery's work and team.

In the first year, we did our best to keep supporting our people. But it got harder to keep in touch. The team of facilitators left to forge their own routes.

I hired two of the lads we'd worked with and built online programs for the public. We had a lot of fun doing that and bonded as a team. We built a loyal community of people who loved the work and loved the boys. But loyalty doesn't pay the bills, and by April 2022, we had to let them go their own ways.

I felt like I was holding on with my fingernails. I suffered from the indifference of the Criminal Justice System. My head hurt with the angst of trying to make it all work.

In between all of that, my husband and I moved house. We downsized to a cottage in the Warwickshire countryside. One afternoon in April 2022, I was making a cup of peppermint tea, surrounded by unpacked boxes, when it struck me, "I don't work in prisons!" For two years, I'd ducked and dived and tried to find ways of working with the new system. And for two years, the work had not been there. I watched the blue tits flying in and out of the bird box on the wall of orange bricks. Sounds of sheep in the field opposite our home filled the air. Tepid spring sunshine highlighted the dust on the windows. Relief washed through my body, and tears pricked my eyes. "Wow," I said, "so what's next?"

I didn't find it easy to let go of the prison angel identity. I thought I'd got a handle on my ego around the work. I thought I was the person who could walk away when it was time to walk away. Turns out I'm not, that even I, with all that I know about how our psychological experience works, can't just lean into the now without a fight.

So, with the thought "I don't work in prisons." I stopped trying to rescue something that was over and started looking at new opportunities.

May 2023

Beyond Recovery has done a small amount of prison work in HMP Portland and is willing to work in prisons, but I no longer chase the contracts and dig the ditches for sparse funding. We partnered with an addiction organisation in Bristol to provide aftercare programs for people with gambling-related harms; we have a growing team of volunteers that support prison residents on our distance learning program; I still write a monthly column for the Insidetime newspaper; and we train people who work with marginalised communities in our evidenced based Insight to Well-being curriculum.

Derrick Mason – started his own business, sharing the understanding that changed his life with different populations and is a sought-after speaker at events. At the time of writing, he is a director of three different charities.

Omar Wilson – took a job to support his young family. He is a sought-after speaker and is regularly requested for presentations and group work. Omar was the lead facilitator during our work at HMP Portland this year and has an impact on even the hardest-to-reach people.

Both guys do work for Beyond Recovery as it comes up, and we remain very close.

The pre-COVID Beyond Recovery team went on to start their own practices and charities and are thriving.

And me? I finished this book and created mentoring programs for coaches and facilitators; I collaborate with a specialist research team on why people at the edges of society need access to programs like Beyond Recovery, and I'm building a digital business of online well-being courses.

I realise, as I have so many times throughout this journey, that human potential is infinite. That we rise and rise again, no matter how many times we get knocked down. That opportunity is the other side of the coin to disaster. That circumstances do not define us.

This book is not about transforming the lives of people in prison. It's not even about me. It's about our inbuilt emotional resilience and your ability to bounce back regardless of what life throws at you; it's about the journey and not the destination, and it's about the hope and potential that life offers every single person.

One last thought: There are Angels everywhere. They may be your neighbour, your brother, your mother, your colleague or even yourself. I invite you not to define the angels you meet by their past or even their current behaviour.

This book offers the possibility to look past the obvious to the beauty within. To be kind to yourself and patient with others. And to look for the thing that connects us all. The spirit of love and compassion. And if all else fails, remember the words from this old Indian proverb: *"In the end, everything will be OK. If it's not OK, it's not the end."*

Appendix

The Three Principles of Mind, Consciousness and Thought

When the study of psychology became popular around 1890, it was as much about the 'psyche' as it was about the cognitive processes. Suffice to say that later evolutions of understanding the mind ditched the spiritual as being the realm of the church and concentrated on the psychological (mental and behavioural processes).

Dr George Pransky, a psychiatrist who has researched the Three Principles, has documented the specific break-throughs[67] discoveries by Sidney Banks and why they matter to the field of psychology.

Universal Mind

This refers to the intelligence behind life. The whole. The Life force that exists in every living thing. The same energy that has flowers turning to the sun works through us. In the Missing Link, Sidney Banks states:

"Mind is the creative power, the essence, and the intelligence behind all life."

George Pransky says: "This matters because it states that mind is spiritual in nature rather than biological and that it is the source of all life and the fundamental intelligence behind all life."

Universal Consciousness

Consciousness enables our awareness. It allows us to perceive what's going on. It informs our filters. It changes, expands and contracts as we go through our day. It provides our experience of thought. It is our special effects system.

Sydney Banks describes it as "Consciousness brings thought to life via the senses."

George Pransky says: "This matters because it explains why thought does not look like thought but rather like an independent, freestanding reality captured by the senses just as a camera captures a scene. Thus, when people discover the nature of consciousness, they are empowered to take even the most compelling experiences in stride rather than overreacting to them."

Universal Thought

Thought gives us the power to navigate through life. It is the tool we use for decision-making, creating feelings, and experiencing life. Realising the fact that we think automatically promotes psychological well-being, regardless of the content of our thoughts.

Sydney Banks writes: "Thought is the gift that human beings and other creatures possess to create subjective, momentary images and words in their minds."

George Pransky says: "When people discover that well-being comes purely through realizing the simple fact that they think, they are no longer tempted towards the effortful and ultimately unrealistic task of 'managing' their thinking in the pursuit of wellbeing."

The Life-Changing Potential
of the Three Principles

In my experience of sharing this paradigm within English prisons for over five years, deep psychological change occurs when humans wake up to their innate well-being, regardless of their circumstances. In simple terms, 'when we feel better, we do better'.

One study[68] on my work found that men who had received the Insight to Wellbeing classes had higher levels of self-control, well-being and pro-social behaviour in addition to lower levels of aggression compared to the control group (people who were in the same prison but didn't receive our classes).

In schools[69] in Tampa, Florida, children waking up to their innate health experienced an increased ability to regulate their emotions, and increased decision-making and problem-solving skills. Plus, increased personal resilience and compassion for others!

Dr Anthony Kessel describes the Three Principles as a Superpower[70] that can make work-related stress appear very different and make relating to others more natural:

"Stress and anxiety are seen as the experiential manifestation of thoughts that do not need to be feared and can be dropped. Rapport is not a strategy to be applied to others, but a natural consequence of being completely present in the room, listening with respect and being prepared to learn. Influencing others no longer takes the form of how you get people to do what you want, but is about genuinely connecting, presenting your position thoughtfully and being prepared to be influenced by those around you. Conflict, promotion, and change management all appear different."

Notes

67   https://www.pranskyandassociates.com/post/the-specific-breakthrough-discoveries-of-sydney-banks

68   https://www.preprints.org/manuscript/202206.0023/v1

69   https://sparkcurriculum.org/spark-evidence-based-curriculum/

70   https://beyond-recovery.co.uk/2018/04/30/kessel/

Enjoyed Wing of an Angel?

If you loved the book and have a moment to spare, please leave a review on Amazon or Goodreads.

I'd appreciate it dearly, plus it will help spread the word and inspire others to live to their full potential. Thank you!

Join my Bytes of Insight Membership Group

It's free; you'll get a short weekly update packed with goodies, insights, personal updates and advance notification of upcoming events, workshops, member-only webinars and books.

https://jbhollows.ck.page/bytesofinsight

Taking Inspired Action

If you'd like a short course on creating your own inspired life, sign up for this free programme to guide you on your journey. https://jbhollows.ck.page/inspiredaction

BEYOND TV

For interviews and reflections on the deeper side of life and living in our true nature, there are plenty of free resources on my YouTube channel
https://www.youtube.com/@BeyondTVchannel

Connection

I love hearing from people and their journeys. Email me with your thoughts and stories at jacqueline@jbhollows.co.uk or check out some free resources at www.jbhollows.co.uk

Acknowledgements

To all the people I've met in prison. I'm honoured to have been a small part of your stories; your courageousness inspires me; your potential ignites me.

This book has been brought to life with many hands, hearts and minds: Genny Abbot, Jane Tucker, Rob Hollows, Judy Banks, Jules Swales, Wendy Davey and many beta readers whose sharp eyes helped to craft the story and stop me waffling!

Maria Iliffe-Wood believed in me and this project even before it was a book, before she had a publishing press, and before I had a clue that I could write. Jules Swales shaped the story from my scribbles, championed the cause and helped me find my voice, in addition to the essential developmental reviews.

The saying 'it takes a village' couldn't be truer when I think about the incredible people who have been guiding lights in the creation of Beyond Recovery and its mission to revolutionise the way we view and treat addiction, mental health and offending behaviour. So many have supported, donated, advised, visited, cheered, and shared the incredible journey of uncovering the light that dwells in the hearts and minds of incarcerated people. A few are mentioned below, and there were many more whom I hold dear in my heart forever.

David and Kathy Hollows, Alison and Neil Stones, Dazzle and Lollie Williams, Andrew Hollows, Rhys Thomas, David Kowitz, Aaron and Lila Turner, Lou Scott, Julian Fraser, Chris Mander, Emma Wilkins, Jan Anderson, Julie-Anne Bleasdale, Brooke Wheldon-Reece, Jamie Fiore Higgins, Joanne McKinnon (RIP), Simon Morgan (RIP), Christopher Cart (RIP).

Derrick Mason, Omar Wilson, and Chris Mavinga, you are a light in my life. The reason for everything. Thank you.

Thank you to the people who got me started and kept me going: Paul O'Connell, Michael DeGroot, Russell Johnson, Scott Davidson and Ian Fulton.

The incredible facilitators that came on this journey with me. We've laughed, cried, and grown together. I really couldn't have done it without each one of you. Paul Lock, Anna Debenham, Susan Marmot, Liliana Bellini, Jacquie Moses, Al Milledge, Gary Burton, Stella Popowicz, Jean Floyd, Nicky Drew, Dave Robinson, Liz Newton, Pete Williams, Sam Herman, Neeta O'Keefe, Liz Babb, and (for always having our backs) Debbie Hemming.

The wonderful 'Buddies' – Carola Mills, and all the volunteers on our Distance Learning Scheme who continue to write to prison residents and sprinkle the fairy dust.

The pioneers of the Three Principles, affectionately known by the guys as the GOATS (Greatest of All Time) have taught me, supported me and helped me in more ways than I can mention. I'm humbled by your friendship: Jan and Chip Chipman, Dicken and Coizie Bettinger, Michael Neill, Linda and George Pransky, Mara Olsen-Gleason, Mark Howard, and Linda Sandel Pettit.

Special thanks to Jack Pransky, who wanted to 'put me on the map'; your invitation to create a research project opened doors I didn't even know existed. Elsie Spittle, Mama, you taught me to love the silence. Joe Bailey, your books ignited the hope within me, and your friendship has been a guiding light.

Bill Pettit your steady hand, always pointing me towards the spiritual nature of this work, your unwavering guidance and the many laughs (and sing songs) along the way.

Huge gratitude to Prof Tom Kelley and your team for our first three research papers and for your dedication to evidencing the Innate Health understanding. Ron McVety, for your vision and insight into creating Innate Health Research as a platform for distributing Syd Banks's understanding to the world. Jeanne Catherine Grey, Dani Palade, Anita McGinty and Nici Butchart are pioneering a way of showing that desistance is not only possible in criminology but highly desirable. You guys' rock.

Especial gratitude to Shaul and Chana Rosenblatt and all the sweet Rabbis that came to visit. We've appreciated your support, kindness, and wisdom along this journey. Shaul's visit to discuss religion with a couple of the guys and the session that we ran with the fellas from the Rabbinic Training Academy are high on my list of favourite visits of all time.

To Judy Banks, you know why.

The beautiful souls on Salt Spring Island took us into their hearts, welcomed us into their homes and made us feel blessed on our visits there. People who'd learned from Syd Banks directly and just went about their lives in a more harmonious way. No fanfare, no social media, just beautiful living. I learned so much from being in your company, over shared meals, shared stories, and lots of shared laughter: Jane and Tom Tucker, Karen and Mark Miller-Williams, Jerry Lee and Robin Allen, Marika and Richard Mayer, Christa and Bob Campsell.

My precious son Dazzle. My heart bursts with love for you. Your constant appreciation and support has me level up every time.

Our grandchildren, Miyah Rose and Odysseus, wishing you a life of freedom from judgement and the space to express your beautiful minds.

Mr Sydney Banks. I'm grateful that you walked this world. I give thanks every day to you and the pioneers that brought this understanding into my life and the life of so many others.

My darling Hollows. Beyond words. Always.

Permissions

Dedication page: Rumi Extract as interpreted by Coleman Barks

Lord Michael Young quote reprinted with permission of School for Social Entrepreneurs. https://www.the-sse.org/about-school-for-social-entrepreneurs/

Quotes by Sydney Banks reprinted with permission of Judy Banks.

Sally's Story – printed with kind permission of Sally Wyse

Lord Robin Corbett quote reprinted with permission of Lady Val Corbett.

Derrick's Story – printed with kind permission of Derrick Mason.

Christine Heath quote reprinted with permission from Christine Heath

Rabbi Shaul Rosenblatt quote reprinted with permission from Shaul Rosenblatt.

About the Author

Jacqueline (JB) Hollows is an author, a social entrepreneur, and a mental well-being mentor. Her tagline 'Doing Life Perfectly Imperfect' sums up her attitude of embracing the messiness of life's journey and her ability to see the perfection in everyone she works with. From a career in IT to pioneering well-being programs in prisons, to co-authoring research papers to publishing books, to pivoting as a digital creative, Jacqueline embraces change and brings others along with her. She hopes to ignite the potential in you with her inspiring memoir *Wing of an Angel*.

In 2015 Jacqueline founded a non-profit organisation, Beyond Recovery CIC (BR) to deliver resilience programmes to people in the UK prison system. She also trained and nurtured a team of Well-being facilitators. BR's mission is to revolutionise the way we see addictions, mental health and offending behaviour and to eliminate stigma.

Jacqueline also runs mentoring programmes to develop

practitioners and is passionate about working with emerging leaders and women who want to fulfil their powerful potential. She runs online courses and well-being retreats at her home in Warwickshire, England.

An author of several research papers evidencing the Three Principles approach, Jacqueline is actively involved in creating equitable access to the life-changing opportunities that arise from realising the work of Mr Sydney Banks, a philosopher and theosopher that uncovered the fact that mental well-being is innate and available within every human being.

Jacqueline is also a regular contributor for a prison newspaper: *Insidetime* (readership c60,000). And writes on Medium as well as creating inspirational content for her YouTube channel Beyond TV.

Since discovering a passion for writing JB Hollows has contributed to a number of anthologies and is a published author of two books as part of a collaboration of writers: *A Different Story;* and *Stories from the Muses.*

Also by JB Hollows

The following books include contributions from JB Hollows:

A Different Story: How Six Authors Became Better Writers
Stories from the Muses: Become a Better Writer

 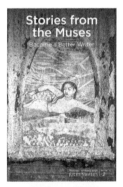

Beyond Recovery CIC[71]

Beyond Recovery is a grassroots social enterprise with a mission to end stigma and revolutionise the way we view and treat offending behaviour.

Founded by Jacqueline Hollows in 2015 from her passion for uncovering the potential in people with lived experience of addiction and prison. Jacqueline's childhood was littered with neglect and abuse, which shaped her life for many years as an adult. When she saw the true cause of the issues, she could forgive and transcend her past. She wants to be able to provide the same hope and awareness to others.

People who commit crimes are sent to prison. Punishment is the lack of liberty and the knock-on effect this creates in their lives. What is not addressed is the mental well-being and lack of self-efficacy, which is at the heart of all criminal behaviour. 60% of prison residents have low literacy standards, 45% have anxiety or depression. High percentages have a history of social exclusion and disruptive backgrounds.

BR offers a simple solution: uncover the well-being, resilience, and potential of prison residents through an understanding of the mind and human experience. It is low-cost, effective, and profound. Having worked with over six hundred people, the BR team have seen that when levels of well-being increase, risk factors are reduced, psychological and emotional well-being is increased, and individuals are able to access their own creative solutions to any issues, regardless of the circumstances.

The work of BR, with this innovative paradigm, has been evidenced in several academic research papers.

Post COVID-19: BR has pivoted to create distance learning programmes and work with people on release rather than in custody. This has given them the opportunity to scale and reach more people across the UK. In addition, BR created a ground-breaking curriculum which can be taught to organisations that have greater access to the people we want to serve.

Two of the people whom BR worked with in the early days have gone on to become directors of Beyond Recovery and have started their own mentoring businesses.

To scale, BR has had to balance financial stability with social impact. To that end, they have established several online programmes and mentoring packages in addition to their Train the Trainer programme. This suite of offerings has the ripple effect of affecting the broader community of the prison leaver. Enabling BR to reach and recognise the limitless potential of their beneficiaries.

Notes

71   https://beyond-recovery.co.uk/

Glossary

Banged Up
Slang for being locked in their cells.

Barricade
Piling all the furniture in front of a cell door to prevent officers entering.

Behind the door
Slang for being locked in their cells.

Bro or Bruv
A friendly term to a peer.

Burn
Slang for tobacco.

Buttie
Slang for a bacon sandwich.

Custody
Held in prison.

CSU / The Block / Seg / Segregation Unit
The Care and Support Unit – is a place where prisoners are isolated for infractions such as violence. It is used to protect prisoners who need to be segregated and punish prisoners by isolating them. More commonly known as The Block or Seg (segregation).

Closed Visits
The family is only allowed to see the prisoner behind a screen and speak through a communication system such as a telephone. High-risk

prisoners, or those likely to smuggle drugs into the prison, must have closed visits.

Complex Needs
A person with complex needs will have several issues, such as addiction, mental health diagnosis and trauma backgrounds. Sometimes referred to as Dual Diagnosis. Many agencies cannot deal with all the issues, so the people keep getting batted around and not being helped.

'D' Cat (or Category D, C, B, A)
Prisons are categorised from A to D depending on the offenders' risk to the public. A is the highest risk, and D is the lowest (usually an open prison).

Fam
A friendly term to a peer.

First Generation Teachers
People who knew and were taught by Sydney Banks – the enlightened man who uncovered the Three Principles understanding. Also known as the OGs.

Flat packing
Prisoners who act out by smashing up their cells will remove sinks and fixed items from the wall and use these to barricade themselves in. Referred to as 'flat packing' by the guys in prison.

Food
Slang for drugs.

Harm Reduction
A particular philosophy known as 'harm reduction', where instead of getting people clean, you keep them on medications and teach them about how different substances interact with each other physiologically. https://www.hri.global/what-is-harm-reduction

HMP Onley
A Category C Men's prison, operated by Her Majesty's Prison Service, that houses up to seven hundred and fifty prisoners. The prison is named after the lost village of Onley, which is located next to the prison. Onley Prison is in the county of Northamptonshire, close to its border with Warwickshire in England.

IPP

Indeterminate Public Protection. The term is no longer used, as it creates a feeling of hopelessness. Residents will often give up, thinking they will never be released; therefore, their state of mind and behaviour deteriorates.

KoW or Keep on Wing

The prisoner is not allowed to leave the wing for security reasons.

Lockdown

Some threats to the prison, like a missing man, or someone on the roof, or a threat to life will result in the whole prison going into lock down – all men will be locked up and accounted for and all staff have to stay put, unable to leave or even move around the prison until the issue is resolved.

Market Gardens

An area in prison for growing produce that is used in the prison kitchens. One of the most trusted jobs, only given to men who are 'low risk' due to their being tools such as metal spades.

NHS

The British National Health Service.

NLP

Neuro-linguistic programming is a way of changing someone's thoughts and behaviours to help achieve desired outcomes for them.

On Remand

In custody, pending trial.

PA

Personal Assistant.

Paper

Slang for money.

Research Project

A Research Project is a scientific endeavour to answer a research question. Jack suggested that I measure the impact of our program against people who were not receiving the program but who were in the same circumstances (called a Control Group).

Road
Working in the criminal lifestyle.

Road Families
Families where fathers and uncles are all embedded into the criminal lifestyle.

ROTL
Release on Temporary Licence – a prisoner is allowed release for work-based activities.

Safer Custody
A department in prisons dedicated to looking after the safety of the prison, staff, and residents.

Smart Recovery
An international non-profit organization that aids individuals seeking abstinence from addiction. SMART stands for Self-Management and Recovery Training. The SMART approach is secular and science-based, using cognitive behavioural therapy and non-confrontational motivational methods https://www.smartrecovery.org/

Support Worker
Works with people who need help at university, taking notes in class, helping with research, organisation, and deadlines.

Tariff
The length of the prison sentence.

TEDx
TED is a non-profit organisation devoted to spreading ideas, usually in the form of short, powerful talks (eighteen minutes or less). A TEDx event is a local gathering where live TED-like talks and performances are shared with the community. The difference between TED and TEDx events is that the former takes more of a global approach while the latter typically focuses on a local community that concentrates on local voices. Officially, the 'x' in TEDx stands for 'independently organized TED event' – but it's more of a TED multiplied.

The 12-Steps
Also known as Alcoholics Anonymous or AA. The AA program has helped a lot of people all over the world find sobriety and serenity. It was co-founded from an insight by Bill W (Wilson).

The Green
Birmingham Prison, also known as HMP Winson Green (or The Green).

The Two's
Prison landings are referred to by which level they are on. The second landing is the twos.

Tornado Units
Tornado teams are units of elite officers sent into prisons to bring riots under control. They are usually made up of fifty officers who dress in RoboCop-style black boiler suits. The squads are armed with batons and protected by shields.

Virtual reality
A simulated experience that can be similar to or completely different from the real world. Applications of virtual reality can include entertainment and educational purposes.

Wings
The blocks or units in a prison are often referred to as "wings". This is where the prisoners reside in cells. In some prisons, they are labelled alphabetically A, B, and C so that they can be referred to phonetically as Alpha, Bravo, Charlie over the radio to aid clarity of location.

Bibliography & Resources

References

Drink driving statistics https://www.quittance.co.uk/uk-drink-driving-statistics

Michael Neill's website https://www.michaelneill.org/

Harm reduction https://www.hri.global/what-is-harm-reduction

The Three Principles of Mind, Consciousness & Thought as realised and taught by Sydney Banks https://sydbanks.com/

SMART Recovery https://www.smartrecovery.org/

Anna Debenham https://theinsightalliance.org/

60% of the prison population have literacy issues – https://literacytrust.org.uk/

Valuing Volunteers by CLINKS https://www.clinks.org/sites/default/files/2018-11/Valuing%20volunteers%20in%20prison.pdf

SSE—The School for Social Entrepreneurs https://www.the-sse.org/

more London https://en.wikipedia.org/wiki/More_London

3PUK Conference Videos https://www.youtube.com/channel/UCwYghuJFy3nctWGuKKPqgDg/videos

Three Principles Foundation videos https://www.youtube.com/c/ThreePrinciplesFoundationSydneyBanks/videos

Innate Health Research https://innatehealthresearch.org/

Three Principles Global Community Research https://3pgc.org/evidence-of-impact/

Dr George Pransky – The Specific Breakthroughs of Sydney
Banks https://www.pranskyandassociates.com/post/
the-specific-breakthrough-discoveries-of-sydney-banks

Beyond Recovery CIC https://beyond-recovery.co.uk/

Conferences

One Solution, Chicago https://onesolutionglobal.org/

Understanding the Human Mind, Prague https://porozumenimysli.cz/

The Viva Event, Spain https://thevivaevent.com/

Videos

The Chicks, Jacqueline Hollows https://youtu.be/76xR5wN1ocE

Volcano moment, Jacqueline Hollows https://youtu.be/tqidMLuVa1s

Syd Banks Experience https://sydbanks.com/longbeach/

The Chipman's in Onley, Jacqueline Hollows https://youtu.
be/76xR5wN1ocE

Sai Weng lost his horse, Alan Watts https://youtu.be/sWd6fNVZ20o

David Saunders presenting at the 3PUK conference https://youtu.
be/5PKQ3wQxXi4

Visitors: Steph & Kaye https://youtu.be/uQW5rB9fHNg

Craig Wyman https://www.youtu.be.com/watch?v=pQDC7Zm1vDw

Steve Jobs commencement speech https://youtu.be/UF8uR6Z6KLc

Books

Healthy thinking/feeling/doing from the inside out Jack Pransky
https://www.goodreads.com/book/show/22611463-healthy
-thinking-feeling-doing-from-the-inside-out

The Serenity Principle Joe Bailey https://www.goodreads.com/book/
show/287080.The_Serenity_Principle

And Death Came Third Andy Lopata & Peter Roper https://www.
goodreads.com/book/show/11368402-and-death-came-third

*Modello: A Story of Hope for the Inner City and Beyond: An Inside-Out
Model of Prevention and Resiliency in Action* Jack Pransky https://
www.goodreads.com/book/show/19441227-modello

12 Steps Bill Wilson https://www.goodreads.com/book/show/834926.
Bill_W

Beyond Recovery Research Papers

Published Research Papers:

Kelly, T., Hollows, J., Lambert, E., Savard, D. & Pransky, J. (2017) Teaching Health Versus Treating Illness: The Efficacy of Three Principles Correctional Counselling with People in an English Prison International Journal of Offender Therapy and Comparative Criminology 1–26 https://journals.sagepub.com/doi/abs/10.1177/0306624X17735253

Kelly, T., Hollows, J., Lambert, E., Savard, D. & Pransky, J. (2018) The Efficacy of Intensive Three Principles Correctional Counselling for Improving the Mental Health/Resilience of People in an English Prison Journal of Offender Rehabilitation https://www.tandfonline.com/doi/abs/10.1080/10509674.2019.1648352

Kelly, T., Hollows, J., Lambert, E., Savard, D. & Pransky, J. (2021) The Efficacy of Three Principles Correctional Counselling for Improving the Mental Health and Self-Control of People Incarcerated for Sexual Violence Journal of Violence against Women https://journals.sagepub.com/doi/abs/10.1177/10778012211022783

Catherine, J.L., Denkers, A., & McGinty, A. (2022) *Innate health: A novel examination of what explains well-being, prosocial behavior, and aggression among men living in a UK prison.* Manuscript submitted for publication. Preprints. https://www.preprints.org/manuscript/202206.0023/v1

Catherine, J.L., Palade, D., & Denkers, A. (2020) *Evaluation of the effectiveness of the Three Principles Correctional Counseling interventions for imprisoned young men with a history of violent offence at HMP Nottingham.* Report delivered to HM Probation & PCC VRU Nottingham.

Catherine, J.L., Hollows, J., Denkers, A., Palade, D., & Scott L. (2020) *Evaluation of the effectiveness of the Three Principles Correctional Counseling intervention for imprisoned men within the incentivized substance free living initiative at HMP Nottingham.* Report delivered to HM Prison and Probation Service.